SALT LICKS
AND OTHER PLAYS

## Sunday Brunch at the Gymkhana

*Rights of Admission Reserved*

## Salt Licks

*An act in two plays. A play in two acts*

## Gold and Silver

*A coupe on the Grand Trunk Express*

## Head Start

*A romp in the garden*

## Evening Shadows

*An original adaptation in English of Sandhya Chhaya by Jaywant Dalvi*

Vitasta
LET KNOWLEDGE SPREAD

BANGALORE
LITTLE
THEATRE

## COMMENTS ON THE PUBLICATIONS

*Glocal is the word that comes immediately to mind when I think of BLT's long history and ambitions. One can be local in one's view, without being insular, and one can be global, pulling voices from elsewhere into the context one inhabits, without becoming deracinated. BLT's house is strong because it has been built in the here and now; it is doubly strong because its windows have been open to the oxygen from elsewhere and from other times.*

*Ecosystem is another word I would use to pinpoint BLT's aspirations. It has understood that its strength is derived from the strength of the field in which it works. Whatever BLT knows, it has shared, and this sharing has taken many forms – from the training it has imparted to budding actors and directors to the support it has provided to fledgling theatre groups. The same commitment has propelled BLT's initiative to publish multiple volumes of plays that have been spawned by its admirable play development programme. There is a hunger for strong dramatic texts in India, where theatre production has grown far more rapidly than playwriting. In that context, these volumes will be seen as yet another precious gift that BLT has given to the theatre community.*

**Anmol Vellani**
Theatre Director and past Director of India Foundation for the Arts

*I am delighted that you are presenting all these plays that are at one and the same time enjoyable, revealing and memorable!*

**Roddam Narasimha**
Science Historian and Professor,
Jawaharlal Nehru Centre for Advanced Scientific Research

*This initiative would allow theatre practitioners from other parts of the world to access this work and look at the possibilities of staging these plays in multiple languages and in multiple cultural contexts.*

**Vidyanidhi Vanarase**
Founder-Dirtector, International Association for Performing Arts and Research

*This volume addresses the critical need for more actable and accessible versions of classic Indian plays in English. Good plays around important historical ideas are unfortunately scarce. The second admirable volume helps correct that deficiency.*

**Ira Hauptman**
Professor of Drama, Queens College, CUNY, New York

*We have eagerly awaited the publication of these volumes. They have finally arrived. They will reach performers and audiences right across national borders and far beyond.*

**Sai Paranjpye**
Theatre personality and award winning film director

*An international leader in our field, especially its serious investment in new play development, including the publication series that can benefit all of us theater makers across the world.*

**Bill Rauch**
Artistic Director, Perelman Performing Arts Center at the World Trade Center, New York City

*The new publication series produced by the Bangalore Little Theatre are an important and most welcome addition to world theater knowledge. Bravo!*

**Arthur Giron**
Founding Member of Ensemble Studio Theatre, New York, formerly Head, Graduate Playwriting Program, Carnegie Mellon University

*Bangalore Little Theatre has reached veteran status in Indian theatre with their powerful theatrical interventions in the community, spanning 60 years...these volumes enrich our understanding of the capacity of theatre to create spaces for potent ideas, that demand our engagement.*

**Yvette Hardie**
President: ASSITEJ (International Association for Theatre for Children and Young People)

*This work is not only important for India, it also makes plays from Indian writing known across the world. It is a very important and necessary project.*

**Ursula Werdenberg**
Dramaturg-Playwright,
Secretary General of The International Playwrights' Forum

*My warmest congratulations. This is a significant milestone and a wonderful achievement that gives readers an opportunity to think about our pasts and our presents through a history of ideas.*

**Anuradha Kapur**
Past Director, National School of Drama

*These are a valued resource .... they celebrate authors past and present and their translators as well, making the local, global.*

**Richard Crane**
Playwright-Director,
Co-founder of Brighton Theatre

*Your contribution to the goals of the International Playwrights' Forum, to the artistic treasures of your country, as well as for universal culture in general is indescribable indeed.*

**Gad Kaynar (Kissinger)**
Professor, International Theatre Institute
The Yolanda and David Katz Faculty of the Arts, Tel Aviv University

ये नाम केचिदिह नः प्रथयन्त्यवज्ञां
जानन्ति ते किमपि तान्प्रति नैष यत्नः ।
उत्पत्स्यते तु मम कोऽपि समानधर्म
कालो ह्ययं निरवधिर्विपुला च पृथ्वी ॥

*Those who deride or ignore my work –*
*let them know: my efforts are not for them.*
*There will come along someone who shares my spirit:*
*the world is vast, and time endless.*

***– Bhavabhuti***

*Bangalore Little Theatre is privileged to receive a substantial grant from **Kusum** and **Mohandas Pai** towards education and institutional development programmes, which include the publication of these plays.*

Published by,
**Renu Kaul Verma**
Vitasta Publishing Pvt Ltd
2/15, Ansari Road, Daryaganj
New Delhi 110002
info@vitastapublishing.com

**ISBN** 978-93-90961-16-0

MRP ₹450
First Edition 2022



Editors: Kanagam King, Papri Sen Sri Raman
Layout: Deepak Mote, Goutam Hegde
Illustrations: Supriya Kannan
Printer: Vikas Computer and Printers

# CONTENTS

# FOREWORD TO THE SERIES

Bangalore Little Theatre is an enormous exercise in imagination. It remains an aspiration for theatre performers and a source of inspiration for practitioners. The passion, perseverance, toil and grace is the hallmark of this intimate Institution, which has embarked on many pathbreaking initiatives, programmes and productions. If the History of Ideas programme was unique, the translation and adaptation of Indian classics in English is a huge service. In the programme Vijay Padaki has presented a pertinent model, wherein the play scripts transcend the cultural specificity and period in time to speak in a universal language that addresses our contemporary concerns. Although we read the text in English, we experience the content in the original. A truly remarkable feat.

BLT has had a strong play development programme for a long time. It is most appropriate that the plays are being published now. Several volumes of plays can be expected in print very soon. This is a huge contribution to the institution of theatre in India. We can be sure they will be received with enthusiasm world-wide.

**Feroz Abbas Khan**
*Theatre director and award winning film maker*

# SPECIAL MESSAGE

For nearly 60 years, Bangalore Little Theatre has been instrumental in promoting theatre arts in Bengaluru and across the country. The ambitious project of publishing their most successful plays in a multi-volume anthology marks a great point in their story – another marker of the tremendous success they have attained.

In translating to English and adapting the plays for the modern stage, Mr Vijay Padaki (BLT) is conserving the best of Indian theatre. Each play is especially relevant to contemporary situations, from environmental concerns to resurgent regional identities, to introspecting the carnage of wars and finally the complexities of court politics.

I am certain that such a project provides us the perfect opportunity to understand, perhaps for the first time in recent years, the sheer wealth of Indian theatre spanning different cultural and linguistic traditions in the subcontinent. In producing such plays, and putting them together in this volume, BLT has undertaken a public service, one which every Indian living in the 21st century can profit from, for a long time to come.

With this, I wish BLT the very best for this and their many future endeavours.

**Shashi Tharoor**
*Member of Parliament for Thiruvananthapuram*

# PUBLISHER'S NOTE

The last play in Volume 6 is ***Evening Shadows***, an English language adaptation of *Sandhya Chhaya*, by the Marathi playwright Jaywant Dalvi. From Marathi, it was translated for the Hindi stage by Nadira Babbar. It is from this Hindi play that the present English adaptation has been created. India's repository of plays in regional languages is rich and deep. As far as translations into the English language go, we have only begun to skim the surface, as presenters of India's diversity in the literary world. No doubt, deep sea diving into our ocean of languages will yield a rich harvest of creative writing; we have not even begun researching our linguistic heritage on regional stages yet, but one day in the future, yes, we hope translation readers will have the satisfaction of finding Indian plays on the global stage.

The first play in Modern India was a play in Bengali, written in 1860 by **Michael Madhusudan Dutt**. It was called, *Buro Shalikher Ghaare Roa*. At the same time, a writer called Dinabandhu Mitra wrote a play in Bengali in 1860 called *Nil Darpan*, describing the plight of Indigo farmers in Bengal exploited by the East India Company. This play has the distinction of being one of the most contemporary chronicles of history. The Sepoy Mutiny took place in 1856-57. Soon after, the Indigo farmers rose in revolt in 1859. In 1860, there was a play on the protest; a very close look at events unfolding at the time, very near the truth of the matter.

Michael Madhusudan translated it into English. This was the first English rendition of a regional language play in modern India. A missionary called Rev James Long printed the English version and was prosecuted and jailed for it. When **Girish Chandra Ghosh** established the National Theatre in Calcutta (Kolkata) in 1872, the first play ever commercially staged was *Nil Darpan* in Bangla.

We have come a long way in publishing regional theatre in the English language. But we have not yet fully explored the possibility of translating regional language plays into English, which today claims to being more of an Indian language than English. It is no longer exclusive to England and India's brand of In-glish is very popular, so popular that Hinglish is part of the English language vocabulary.

This series of play books began with ***The Toy Cart of Clay***, an adaptation of the Sanskrit Classic ***Mrichhakatika*** by Sudraka; ***The Anklet***, an adaptation from Ilango Adigal's Tamil Classic ***Silappadikaram***; ***Kurukshetra Burning!*** based on ***Smashana Kurukshetra*** in Kannada by Kuvempu and ***The Echo***, an adaptation of ***Chomana Dudi*** in Kannada by Shivarama Karanth.

We at Vitasta hope to bring to its readers more such books of plays from India in the coming years.

# SALUTATIONS

Volumes 1-3 of the publication project were pushed through in very little time to meet the deadline of 17 December 2019, kicking off the Diamond Jubilee year of BLT. It was on that date in 1960 that BLT had its first public performance. From the original plan of a token release of one volume we went on to release three volumes! The people who went out of the way to make this happen were Papri Sen Sri Raman, Kanagam King and their team at Vitasta Publishing. BLT commissioned the publication of six volumes of plays to Vitasta. It has been a great pleasure working with the Vitasta team, ever meticulous in editorial inputs and ever patient with the BLT team. It has been a great learning experience working with Papri and her team.

It is well known that the huge collection of play scripts in BLT had remained unpublished for years. We are thankful to the Managing Committee of BLT to take on the publication task with determination in 2019 – and for pushing us into its execution. There has been an even more powerful hand behind the publications project, invisible but relentless in drive over several years. Rupande Padaki, known to all of us as Rupa, was in many ways responsible for the publications to be taken up. She succeeded at last.

**Deepak Mote • Vijay Padaki**

# PREFACE TO THE VOLUME

It may be worth extracting a few lines from the Preface to Volume 1. It was about the Cantonment context just after Independence when Bangalore Little Theatre was created.

> It can be said that English language drama in India was essentially a colonial cultural legacy. The very term colonial legacy has, inescapably, a negative connotation...In 1960 a small group of committed persons in Bangalore sought a theatre experience that could be a genuine alternative to the order of the day that was called BBC Theatre – British Bedroom Comedy.

When BLT was created we had a remarkable collaboration of expatriates serving in Bangalore and local artists already engaged in the theatre. They had a vision of a Community Theatre best described by the slogan invented 25 years later: *Think Globally, Act Locally.* The plays in Volume 6 salute some of the expatriates in BLT in the formative years who gave the group a distinct pride in its Indianness:

- **Scott and Margaret Tod**. Scott was an Electrical Engineer seconded to Indian Telephone Industries, but also a trained Director in the Little Theatre movement in England. Margaret was a trained actress and a fine trainer. On arrival they found a British expat community active in amateur theatre. They chose not to join them and, instead, joined others in founding BLT.
- **Gordon and Esther Muirhead**. Gordon, a solicitor, was attached to King & Partridge in Bangalore. Esther was the Representative in India for Oxfam and War on Want before they opened offices in India. They were both committed Gandhians. During the partition riots, one served in the refugee camps in the Western border, the other in the Eastern Border.
- **Glynn Wood.** He was sent to Bangalore as Director of the American Cultural Centre (USIS). Young and active in athletics, he endeared himself to the college campuses in Bangalore and Karnataka. He went on to do his Doctoral studies on the political history of Karnataka and became a Professor of Political Science. He was a distance runner. Back home he introduced President Jimmy Carter to distance running.
- **David and Doreen Horsburgh.** David served in the Royal Air Force during the war, decided to settle down in India, found his calling in education and joined the Krishnamurti Foundation school in Rishi valley. He developed the now famous Methods of English Language Teaching (MELT) for British Council. Later, he created Neel Bagh, an education

centre in rural Karnataka. Doreen was proficient in arts and crafts and a great asset in backstage departments.

- **Jean Thomas.** Her husband, Rev Lowerth Lewis Thomas, was a House Warden in Bishop Cotton Boys School. Jean was committed to education excellence and was the first woman director in BLT. The production was *A Man For All Seasons,* the very first in India.

There were others. What characterized the first generation expat members of BLT was their genuine love of India and their commitment to a truly cross-cultural theatre.

The plays in Volume 6 reflect on the continued Western orientation of Indian communities till today. As a character in *Salt Licks* says: 'Go West, young man, to rediscover the East. And don't be in a hurry to get back'. The first play in the publication series refers to a peculiarly Bangalore society of elders fixated on the Raj, calling themselves the Empire Loyalists. If it was 'Great Britain' at one time, it was the American Dream later. In the pre-liberalized economy, young people went to extremes to get admission in American colleges and universities. Any university, any course, any location, it was only important to get there first. And yet... there was something so human in their dreams. The plays have stayed away from moralistic social commentary. They embrace the social context of the times. They celebrate the human spirit.

The plays in this Volume can be called the early plays. The stories are set in the period early 'seventies to early 'nineties. The ubiquitous 2-in-1 music system in the plays has to be understood better by contemporary audiences. Two of the plays were early experiments in form: *Salt Licks and Head Start.* They are constructed as 2-part plays. Either part can be performed by itself as a one-act piece. Together they make a full-length play. People have preferred to do the two parts together. End of experiment! *Gold and Silver* was written originally as a radio play at the time of an exchange project with the Royal National Theatre. It was required to be within 45 minutes, so it can be called a long short play. *Sunday Brunch at the Gymkhana* is a proper full-length play of two hours duration. That means theatre groups today will not touch it. It is a true post-Raj Angrezi play. *Action Stations* was written at about the same time, with a similar post-Raj setting, but it has been put into Volume 7. *Evening Shadows* is an original English language adaptation of *Sandhya Chhaya* by the Marathi playwright Jaywant Dalvi. The loneliness of an elderly couple is compounded by the son not returning from America.

While the play scripts in this Volume have been dedicated to various expats who contributed significantly to BLT in the formative years, I would like to add the name of another dramaturg who was responsible for opening up the world of drama to me. Dr James Russell Macphail was the Professor of English Literature and Drama in Madras Christian College, and later the Principal. He was an authority on Shaw, a contemporary of his, and got us to understand Shaw like no other Director has done after that. Way back in the 'fifties he had introduced the work of two dramatists to me, unknown to us at that time, and said that I should look out for them, that they would be the torchbearers of a new wave in Western drama. The names were Samuel Beckett and Bertolt Brecht. I was so fortunate to have had a teacher like JRM.

Many thanks to Asha Mathew, Minti Jain and Murtuza Khetty for the help in editing the manuscripts for this Volume.

**Vijay Padaki**
*Series Editor*

# STAGE DIRECTIONS
with the actor facing the audience

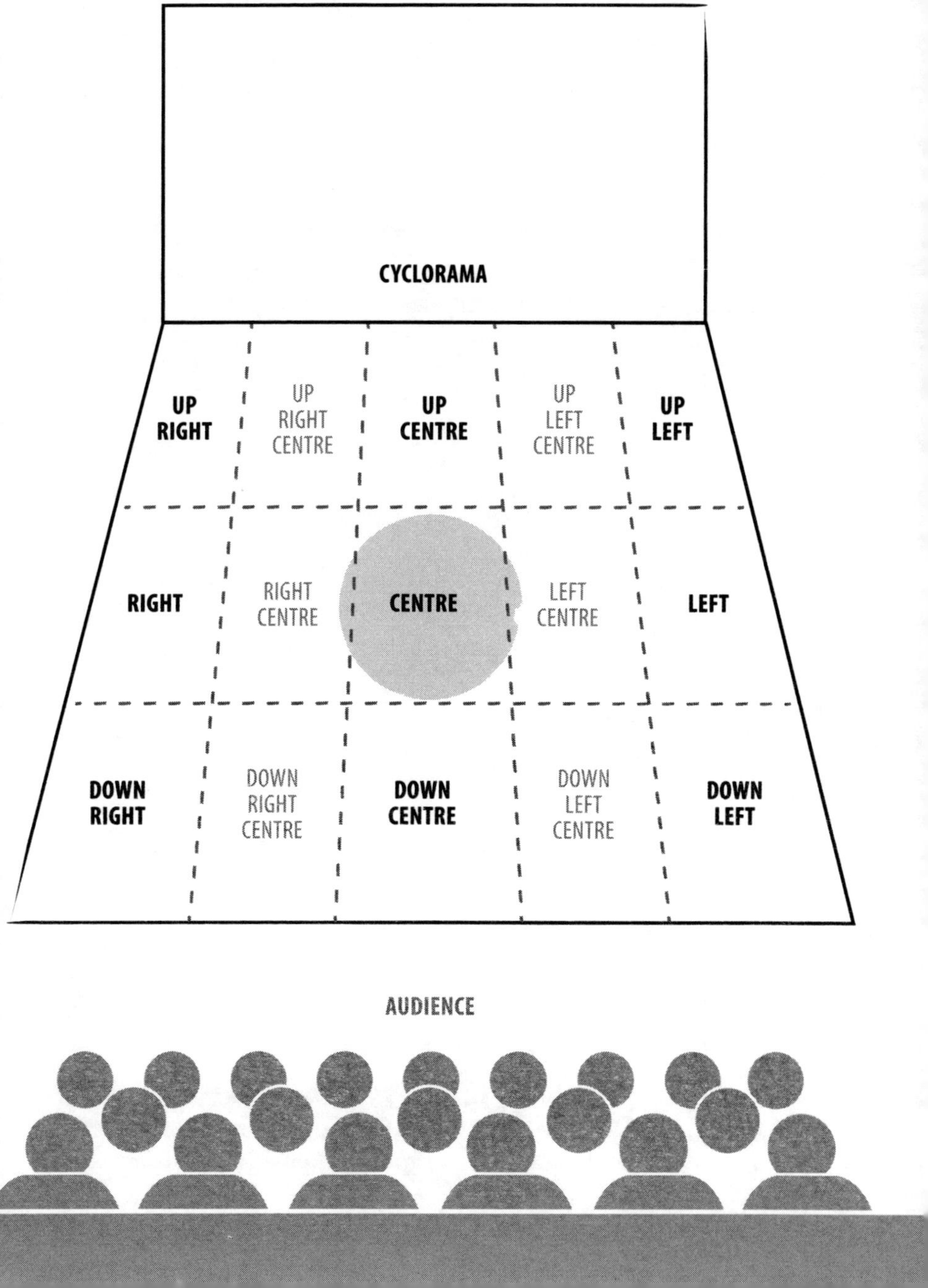

# Sunday Brunch at The Gymkhana

*Rights of Admission Reserved*
***Vijay Padaki***

FOR
**SCOTT AND MARGARET TOD**

## CHARACTERS IN THE PLAY

MUTHU ........ *A steward at the Club*
SEBASTIAN ........ *A bearer*
DAISY AND HARISH ........ *Couple, members of the Club*
SHWETA AND UDIT ........ *Couple, members of the Club*
JINI AND JEEVAN ........ *Couple, members of the Club*
MANI ........ *Executive Secretary of the Club*
KEVIN J MASCARENHAS ........ *A judge*
THELMA ........ *Kevin's wife*

## INTRODUCTION

The script does not provide detailed portraits of the characters in the play. These should become evident in the unfolding of the play. The performing group is encouraged to arrive at its own interpretations. A sensitivity to the social context would be preferable over formula characterisations.

The content of the play might appear familiar to some. It cannot be helped, I suppose. It is the Indian subcontinent gymkhana syndrome. Here is the standard disclaimer: The play is not about any particular club, nor about any particular people, as tempting as it might be to draw some comparisons, and any resemblance...etcetera, etcetera.

The characters of Muthu and Sebastian need special attention. It will be seen that they speak our kind of English, quite fluently, when they are talking to one another. They speak another English when they are talking to members of the club. In readings of this play, this has been recognised as a fascinating feature of the play – Muthu and Sebastian pandering to the needs of the members. Their self-fulfilling prophecies? I have been urged to retain it. It is retained. When Sebastian discovers himself towards the end of the play, his language also changes.

A single intermission is suggested at the end of Scene 6, making Part Two slightly shorter than Part One. The performing group may wish to bring the intermission forward to the end of Scene 5. This will make the second half slightly longer than the first. No more than one intermission should be necessary.

There are four areas of action in the play:

- An indoor space in the Club – with multiple uses.
- The lawn service area of the Club.
- The office of the Club's Executive Secretary.
- The verandah in the home of Justice Kevin J Mascarenhas.

The production should not require elaborate sets, or a realistic depiction of the areas of action. Intelligent use of the available stage space, supported by a good lighting design, should do.

### Language Notes

*Dhamaal:* Ruckus
*Mirch masala:* Chillies and spice. Spicing up
*Zara:* A little
*Dabba:* Box, container
*Choodiyaan:* Bangles.
*Send them bangles:* A mocking expression for men who are not man enough
*Chaddi friends:* From undies. Thick friends
*Tamasha:* A show, drama, usually connoting hullabaloo
*Zanana-mardana:* Separation of women's place from men's place.

# PART ONE

## SCENE 1

***The club: indoor space.***
*In the dark, the sound of a Chairman's gavel striking the table.*

**CHAIRMAN'S VOICE**
Ladies and gentlemen, the counting has just been completed. The vote is clear. The ayes have it.
*(Cheers and cries of hear, hear! accompanied by thumping on tables.)*

**CHAIRMAN'S VOICE**
This meeting is now adjourned. Thank you, ladies and gentlemen, for your kind attendance.
*(The sound of the gathering fades out.*
*The lights come on to reveal an empty top table set up for a meeting. The court of arms of the club is attached to the edge of the table in the middle. Stacks of chairs and other paraphernalia on one side reveal a clearing up process is on. Steward Muthu is instructing Sebastian.)*

**MUTHU**
Use both hands. Lift it slightly, it will come off. That's right. Now, carry it straight to the lounge. Don't stop anywhere. Go straight to the lounge and fix it in its place on the wall. Take some help if you like.

**SEBASTIAN**
This is not my job. I have to be on the lawn. I'm a bearer in this club, not a coolie.

**MUTHU**
Your job is what your steward tells you to do. And he is telling you to hurry up to the lounge. We don't want a blank space on the wall when the lounge starts filling up.

**SEBASTIAN**
With all the cobwebs seen.

**MUTHU**
Yes, remember to wipe the wall clean before fixing it.

**SEBASTIAN**
Can I go to my duty spot directly from there?

**MUTHU**
How much tip money are you going to lose by being five minutes late?

**SEBASTIAN**

The early ones are the thirstiest. And in the greatest hurry.

**MUTHU**

Okay, go on now. Be careful. Hold it with both hands. It's eighty years old, very precious.

**SEBASTIAN** *(As he leaves)*

It's eighty years old, very precious!

*(The lights expand to reveal Jini seated alone in a chair that has not been removed yet. She is joined by Jeevan, who draws up a chair next to her. They sit in silence for a while. Muthu goes up to them.)*

**JEEVAN**

I am sorry I couldn't come in earlier. I was waiting for all of them to leave the hall.

**JINI**

You have heard the verdict, of course.

**MUTHU**

I lock up now, madam. Good evening, sir.

**JINI**

I will leave in a minute, Muthu.

**MUTHU**

No problem, madam. I will come in five-ten minutes after checking bearer attendance.

**JINI**

Thank you, Muthu.

**MUTHU**

Madam... I am sorry.

**JINI**

It's all right, Muthu, you are doing your job. Lock-up time is lock-up time.

**MUTHU**

Not that, madam. About this meeting.

**JINI**

Oh, that.

**MUTHU**

I am sorry, madam.

**JINI**

Why, Muthu?

**MUTHU**

Why, madam?

**JINI**

I mean, why are you sorry?

**MUTHU**

How to answer, madam?

**JINI**

You are sorry, are you not?

**MUTHU**

Never happened like this before.

**JINI**

You are sorry because...

**MUTHU**

It is not good for lady member of club to be treated like that.

**JINI**

Like what? *(The Executive Secretary enters, looking for Muthu.)*

**MANI**

Muthu, please report at once at... *(He sees Jini and Jeevan)*
Oh, you are still here.

**MUTHU**

Excuse me, madam, I have to... You can sit here, madam, no problem. *(He leaves.)*

**JINI**

Good evening, Mr Mani.

**MANI**

I am sorry, you have to vacate the room now.

**JINI**

Good evening, Mr Mani.

**MANI**

You must understand that the rules and customs of the club are not...

**JINI**

It is an honourable custom to return a greeting – honoured in this club too, I hope.

**JEEVAN**

Good evening, Mr Mani.

**MANI**

Good evening. I am sorry, but you have to...

**JINI**

Why, Mr Mani?

**MANI**

Why?

**JINI**

Why are you sorry, Mr Mani?

**MANI**

I don't know what you are getting at, but it must be clear that...

**JINI**

You are sorry, are you not?

**MANI**

The time for your games is over. It is good bye time now. What do you mean am I sorry or not?

**JINI**

Just checking.

**MANI**

I hope you will leave quietly, without creating problems – problems for yourself, really.

**JINI**

I wish to order some drinks and snacks. We will have it here. Will you join us?

**MANI**

The General Body Meeting has just passed a resolution...

**JINI**

The Extraordinary Meeting of the General Body voted on two counts, Mr Mani. First, to reject the resolution proposed by me. Second, to direct the Executive Committee to issue a show cause notice to me as to why my membership should not be terminated.

**MANI**

You cannot order anything from the bar or dining room. And you cannot remain in this room. *(He starts to go)*

**JINI**

I am not an ex-member yet, Mr Mani. I enjoy all the rights and privileges of the club, as dubious as some of them might be, until I am actually declared non-existent.

**MANI**

We shall see.

*(He strides out.*

*Jeevan takes Jini's hand in his. She smiles.*

*Fade out.)*

## SCENE 2

***The Club: The lawn service area***

*Daisy, Harish, Shweta, and Udit are seated around a table. Sebastian is waiting on them.*

**UDIT**

Bring us our order now. There are some others joining us. *(He slips Sebastian a note)* So don't take long.

**SEBASTIAN**

I join one more table?

**SHWETA**

Yes, good idea. *(Sebastian starts to go)*

**UDIT**

No, Sebastian, no need. Just two chairs will do.

**SEBASTIAN**

Yes, sir. *(He starts again)*

**UDIT**

Not just now. There is time. You just get our first order now.

**DAISY**

Please hurry.

**SEBASTIAN**

Yes, madam, I get immediately.

**HARISH**

Immediately after half an hour.

**SEBASTIAN** *(Grinning)*

You watch now, sir. *(He leaves.)*

**SHWETA** *(To Udit)*

How much did you give him?

**UDIT**

Oh, the usual.

**DAISY**

What a way to start the evening.

**SHWETA**

There's more to come. We're shifting indoors after J and J get here.

**HARISH**

What's keeping them, I wonder. They are usually so punctual.

**DAISY**

Frightfully punctual.

**HARISH**

Trying to get a parking space – without a tip, that is.

**UDIT**

Nothing works here without a tip.

**HARISH**

The membership rules say something else.

**UDIT**

It's a big joke. 'No tips to anybody, anywhere.'

**HARISH**

They should just standardise them. It should be clear to everybody exactly what should be paid for what sort of order in which part of the club.

**DAISY**

At what time of the day.

**SHWETA**

And then somebody like Udit will top that with another crisp blue note, and we'll start all over again.

**UDIT**

Okay, okay. You do it your way when you are by yourself. Go by the rule book.

**HARISH**

The rule book of the club is that thick.

**UDIT**

And keeps getting thicker each year.

**HARISH**

Rules are made to be broken – especially if they don't serve a purpose.

**UDIT**

When you want service here, you'll turn to me anyway.

**DAISY**

Fine, Udi, you've made your point.

**HARISH**

Do you or do you not want a table before J and J arrive?

**DAISY**

The point is made! Pah!

**SHWETA**

And let's not get into another one of these... what do you call this... ?

**UDIT**

Fish market arguments...

**HARISH**

Lok Sabha debates...

**DAISY**

Short of hurling chairs and microphones...

**SHWETA**

Let's not get into that, please. Not on an occasion like this. We are here to welcome J-J as new members. Let's all have a nice...

**UDIT**

They are not really new members.

**HARISH**

Neither Jeevan nor Jini.

**SHWETA**

I know. Not new in that sense. But you know what I mean. She was neither here nor there for such a long time. Even after remarrying, she had to wait so long for her membership to be made pukka.

**UDIT**

Couldn't be helped. As a divorcee, she could have asked for her own membership. She didn't.

**DAISY**

Do you think the Club might have... ?

**HARISH**

Not the Club. She. She didn't.

**SHWETA**

Anyway, all that is in the past. The fact is Jini is a good old friend of ours. Jeevan is a good old friend of ours. Jini is now a full member once again. And we are all meeting for a nice evening, a nice dinner, a nice time. So...

**DAISY**

There's Jeevan now. I don't see Jini. Where's Jini?

**SHWETA**

So...

**UDIT**

So, we must make sure we have that table before they join us.

**HARISH**

There's Jini – coming from the billiard room corridor. I thought they were getting here together.

**SHWETA**

So, we make sure we are at the table together after we've got it.

*(Jeevan and Jini enter. They are greeted by the four others. There is warmth in the chatter and the banter. Finally, Daisy speaks up.)*

**DAISY**

What took you so long?

**JINI**
You won't believe this...

**SHWETA**
But Jeev went round and round looking for a parking spot!

**UDIT**
Instead of leaving the car and the keys with the attendant.

**JINI**
No, listen...

**HARISH**
And he was going to take so long that he sent you off to the billiard room for your first lesson.

**JEEVAN**
Actually...

**DAISY**
Actually, you got terribly late getting here, and you were looking for a terribly original excuse.

**JEEVAN**
No, we found a place to park at the rear, and we were going to walk through the lounge area.

**JINI**
We stepped into the men's bar...

**JEEVAN**
Just behind the lounge. We were only going to walk through.

**JINI**
And you should have seen the dhamaal! First, all conversation came to a sudden stop. All joking, all gassing, everything. And then, Jeev made the mistake of going up to one of them...

**JEEVAN**
A Committee member, Sam. Sampath. I was only going to say Hi, and enquire about his recovery from the viral flu last week.

**JINI**
That was it. They pounced on him, all together, a chorus of protests.

**JEEVAN**
How could a woman ever... ?

**JINI**
How dare a woman... ?

**JEEVAN**
How could Jini accompany me in the men's bar?

**JINI**
I tried to explain.

**HARISH**
Jini went into the bar with you?

**JEEVAN**
Not really, we were only...

**UDIT**
It's not allowed. Everybody knows that.

**JINI**
Oh, come on. We were only walking through.

**HARISH**
It's the rule.

**JINI**
Okay, it was a mistake. A first offence, a little goof. Jeev said he was sorry.

**JEEVAN**
We both did.

**JINI**
Did I? Maybe I did. I don't remember. I didn't hear myself. They wouldn't have either... the din there with all that howling and barking and snapping.

**JEEVAN**
It took some time to pacify them.

**JINI**
And the jeering and the quips with double meaning.

**JEEVAN**
Anyway, they agreed to let it pass.

**JINI**
But not let us pass through.

**SHWETA**
You are lucky.

**DAISY**
Somebody could have taken it into his head to make a big thing of it.

**SHWETA**
Anything is possible after two whiskeys.

**JEEVAN**
Jini left immediately.

**DAISY**
It must have been embarrassing.

**JINI**
At the least.

**JEEVAN**
I came through the lounge anyway.

**JINI**

He still doesn't know how Sam is after the viral flu.

**UDIT**

There's Sebastian. *(Calling)* Sebastian! Okay, Jeevan, what will it be? The usual?

**JEEVAN**

Actually...

**JINI**

Being a rather special evening...

**JEEVAN**

We have ordered for a...

**JINI**

For a change... *(Jeevan and Jini stop, look at each other and laugh)*

**JEEVAN**

Go ahead, Jini.

**JINI**

For a change, at least on a special occasion, do you think it would be a good idea for the lady to be asked first?

*(A half apology from Udit, a half successful cover-up from Harish, and a rally round Jini from Daisy and Shweta together.)*

**JEEVAN**

Actually, that won't be necessary.

**JINI**

We have ordered two bottles of champagne.

*(General cheer with appropriate exclamations.)*

**UDIT**

Wah! Champa-gini, with the compliments of J and J.

**HARISH**

Indian or imported?

**UDIT**

Bangalore stuff or asli maal?

*(The girls protest but are overruled by the two men. There is more joking, all fun.)*

**HARISH**

Okay, okay, we need to make sure we have a table first. Why don't you all wait here? Udi and I will go in and look into it.

**UDIT**

And do something about it.

**JEEVAN**

I'll come with you.

**JINI**

Before we start on dinner, can we all get a photo taken?

**UDIT**

Photo? Who has a camera?

**JINI**

I've brought one. It's in my bag.

**HARISH**

Sure. All six of us. We'll ask somebody to take the picture.

**JINI**

Next to the stuffed tiger – in the lounge. We'll all stand behind the stuffed tiger.

**HARISH**

Right. Let's move now. *(The three men go out.)*

**SHWETA**

So... you got your first taste of the membership thing?

**JINI**

Tribal initiation rites.

**DAISY**

Your first lesson.

**JINI**

Obedience school.

**SHWETA**

Anyway, it's all part of the game, I suppose. Nothing we can do about it.

**JINI**

Just learn the hand signals. The signals for 'Sit' or 'Down'. And when you are not allowed in, the hand signal that says 'Stay!'

**SHWETA**

Shake hands!

**JINI**

What a woman does seated and a dog on three legs.

**DAISY**

Have you heard the one about the woman who took her Pomeranian to the vet... ?

**SHWETA**

Complaining about a running nose?

**JINI**

You know, the whole thing is quite comic, really.

**DAISY**

All doggie jokes are. Some are naughty, of course.

**JINI**
No, about the club, I mean.

**SHWETA**
The rules?

**JINI**
The regulations. What you can't do, the don'ts, the no-nos. Thou shalt not, and thus it shall not be.

**SHWETA**
Some of them are funny, I agree. Maybe a hundred years ago...

**DAISY**
When arrogant Brit soldiers and their stuffy Indian chamchas pretended to be rubbing shoulders...

**JINI**
Comic. Really comic.

**DAISY**
You know, I think a lot of people will agree that there are club rules – okay, regulations – that are quite outdated.

**JINI**
Comic.

**SHWETA**
Oh, yes. Any number of jokes about them.

**JINI**
For instance...

**SHWETA**
For instance, at the dining room you simply cannot keep your quarter plate on the right side, even if you are eating roti from it.

**DAISY**
Even if you are right-handed.

**JINI**
Or your glass on your left side.

**DAISY**
Even if you are left-handed. You can easily do a skit on them the next time there is a Variety Nite.

**SHWETA**
Yes, but you know, Daisy, we joke about these things among ourselves, in small groups. It's never talked about in any large group.

**DAISY**
They are planning something on Independence Day. Maybe we should find out.

**SHWETA**

We should try and get a few others to join us. Do you think they will?

**JINI**

Shweta, Daisy, why are club members such carbon copies?

## SCENE 3

***The Club: Office of the Executive Secretary.***

*Muthu is arranging papers for Mani, putting up some of them on priority, putting others down below or away. The discretion and the skill for this have been acquired over at least twenty years, with no mention in his job description. The phone rings. Muthu picks it up.*

**MUTHU**

Secretary office... Yes, sir. Please be on line, sir. *(To Mani)* President on line, sir.

**MANI** *(Springing to life)*

Hello, good morning, sir. Very well, sir, very well... Yes, sir, today is the last date for masonry and painting contract tenders, sir. Twelve noon.

*(Muthu gives him a set of envelopes.)*

We have received six tenders, sir. All kept sealed, sir... What was the name, sir? I'm sorry, sir, but two covers don't have the contractors' names. Maybe... Okay, sir, no problem. Do you want the names of the four others, sir? No problem, sir. It is still 10:30. I can even wait till lunch time, sir. Yes, sir... Sir, the agenda papers for the next Committee meeting were ready two days ago.

*(Muthu hands him a set of papers.)*

No problem, sir, I'll send them to your residence for signatures... Yes, sir, I will include it with the papers... Five nominations, sir.

*(Muthu hands him a set of forms.)*

One outstation gentleman, sir, IAS officer on central posting. Four local, family members, sir... Next Friday, sir? Right-o, sir, I will inform the other Committee members... Yes, sir, there is one other matter for the Committee.

*(Muthu hands him a folder)*

There are six offers of donations, sir... Yes, sir, all new companies in Bangalore, all foreign companies, sir... Don't put up in meeting, sir? Okay, okay, sir... Yes, sir. Straight away, sir.

*(He puts the receiver down and speaks to Muthu)*

You heard that, Muthu? Next Friday. Make the usual arrangements in the President's office. Five o'clock sharp.

**MUTHU**

Five members, sir?

**MANI**

Not five members, Muthu. Five candidates for membership.

**MUTHU**

Sorry, sir. Five candidates.

**MANI**

Three men and two women. You won't recognize them on Friday. They will bathe and spray their underarms and dress smartly. They will speak with honey on their tongues from the moment they enter the club. They will have smiles fixed on their faces for four hours, till their membership is announced by the Committee. And then...

**MUTHU**

Sir is having bad experience.

**MANI**

Ten years, Muthu, I have seen a lot in ten years. Not like those Honorary Secretaries. They come and they go – in today, out tomorrow. They attend meetings, give their vote of thanks. They pose in group photographs. They can't even prepare minutes of meetings. They sign on minutes, I prepare. Honorary Secretaries, they come and go. The bloody Executive Secretary runs the show.

**MUTHU**

You know club like own house backside, sir. You are here long time.

**MANI**

Not as long as you, Muthu. How long have you been in the club? Fifteen years? Twenty years?

**MUTHU**

Oh, twenty-five, thirty years, sir. Don't know, don't remember. Maybe thirty-five years, sir. I join as tennis court boy when father was marker.

**MANI**

Those days were good, no? Club members must have been real gentlemen those days.

**MUTHU**

Also good ladies, sir.

**MANI**

Not like the kachda people nowadays – all show outside, bloody city market mentality inside. What do you say, Muthu?

**MUTHU**

What to say, sir?

**MANI**

You see their real colours on Sundays – Sundays and holidays – at the parking area, in the lawn service, in the dining room, the billiard room, the bar, everywhere. Everybody thinks he is the brother-in-law of the Maharajah's son-in-law.

**MUTHU**

Some people like that, sir. Some people good. *(Sebastian comes in and goes straight to Muthu. He notices Mani and controls himself.)*

**SEBASTIAN**

They said you were in Secretary sir's room... Sorry, sir, good evening, sir...

**MUTHU**

What are you doing here?

**SEBASTIAN**

What I am doing here? Talking to you.

**MUTHU**

You should be on bearer duty.

**SEBASTIAN**

I am on bearer duty.

**MUTHU**

Here?

**SEBASTIAN**

Here.

**MUTHU**

Sebastian, the members will be waiting. They will get impatient, annoyed.

**SEBASTIAN**

They are impatient. They are annoyed.

**MUTHU**

What?

**MANI**

Sebastian, get back to your service area at once!

**SEBASTIAN**

You are ordering me, sir?

**MANI**

That is an order.

**SEBASTIAN**

Please, you give in writing, sir.

**MANI**

What? You are telling me...

**SEBASTIAN**

I am telling, my job is taking order from Steward Muthu. You give order you come through proper channel. Or you talk to Union.

**MANI**

Your duty is to the club first. The club service comes first.

**SEBASTIAN**

See, Secretary sir, everybody having duty serving club. You are giving fifty tables – total fifty tables. You are giving admission five hundred members. How they will fit? On my head, anh? Everyday more members. Coming like babies in Mother India. There must be some family planning or no?

**MANI**

Sebastian, I am warning you. If you don't go back to the service area at once, I will have to take action.

**SEBASTIAN**

You take action, sir?

**MANI**

Disciplinary action.

**SEBASTIAN**

Action for what, sir?

**MANI**

Disobedience. Neglecting duty.

**SEBASTIAN**

You are having proof, sir?

**MANI**

I have a witness here, Muthu.

**MUTHU** *(Acutely embarrassed)*

Very sorry, sir... you leave now. I take care...

**SEBASTIAN**

Yes, you leave, Secretary sir. This not good time discuss club management matter – like spending four lakh rupees on new block renovation. That is new building, no? Only five years.

**MANI**

None of your business!

**SEBASTIAN**

And choosing masonry-painting contractor for renovation job. Whose business, sir? *(Mani storms out. Sebastian calls after him)*

We are all doing duty, sir!

**MUTHU**

Sebastian, you have hot coals in your head. Always overheated.

**SEBASTIAN** *(Grinning)*

You should know how to put these buggers in their place.

**MUTHU**

You'll go back to your duty now?

**SEBASTIAN**
Of course I'll go back. Who said I was not going back.

**MUTHU**
They will be waiting.

**SEBASTIAN**
Good if they wait a little, no?

## SCENE 4

***The Club: The lawn service***
*Daisy, Shweta, and Jini are at a table.*

**JINI**
Yesss!

**SHWETA**
What do we call the skit?

**DAISY:**
We must give it a nice catchy name.

**SHWETA**
How about 'What Are Big Boys Made Of?'

**DAISY**
How about 'Puppy Dog Tails?'

**JINI**
The skit is not only about men's hang-ups, you know.

**DAISY**
That's right. It's about us too.

**JINI**
Not just us as of now, but what we ought to be.

**SHWETA**
With our own mirch masala.

**DAISY**
What would they do without our masala dabba?

**SHWETA**
That's it. We could call the skit 'Masala Dabba'.

**DAISY**
If Nisha Singh joins us, we can call it the Bangalore Spice Girls' Show.

**SHWETA**
The Bangalore Spice Girls present Masala Dabba?

**DAISY**
Too much copycat. We should avoid the name Spice Girls.

**JINI**
Turn it around. 'Girls spice'. As a single word, girlspice.

**SHWETA**
We are spending too much time on the name. We can take a final shot later on.

**DAISY**
'The Girlspice Bar'! That sounds good.

**SHWETA**
Okay, we can think about that.

**JINI**
Better than 'The Millennium Bar'.

**SHWETA**
Right now we must think about the end. The ending is weak.

**JINI**
Actually, the entire second half needs reworking.

**DAISY**
The first half is great!

**SHWETA**
Okay, we have a 'Women Only' bar. We can give it a nice name later on. Jini's Girlspice sounds good. We have women members in the bar. We have a woman bartender.

**DAISY**
And we have a pretty looking boy-man serving peanuts and chips at tables.

**SHWETA**
A proper that type boy-man.

**DAISY**
I know who you have in mind to play the part! *(They giggle)*

**SHWETA**
The way he walks up to the table and says, 'Good evening, ladies. And how are we this evening?'

**JINI**
That's another detail we can come back to later.

**DAISY**
About the boy barmaid?

**JINI**
No, I mean about the skit picking on people. Also, we can think about whether a man plays that part or one of the girls plays the part of a – what did you call it – a boy barmaid.

**SHWETA**

Or it's a character – a girl who wants to cross dress as a man, and the Girlspice bar allows her to do it.

**JINI**

An interesting angle.

**DAISY**

Can I play the part? Can I?

**SHWETA**

And you'll dress and talk like... ?

**DAISY**

Three guesses.

**SHWETA**

Not Harish, I'm sure.

**DAISY**

Idea achcha, but zara practical difficulty.

**SHWETA**

Not Udit, I hope.

**DAISY**

Zara technical hitch. How will I get his... ?

**JINI**

Zara concentration, please.

**SHWETA**

I think we should leave the opening scene intact. The bar scene in the evening.

**DAISY**

Enter Jini with Jeevan. We will all pounce on them. How dare Jeevan step into the Women's Bar!

**SHWETA**

We will surround Jini and give her a proper treatment.

**DAISY**

With jokes about Jeevan, double meanings and all.

**JINI**

Who will play the part of Jeevan?

**DAISY**

Good question.

**JINI**

Actually, it may not be a good idea to refer to Jeevan and me directly. It can be misinterpreted.

**SHWETA**

She is right. This is not a skit about – you know – what do we call it?

**DAISY**

A complaint – a grievance.

**SHWETA**

Right. No particular grievance. It is about the system, that is so...

**JINI**

Comic

**SHWETA**

That's right. So we'll find a way to do that scene without suggesting that it is about Jini and Jeevan.

**DAISY**

Do we keep the joke about a set of bangles for the husband?

**SHWETA**

Not in that way. It is too common, no? Every TV serial has the joke about choodiyaan bhej do saale ko.

**JINI**

Whatever we do, we should not end up making fun of women ourselves – you know, reinforcing silly ideas about women and how they are supposed to be.

**SHWETA**

Good point. We need a link now between the first and second scenes.

**DAISY**

The second scene should really hit them! The Independence Day floor show at the Women's Bar.

**SHWETA**

Okay, so we will have the huge cake rolled into the bar.

**DAISY**

All the girls singing a specially composed verse of Surangani.

**SHWETA**

And out of the cake will pop out – tantarra...

**DAISY**

Tantarra tantarra tantarra...

**JINI**

Look, the idea is absolutely terrific. The build-up and the surprise package inside the giant cake will definitely have them falling off their seats. But...

**SHWETA**

They won't think it's too bold?

**JINI**

They shouldn't. We don't think it's too bold, do we? That's not the point. The point is to make it work. We have to handle it like a military mission.

**SHWETA**

That's the challenge – keeping it top secret. Till it is actually done.

**DAISY**

That, and the link to the opening scene.

**JINI**

That, and taking the joke forward. And bringing the skit to a proper end.

**DAISY**

You mean a message or something?

**SHWETA**

Not really a message, you know. Not like giving generously to cyclone relief in West Bengal.

**JINI**

Floods in West Bengal. Cyclones in Orissa.

**DAISY**

Wherever. But not a message.

**SHWETA**

We can't do something like that. We are not good at that.

**DAISY**

Anyway, it is for Independence Day.

**SHWETA**

The link between the first and second scenes can come from that, you know.

**DAISY**

From what?

**SHWETA**

From Independence Day. We can get the women members in the bar to make an offer to Jini and Jeevan...

**JINI**

Or whoever...

**SHWETA**

Or whoever, whichever the couple walking into the bar – they can be made an offer. They will be excused if they agree to do something the women decide.

**JINI**

Like a game of dare.

**DAISY**

If they choose not to, they will be given due punishment.

**SHWETA**

As per the rules and regulations of the Women's Bar.

**DAISY**

Fair chance. Better than the dumb customs of the Men's Bar.

**JINI**

Right. I think it's falling into place. *(The three girls feel good about the plan. There is great enthusiasm about starting work on it. Harish and Udit enter.)*

**HARISH**

Let's go. It's all fixed up. *(Shweta and Daisy can't help grinning.)* What's the joke?

**JINI**

Where is Jeev?

**UDIT**

He is holding the table. What's the joke?

**JINI**

Well...

**SHWETA**

We were planning a skit.

**UDIT**

A skit?

**DAISY**

For Independence Day. For the evening variety show on Independence Day.

**HARISH**

You are sure you want to do something like that?

**UDIT**

What is the skit about?

**DAISY**

It is about...

**SHWETA**

It is about us. It is about laughing at ourselves.

**UDIT**

Yourselves or all of us?

**SHWETA**

Well, you could say it is mostly about us, but...

**HARISH**

Come on, come on, let's not waste time on silly things now. We have to place our orders still. *(He leaves)*

**UDIT**

That's right. Don't get into things that are a waste of time. Let's go now.

**SHWETA**

You go ahead, Udit. We will sign up here and come. Sebastian is coming with the bill.

**UDIT**

Okay, but hurry up. *(He leaves)*

**DAISY**

What do we do now?

**JINI**

We could write a skit on three women plotting to do a skit without the knowledge of their husbands.

**SHWETA**

And their husbands finding out.

## SCENE 5

***The Club: Indoor space***

*In the dark, the sound of clapping and applause, followed by the voice of a master of ceremonies.*

**VOICE**

And finally, ladies and gentlemen, before we conclude the Independence Day Variety Show, and move on to the lawn for the very special buffet, spread out for us by the club kitchen staff, please join me in showing your appreciation for all the effort and all the talent that has gone into this evening's show. Let's hear it from there. *(Applause)*

We know, we have always known it, and it really does not need to be stated, that your club has lots and lots of talent in its membership. *(Applause)*

We have given the State and the country some of the finest sportsmen in billiards, squash, and tennis. *(Applause)*

We have produced great toastmasters and comperes. And now we know, as if there was any need for proof, that we have with us some fantastic talent in song and dance and drama as well. *(Applause)*

Ladies and gentlemen, it gives me great pleasure to announce the President's award, a very special hamper that you see the boys bringing on to the stage... my, my, look at the size of the hamper, I wonder what treasures the pretty packaging holds within... it gives me very great pleasure indeed to announce the winner of the President's award. Ladies and gentlemen, could there be any guesses? Could there be any doubt? The President's award for the best performance in the Independence Day Variety Show goes to... the skit, 'Girlspice Bar'! *(Long applause)*

Thank you, thank you, ladies and gentlemen. I now invite the ladies team that put up the skit to come up to the stage and receive the award from the President. *(Applause and fade out. The lights come on to reveal Jini and Jeevan as in the first scene.)*

**JEEVAN**

What do we do now?

**JINI**

We have dinner.

**JEEVAN**

Very funny.

**JINI**

No grub at home. So I suppose we eat out.

**JEEVAN**

We can get a bite at KK's.

**JINI**

Or we can eat here.

**JEEVAN**

At the club? You must be... I'm sorry, but I didn't think...

**JINI**

Think what?

**JEEVAN**

Think of that – eating at the club.

**JINI**

Shall we?

**JEEVAN**

Will we get a table?

**JINI**

You mean, will we be served.

**JEEVAN**

Not exactly...

**JINI**

Wouldn't it be a really funny sight? Tables all around us, lots of people, everybody enjoying themselves, chatting, eating, drinking, backslapping, some squealing, some guffawing, and in the middle of this ocean of fun and laughter, an island... Two shipwrecked survivors seated on two sides of an empty table, waiting... Waiting for what?

**JEEVAN**

We still have friends in the club, you know.

**JINI**

We do? Where are they? I don't see them.

**JEEVAN**
They might not be here, in this room...

**JINI**
Where we think it would be nice to see them.

**JEEVAN**
But I am sure when we step out into the lounge...

**JINI**
Where they don't think it would be nice to be seen.

**JEEVAN**
Jini, I haven't seen you like this before. I haven't...

**JINI**
Like what?

**JEEVAN**
Like this. You sound so different – so unlike yourself.

**JINI**
Isn't it best to say what you feel? And not pretend to be saying something you don't feel?

**JEEVAN**
You are hurt.

**JINI**
You found out! Is it wrong to be hurt? Is it wrong to feel hurt over what has happened in the last one hour? The last two weeks? The last three months?

**JEEVAN**
Things moved really fast, didn't they?

**JINI**
We moved fast. Other things just followed.

**JEEVAN**
Tell me – I know you have answered this question before – but tell me again...

**JINI**
Do I have any regrets?

**JEEVAN**
Was it worth it?

**JINI**
Worth what?

**JEEVAN**
All that you have had to go through.

**JINI**
We. What we have gone through.

**JEEVAN**
Was it worth it?

**JINI**
Let us take stock. The wrath of the club management – an irritation, but not really a problem. They did what they were expected to do. That's gymkhana. The service at the club – the bearers don't really care. They have their daily targets in tips to meet.

**JEEVAN**
They have been nice to us. We will see what happens tomorrow.

**JINI**
Friends – yes, we have lost friends. But then, you say we still have some friends left. I'll take your word for it.

**JEEVAN**
They will be fewer, but hopefully closer.

**JINI**
Hopefully. Face – have we lost face? That one I cannot answer readily.

**JEEVAN**
That was the intention of the resolution passed today – to make us lose face.

**JINI**
We should take time to react to that. We may too easily do something because we think we have lost face.

**JEEVAN**
On the other hand...

**JINI**
On the other hand, there are points gained.

**JEEVAN**
That's Jini!

**JINI**
We shouldn't lose sight of the points gained. The system has been shaken. The legacy has been opened up to a fresh examination.

**JEEVAN**
That's my Jini!

**JINI**
And you know something? The best way to look at things afresh is to get ourselves to laugh at them first.

**JEEVAN**
It all started with that Independence Day skit, didn't it?

**JINI**
It won a prize, didn't it?

**JEEVAN**

Who should have ever imagined that evening that...

*(They laugh. He holds out his arms. They embrace. She sobs softly in his arms. Muthu enters quietly, watches for a few moments, and coughs politely.)*

**JEEVAN**

Hello, Muthu.

**MUTHU**

Excuse me, sir, ma'am.

**JINI**

It's all right, Muthu. Do you need something from here?

**JEEVAN**

We are leaving now, Muthu.

**MUTHU**

No, sir, you stay. No problem. This message for you.

*(Hands Jini an envelope and waits)*

**JINI**

Thank you, Muthu.

**MUTHU**

Ma'am, sir, I want...

**JEEVAN**

Yes, Muthu?

**MUTHU**

I am saying... I pray for you. Good night, sir, ma'am.

*(He leaves. Jini and Jeevan watch him go, moved. Jini opens the envelope.)*

**JINI**

It is from Kevin Mascarenhas.

**JEEVAN**

Justice Mascarenhas?

**JINI**

Once the President. He says he could not attend the Extraordinary General Meeting today. He has heard about the outcome... He has invited us to meet him at his home to talk about it.

## SCENE 6

***The home of Justice Kevin Joseph Mascarenhas.***

*The verandah. It is late afternoon, tea time. With him are his wife, Thelma, and Jeevan and Jini. There is a big spread on the table. The good judge speaks as he eats. Jini and Jeevan are satisfied with a single sandwich each. Thelma pours tea for them and finds a plate and a seat for herself.*

**THELMA**

Are you sure?

**JEEVAN**

Quite sure, thank you.

**THELMA**

And you, Jini?

**JINI**

Thank you aunty. We had a late lunch.

**JEEVAN**

And a heavy lunch.

**JINI**

This is fine, thanks.

**JUDGE**

You don't mind if I...

**JINI**

Oh, please go ahead, Kevin uncle.

**THELMA**

Tea time is very special in this house, you know.

**JUDGE**

A proper tea.

**THELMA**

He doesn't have a proper lunch. Just a cup of tea and a snack. A single bonda or vada or whatever is on at the time. All fried stuff anyway.

**JUDGE**

A proper tea is the second most important meal of the day.

**THELMA**

You know the sort of breakfast Kevin has. For over twenty-five years now.

**JUDGE**

A proper breakfast, a light lunch, a proper tea, and a light supper. Keeps your body intact, and your mind active.

**THELMA**

In any case, he will not have any intake in the two hours before going to bed.

**JUDGE**

Except liquids.

**JINI**

How do you manage eating out and parties, uncle?

**JEEVAN**

Nobody even mentions food before ten-thirty or eleven.

**THELMA**

Simple. No intake after half past nine.

**JUDGE**

Except liquids. *(Pause. They all look at the Justice.)*

**THELMA**

Actually most people we know are very understanding. They know. They give Kevin a sneak preview by about eight-thirty or nine.

**JINI**

I know. Mummy always talks about her kitchen being open only to two persons – her own mum and Kevin uncle.

**THELMA**

How is she now, after her return from LA? Gosh, I haven't seen her in over three months.

**JINI**

She's well, aunty. A bit exhausted, but fine.

**THELMA**

And Dicky and the baby? I don't even know her name.

**JINI**

They returned home within three days. You know how it is there. You must register a name before you leave the maternity. She is called Christina Gloria.

**JUDGE**

After her grandmother, of course.

**JINI**

That's right. *(Pause. They look at the Justice.)* I have some pictures from the e-mail. I'll bring them with me the next time.

**THELMA**

Gosh, pictures by e-mail! Can't get used to all this easily.

**JINI**

Not the same as a nice glossy print, of course.

**JUDGE**
Never the same. How can it ever be the same?

**JEEVAN**
It is possible. Only it would cost much more.

**THELMA**
Is it really possible?

**JEEVAN**
It is. But you need to put much more into your computer. At both ends – in sending and in receiving. That's the way we receive design prints in the office.

**THELMA**
In colour?

**JEEVAN**
All colours, all shades, perfectly faithful. *(Pause. They look at the Justice.)*

**JUDGE**
Right! We can begin, I believe. The body has been attended to, the mind is awake again. Where do we begin?

**JINI**
I don't know, uncle. Where do you want us to begin?

**THELMA**
You know, Jini, Kevin and I were very, very upset when we heard. Upset and sorry for you. How could they do something like that?

**JUDGE**
What is the update? Have there been developments since... ?

**THELMA**
Why didn't you get in touch with us, dear? You know we hardly ever come to the club ourselves.

**JEEVAN**
But uncle was a President once.

**THELMA**
That was a long time ago. They made him President because they...

**JUDGE**
Because they couldn't find anybody else. Now...

**THELMA**
You know you are welcome any time here. It must have been so hard, you must have felt so low.

**JUDGE**
Thelma, they are here talking about this club thing not because you and Jini's mum were chaddi friends in school, not because we are friends, but

because I invited Jini and Jeevan here. Yes, Jeevan, you too. You might not have realised it yet, but you are also a key figure in this case.

**JEEVAN**

I had a vague sort of expectation about that.

**THELMA**

I am sorry, dear. I was only saying that you and I also care for Jini. Jini and Jeevan, both.

**JUDGE**

We do. That needs no statement. But we are meeting now to discuss business. So...

**JINI**

So, you tell us, uncle. Where do we begin? What do you want from us?

**JUDGE**

The update first.

**JINI**

You know about the Extraordinary General Meeting and what happened there.

**JUDGE**

I know about that. I want to know a bit more about what happened before that meeting, the events leading up to it. And, of course, the events after the EGM, the developments since then.

**JEEVAN**

The EGM took only two decisions. The first was a vote against the resolution proposed by Jini.

**JINI**

Properly processed, proposed, and seconded...

**JEEVAN**

By Jini and me.

**JINI**

By due process, and submitted to the Secretary as required.

**JUDGE**

Was there a quorum at the meeting?

**JEEVAN**

I suppose so... I don't know.

**JUDGE**

Was there a head count? Were signatures taken in the register?

**JINI**

We can find out.

**JUDGE**

You can, but we should find out without any suspicion of your wanting to find out.

**JEEVAN**

You mean they might...

**JUDGE**

I am not saying they would or they did. They might have, they might not have. I am only saying that some simple facts need to be established.

**JINI**

How do we find out?

**JUDGE**

We will find a way. There were two decisions, you say.

**JEEVAN**

Yes, the first on...

**JUDGE**

But it was a single-point agenda for the EGM. You remember the notice for the EGM?

**JINI**

Yes, uncle.

**THELMA**

I remember too. That's when I tried to call you, to find out what on earth was happening.

**JUDGE**

A single-point agenda. To either accept or reject the resolution proposed by you, after due debate and discussion.

**THELMA**

But why an extraordinary general body meeting for that?

**JEEVAN**

That is what surprised us too. We had no idea the Committee was going to call a whole general body meeting for something like...

**THELMA**

Gosh, I don't know when we had an EGM last. Must have been fifteen years ago.

**JUDGE**

Do you remember what it was for?

**THELMA**

No, dear. I don't think I do.

**JUDGE**

It was to discuss whether women members could be on the Managing Committee.

**THELMA**

Oh, yes, that one.

**JUDGE**

And the decision? You remember that? The argument was that the interests of women and children are already well attended to by the present set-up.

**THELMA**

That wasn't untrue. At least not at that time. Were you an office bearer then?

**JUDGE**

Anyway, the question that could be raised – I am not very sure just now, we'll have to look into it – the question could be raised, Was it proper for the EGM to vote for a show cause notice to you?

**JEEVAN**

Did the second vote not follow from the first?

**JUDGE**

Not by due process, no.

**JINI**

I haven't followed this, uncle.

**JUDGE**

It's like this, sweetie. When the general body elects a Managing Committee, it means the members give the committee a mandate to take decisions connected with the functioning of the club, but within the boundaries of the constitution of the club. You have seen the club's MOA I suppose – the Memorandum of Association and by-laws – the constitution.

**JINI**

I got to see it only when all the tamasha got serious.

**JUDGE**

Every member is supposed to get a copy. Every member should get to read it. Now, if there is a need felt at any time to re-examine the constitution itself – for an even better functioning of the club – there must be a way for all members to know about the proposed reforms, and an opportunity for all members to express their opinion and influence the final decision. That is why such proposals call for a resolution in a general body meeting, with enough notice given to all members to attend the meeting if they have something to say about it.

**JINI**

That was done, all right. There was a three-week notice given for the EGM.

**JUDGE**

For the resolution. And what was the resolution proposed by you?

**JINI**

To scrap the rule forbidding women to enter the men's bar – to allow men and women to be in the bar as equals.

**JUDGE**

So?

**JINI**

That was it. That was the proposal, resolution, whatever else they want to call it.

**JUDGE**

So? How did the EGM take a vote on giving the author of the resolution a show cause notice?

**JEEVAN**

After the vote rejecting the resolution, a proposal was made by a member, I am told, to take some suitable action – a disciplinary action they called it, I think – some sort of action to let Jini know, Jini and all club members, that the club expects everybody to conform. They must conduct themselves in line with respected customs and traditions.

**JUDGE**

A very noble intention indeed. We do exactly that with our children at home, and with other people's children in a school. But...

**THELMA**

You think the actions of the Committee can be contested, dear?

**JUDGE**

I am not saying that. Not just yet. I am only trying to get Jini and Jeevan to be alert, to think through the situation logically, instead of being overrun by despair.

**JINI**

You are right, uncle. Up to the time of the EGM, we were full of josh about the reform we thought we were going to bring about. A sort of turn-of-the-century new climate in the club.

**JEEVAN**

We had many on our side, people who thought it was high time something like this was done.

**JINI**

We thought we had many on our side.

**JEEVAN**

Somehow, we don't know why, after the EGM, it has not been the same.

**JINI**

As you said, uncle, maybe we are not thinking clearly enough about this now.

**THELMA**

Cheer up, Jini. It will work out well in the end. I am sure it will. Kevin will see you through. What do you say, Kevin?

**JUDGE**

That comes later. Right now, we must take note of things that need to be looked at a bit more closely.

**JEEVAN**

The first was the quorum business. What others?

**JUDGE**

Item two. The basis for the second decision at the EGM – to issue a show cause notice to Jini.

**JEEVAN**

What if it is a duly recorded proposal at the EGM?

**JINI**

Duly proposed and seconded. I think that's the way it happened.

**JUDGE**

The principle of the thing! A floor resolution of that kind means the club is attempting to define for itself what good, disciplined behaviour is, and what indiscipline is. Should all members not have an opportunity to take part in the discussion?

**JINI**

But what if there was indeed a quorum?

**JUDGE**

It means that those who attended were interested in expressing their opinion on the resolution – and only that – as informed by the notice. That is 33 per cent of the membership. What if the remaining 67 per cent have opinions on the second decision taken, the show cause notice business, but have not had the opportunity to express them?

**JEEVAN**

Does that mean that the second decision at the EGM was – what's the word – not in order?

**JUDGE**

Maybe. Maybe not. We have to see. Item three. Did this really need an extraordinary general meeting?

**JINI**

It did not?

**JUDGE**

Did it? Worth thinking about that? The question is, who called the EGM? Did you?

**JINI**

No, of course not.

**JUDGE**

I didn't think you did. It was called by... ?

**JINI**

I don't know. The Committee, I suppose.

**THELMA**

You were only asked to put your proposal down formally in the form of a resolution.

**JINI**

By the Secretary, yes.

**JUDGE**

So the next question is, why an EGM? What was so grave and urgent about your proposal? Could it not have been discussed in the next AGM – the regular, annual general body meeting?

**JEEVAN**

It could, I am sure.

**JUDGE**

Is it not possible that an EGM might have been called... for what? Not for the first decision, but actually for the second decision?

**THELMA**

Gosh, Kevin, are you saying the Committee might have... ?

**JUDGE**

Am I saying that?

**THELMA**

No, you are not, but...

**JINI**

All he is saying, aunty, is that the second decision might not have been proper. Right, uncle?

**JUDGE**

Good thinking, sweetie!

**JEEVAN**

There might have been motives, there might not have been.

**JUDGE**

Right again. Item four. This one is more basic. This business of women not entering the men's bar – is it really a constitutional matter?

**JINI**

Meaning?

**JUDGE**

We must be clear about the distinction between customs and traditions on the one hand, and rules and regulations on the other hand. And, further, both of these things can be different from constitutional matters. You see, the law permits an association that is formed – and the club is one such association – to frame its own rules and regulations in line with its constitution.

**JEEVAN**

Forbidding the presence of women in some areas of the club – what would you call that?

**JUDGE**

Worth looking at? If it is there somewhere in print, it would be called a regulation. A don't in a set of do's and don'ts.

**JEEVAN**

And if it is not in print?

**JUDGE**

Then it is not in the realm of Rules and Regulations.

**JINI**

You mean... ?

**JUDGE**

However, there could be an interpretation of a constitutional guideline that is adopted as a rule or a regulation without it being in print. That is a tricky one, but it may hold some water.

**JINI**

If the constitution...

**JUDGE**

If the constitution has written into it a zanana-mardana distinction somewhere.

**JINI**

But that's preposterous!

**JUDGE**

An anachronism, perhaps, but not preposterous.

**JEEVAN**

Can it not be challenged?

**JUDGE**

First of all, we don't know – not as yet – if there is some such provision in the constitution, something that can be interpreted on those lines.

**JINI**

If there is?

**JUDGE**
If there is, it may be challenged not as a club-related dispute per se, but as a matter of wider social justice. This is usually done through a public interest litigation.

**JEEVAN**
So, it can be challenged?

**JUDGE**
Of course, it can be. If it carries, you can be sure that you have won. But you cannot be sure that the Committee or the Secretary has 'lost', not in the usual sense of losing a case.

**JINI**
Why not?

**JUDGE**
Because it can be argued that they were acting in accordance with the constitutional provision as given to them, and in good faith. Unless...

**JEEVAN**
Unless there is reason to believe that they did this with the intention of harming Jini?

**JUDGE**
Malevolent intention. Not easy to establish, but yes, that's the line.

**JINI**
What do you say, uncle? Is it worth going to battle over this, or should we... ?

**JUDGE**
Should you what? Give up? I'm afraid only you can answer that question for yourself.

**THELMA**
Kevin, they will value your advice. She is seeking your advice – on what she should do.

**JUDGE**
Ask yourself another question. What would happen if you did not go to battle?

**JINI**
I don't know. I have to think about that.

**JUDGE**
Do. Also think about how many people would benefit, and in what way, if you gave up. Who would be those people? What kinds of people? And if you did fight and win, who then would benefit? What kinds of people? How many?

**JEEVAN**
Right now it is difficult for us to see crowds cheering our victory.

**JUDGE**
Your turn, Thelma.

**THELMA**
Jini, dear, you know Kevin. He will not admit it, but he is actually telling you what to do without calling it advice.

**JUDGE**
Are you sure you are not getting her to do something by putting my name to it?

**THELMA**
Oh, shut up Kevin. Jini, all I can say is, don't despair. Take time to think about it, by all means do, but when you decide to act...

**JINI**
Go to battle?

**THELMA**
Go to battle – if you decide to go to battle, you can be sure you have both Kevin and me with you. Call us for any help, any time. But you understand, I'm sure, that Kevin can put on his other cap and act only when somebody decides to stand up and voice a question.

**JINI**
Oh, thank you so much, aunty.

**THELMA**
Do you remember the case, two years ago, of the unauthorised construction of a shrine, and an encroachment to boot?

**JEEVAN**
The rioting and the curfew?

**THELMA**
Yes, that one. Well, somebody had to stick his neck out and say sorry, this cannot be, it won't do.

**JUDGE**
It was also blowing a whistle. The so-called shrine was not just religious zeal, as it turned out.

**THELMA**
Whatever. The important thing was that somebody did it.

**JEEVAN**
Or there would be hundreds more of such encroachments by now.

**JUDGE**
There already were!

**THELMA**
Hopefully they will think ten times before trying something like that again.

**JEEVAN**
Hopefully.

**THELMA**
I don't know you as one who gives up, Jini. Do think about it seriously. What do you say, Kevin?

**JUDGE**
I can only repeat what I said earlier. Think of the consequences of giving up.

**THELMA**
Think of what else may be enforced in the name of constitutional correctness. You cannot wear Kolhapuri slippers unless you wear socks. You cannot wear a dhoti unless you wear a tie.

**JEEVAN**
In twenty-first century India.

**THELMA**
Exactly. What next? Where do you draw the line?

**JINI**
Thank you, aunty. Thank you, uncle. I certainly feel much less shaky now. I promise you I will think about the next steps seriously. Really seriously.

**JUDGE**
You haven't completed your report.

**JINI**
Report?

**JUDGE**
The update. What developments after the EGM?

**JINI**
Oh, didn't I tell you? The show cause notice was issued.

**JUDGE**
It was?

**THELMA**
Oh dear, oh dear.

**JUDGE**
When?

**JINI**
Two weeks ago.

**JUDGE**
Two weeks already?

**JINI**
I have till the end of this week to reply.

# PART TWO

## SCENE 7

***The Club: the Secretary's office***
*In the dark, the voice of Mani.*

**MANI**

Yes, sir... yes, sir... Definitely not, sir, I will not give them any phone numbers – home, office, mobile, nothing... Sir, five people on the phone, and one came personally... Sir, three from English papers, one local, and one from a women's magazine... Already done, sir. All committee members have been informed. Nobody will give any interview or make any statement.

*(The lights come on. Mani is seen standing, nervous, talking on the phone.)*

Only the President, yes sir... Only you, or only with your prior approval and permission... Strictly, sir, definitely... Sir, I don't know how it happened. He said he was a landscape design consultant and contractor. He wanted to know if the Club would like to enter the Republic Day garden competition... No, sir, I did not tell him anything sir. I only said we can consider his offer... The landscaping offer, sir, to win the prize. But I told him clearly that he has to put up a proposal, and meet you, and meet the Committee – that there is a proper procedure... No, sir, I only told him, yes, there is some case going on, but I don't know the details. I told him, there is nothing serious, just some mischief, some trouble makers... No, sir, no! I never... yes, sir... yes, sir... right, sir... Sir, they have time till seven o'clock to reply... No, sir, nothing received so far... Definitely, sir. I will call you immediately, sir... No, sir, it will not happen again... Yes, sir.

*(Crossfade. The light picks up Justice Mascarenhas. He is talking to a group of journalists who are unseen.)*

**JUDGE**

Yes, that is right. It was admitted three days ago... Yes, three days ago... That is not for me to say. The petitioners might have decided that they do not want any publicity... Yes, I have seen the report in that paper. It is not the concern of the court how the paper acquired the information... No, I will not comment on the report... Yes, the management of the club has been duly notified... It is a public interest litigation. The litigant is not an aggrieved person, but a voluntary, non-profit organization that is challenging the rules and regulations in an institution on the grounds of discriminatory practice... What discrimination? You are, I take it, male by gender? And your mother tongue? From your accent can I take it that you are Malayalee? Yes? Now, suppose you were told by the security staff outside that you would not be allowed in because you were a Malayalee, and a male to boot?... No, of course not, it is not the same in some sense, but yes, it could also be said that it is not too different... No, I am not saying that. The court has simply admitted the litigation... Yes, prima facie there is something in it worth examining. But it does not mean the case is decided. It will be given the examination it deserves... No, the case of the woman in question is only a vehicle for the litigation. It is not the show cause notice per se that interests the court. Neither the court nor the litigant, I believe... Technically, yes. You can say they are delinked. The litigation will proceed independent of the outcome of proceedings within the club. No, neither I nor the court can have any personal interest in the woman vis-à-vis the management of the club... That is not in order. What you have heard, murky details as you put it, is of nobody's concern but your own. If you – or anybody – wants to do something about them, there is a process available. *(Crossfade to the Secretary's room. Mani is attending to papers in an agitated state. Muthu is helping in his quiet way.)*

**MANI**

That's the trouble with people nowadays. Rights, rights, rights. They want to make a noise about their rights, but they don't want to talk about responsibilities. No bloody responsibility. No sense of duty, no obedience, no nothing.

**MUTHU**

Sir, heat up today.

**MANI**

What else? What else do you expect? The Committee on my head, the President's bamboo from below, that rogue of a Sebastian this side, the show cause case that side – I have to take everything – everything here, on me.

**MUTHU**

Sir, take curd rice, feel better.

**MANI**

Muthu, Mr Muthuswamy, do you know what I want to do just now?

**MUTHU**

No, sir. What?

**MANI**

I want to cut off the balls of Sebastian and hang them from the flag post in front of the porch.

**MUTHU**

Sir very angry with Sebastian?

**MANI**

What do you think? Do I look as if I am going to a birthday party?

**MUTHU**

Sir very angry with Muthu last week. Sir is thinking with Muthu also... ?

**MANI**

You must have the balls first, no? No, Muthu, nobody can get angry with you. I shout at you because I can't get angry with you.

**MUTHU**

Sir get angry with Sebastian because can't shout at him?

**MANI**

Hang you, Muthu. Balls and all, hang you.

**MUTHU**

What Sebastian do now?

**MANI**

You mean he has not told you?

**MUTHU**

What, sir?

**MANI**

He served them tea, coffee, snacks on the lawn in front of all members.

**MUTHU**

You mean...

**MANI**

Who else? Disobedience! I gave him strict orders not to serve them anytime, anywhere.

**MUTHU**

They are not member now, sir? Dismiss?

**MANI**

As good as.

**MUTHU**

When dismiss, sir?

**MANI**

They have time till seven o'clock. No reply from them yet on the show cause notice. Why am I in the office working late today? For them! I will close at seven sharp. I don't have to be here. My office time is till 5:30. I don't have to wait for irresponsible members. They should be thrown out. Let them go to hell. But rules, Muthu, rules. We say seven, we mean seven. The President is very particular.

**MUTHU**

They write about President sir also in paper.

**MANI**

They write whatever comes to their heads.

**MUTHU**
But everyone say...

**MANI**
People will say whatever... What do people say? *(There is a knock. Mani does not respond immediately. The knocking is repeated.)*

**MANI**
Come in. *(Jini and Jeevan enter. Muthu moves to set chairs for them. Mani stops him with a glare. Jini and Jeevan reach Mani's desk and remain standing.)*

**JINI**
Good evening.

**MANI**
Well?

**JEEVAN**
Good evening.

**MUTHU**
Good evening, sir, ma'am.

**MANI**
You have brought a letter?

**JINI**
Letter?

**MANI**
Your reply to the show cause notice.

**JINI**
Ah, yes, the show cause notice.

**MANI**
Yes, that. Muthu, you may leave the room now.

**MUTHU**
Yes, sir.

**MANI**
And please tell Sebastian I want to see him here before I leave for the day.

**MUTHU**
Yes, sir. *(He leaves)*

**MANI**
Yes?

**JINI**
You wanted a letter.

**MANI**
Come to the point, please. Have you brought the letter?

**JEEVAN**

Actually, it was in that connection...

**MANI**

Please stay out of this. The matter in question concerns only her. You have not been served the notice. You should be thankful for that.

**JEEVAN**

You mean I can continue to come and go as I like? I can be served anywhere, I can use all the facilities?

**MANI**

Please!

**JEEVAN**

I can bring guests?

**MANI**

You may think it is very funny. But you must know it is no laughing matter.

**JINI**

Does it appear as if we are laughing?

**MANI**

I repeat. Please come to the point. It is going to be seven o'clock soon. And I have my duty to perform.

**JEEVAN**

Of course. We appreciate that.

**MANI**

There are still some people who are conscious of their duties, their responsibilities.

**JEEVAN**

It is good to know.

**MANI**

The letter.

**JINI**

There is no letter.

**MANI**

No letter?

**JINI**

From us. We have only this letter from you.

**MANI**

That is the notice.

**JINI**

Notice? What is the notice?

**JEEVAN**
We could not follow what was in it.

**JINI**
It was in some strange foreign language. It was not in English.

**MANI**
I am not concerned about your educational background.

**JINI**
We are what we are.

**MANI**
And I must do what I have to do.

**JEEVAN**
All of us.

**MANI**
Is there a letter in reply from you, or no?

**JINI**
So we had to consult people about this. We had to find out what it meant.

**MANI**
We know what you are up to. We will see what happens in the court case.

**JEEVAN**
Court case?

**MANI**
The President will see to it that you are properly...

**JINI**
The President?

**MANI** *(Checking himself)*
No. You will not get any opinion from me on that.

**JEEVAN**
Understandable.

**MANI**
So... you don't have a reply?

**JINI**
Not if we can't make out what to reply to.

**MANI**
I will ask you one more time, and the last time. Do you have a reply?

**JINI**
Well, if you insist...

**MANI**
It is not my...

**JINI**

If you think it is correct and proper and all, I can put something down now.

**MANI**

Now?

**JEEVAN**

It is not quite seven yet.

**JINI**

Could you give us a sheet of writing paper, please?

**MANI**

Certainly not!

**JINI**

On loan? Well, then... Jeev, your pen, please. *(Jeevan gives her a pen. She scribbles on the notice letter and hands it to Mani.)*

There.

**MANI**

You really think...

**JEEVAN**

Did you put the date?

**JINI**

Oh yes. *(She takes the letter back, writes on it again, and returns it to Mani.)*

Thank you. And please thank the President and Committee on our behalf for their kindness and patience. *(To Jeevan)* Shall we?

*(Jini and Jeevan leave quickly. Mani is left holding the notice letter. He watches them go and then looks at the letter.)*

**MANI**

Seen, thanks.

## SCENE 8

***The Club: Indoor space***

*In the dark, the sound of a chairman's gavel striking the table.*

**CHAIRMAN'S VOICE**

Ladies and gentlemen, the counting has just been completed. The vote is clear. The ayes have it.

*(Cheers and cries of hear! hear! accompanied by thumping on tables.)*

**CHAIRMAN'S VOICE**

The meeting is now adjourned. Thank you ladies and gentlemen, for your kind attendance. *(The sound of the gathering fades out. The lights come on to reveal Jini seated alone in a chair, as in scene 1. She is joined by Thelma, who draws up a chair next to her.)*

**THELMA**
I'm sorry, dear.

**JINI**
It's all right, aunty.

**THELMA**
So, so sorry. This shouldn't have happened. It shouldn't happen to you. Kevin was so...

**JINI**
I know, aunty. I know Kevin uncle tried his best. It's not his fault. It's nobody's fault.

**THELMA**
Who ever imagined that he would be relieved of the case. He was dead keen on sitting on the case when it came up for hearing.

**JINI**
He needn't have taken so much trouble.

**THELMA**
Not just for you, dear. He was concerned about you, of course, but he was also keen on this case making a point. Driving the point home, as he said.

**JINI**
Do you think his transfer before the hearing was – how do you say it – engineered?

**THELMA**
Could be. Who knows? At his level it is not easy to be manoeuvred. It was not really a transfer, you see.

**JINI**
No, not a transfer. I read about it. They said it was a special assignment.

**THELMA**
Judges are often asked to do such things.

**JINI**
An independent enquiry by a sitting High Court Judge – that's what it was called, I think.

**THELMA**
That's right. The land scam had the names of many big fish in public life. The enquiry was inevitable. Kevin was so sorry about the timing.

**JINI**
I know that, aunty.

**THELMA**
Poor, poor Jini.

**JINI**

Happy little small fish! They got away, didn't they? How lucky they are.

**THELMA**

It wasn't just luck. You know that, don't you?

**JINI**

I had some sort of feeling about it.

**THELMA**

The club system is powerful – very, very powerful. The moment the special enquiry was announced, it swung into action.

**JINI**

You mean – there was corruption of some kind?

**THELMA**

Dear me, no. Corruption in court, never.

**JINI**

There are other ways, then. The judgement was influenced in some way.

**THELMA**

Jini, dear, have you ever thought of the exact meaning of the word elite?

**JINI**

Elite? I suppose it is a class thing. Those who have made it, those who can buy things – expensive things... those who can buy influence?

**THELMA**

Kevin asked me the question once. He asked me to look it up. I didn't have the time, I said. As if I don't have enough to do looking after him. Then he told me himself. He said the correct meaning of the word elite comes from connectedness – a group of people who are interconnected – and have the means to maintain the interconnections.

**JINI**

The clubbies are fully qualified, then. They really are the elite, aren't they?

**THELMA**

Unfortunately for them, Kevin has stayed apart. He has never been one of them.

**JINI**

Although a President once.

**THELMA**

Although a President once.

**JINI**

Not a particularly popular President, as we hear it.

**THELMA**

How could he be popular? Refusing permission to chop trees for extending the card room, asking Committee members to declare that they had no connections with the contractors to be hired, proposing a fine for littering.

**JINI**

Good old Kevin uncle!

**THELMA**

First and last time President. You know he doesn't even go to the club now. No time, he says. No interest either. A couple of times in the year, the odd reception, that's all.

**JINI**

So... the system won.

**THELMA**

The system has force.

**JINI**

The force is with the system.

**THELMA**

The Justice appointed for this case...

**JINI**

I know. The clubbies were invited to his chamber for a private hearing.

**THELMA**

I didn't know about that.

**JINI**

A private interest in a public interest litigation case.

**THELMA**

What I do know is that when the case was handed over, the Justice showed no interest in knowing what Kevin thought about it. *(Jini is silent. Thelma tries to comfort her. There is a long, awkward pause)*

**JINI**

It's coming back. I thought it was all left behind. Sometimes, when you are half asleep, you have a half dream. You can see yourself in the dream. And you see yourself falling off from some place. You are falling, falling – it seems unending.

**THELMA**

Jini, dear, don't lose heart. I'm sure all is not lost.

**JINI**

What does Kevin uncle say? He must have heard.

**THELMA**

He is very, very upset. But he said the same thing – all is not lost.

**JINI**

Do you know the first thing the new Judge did? The litigation had carefully separated the case from the Committee's show cause notice to me. It was delinked. The first thing the new judge did was to link the two. At the end, he not only dismissed the litigation as having insufficient grounds, but also went on to say that the management of the club had every right to interpret and enforce its rules and regulations as it thought fit. He practically gave the Committee the words to put into the order – the order to expel me from the club.

**THELMA**
I know, dear. It's all very distressing.

**JINI**
It's not about me aunty, believe me. Don't be distressed for me. From the time the order was handed down to me, I have asked myself this question, Who lost? Who won? Am I really the loser? When a public interest case is lost, the real loser is the public. I'll survive, thank you.

**THELMA**
There, there, dear. Get a hold of yourself. Let me...

**JINI**
I'll survive, aunty. Don't you worry about that. There are lots of nice people around me. There is you, there is Jeev, lots of nice people still.

**THELMA**
One of them is Kevin. He could not come himself. He has asked me to give you a message.

**JINI**
Kevin uncle?

**THELMA**
Yes. He says you must not give up now. We must challenge the expulsion order.

## SCENE 9

***The Club: the lawn service***
*It is late at night. Muthu and Sebastian are clearing up – chairs turned on tables, empties carted away, and so on.*

**MUTHU**
Opening stock.

**SEBASTIAN**
Done.

**MUTHU**
Closing stock.

**SEBASTIAN**
Done.

**MUTHU**
Bar billing.

**SEBASTIAN**
Done. Snacks billing, done. Dining room billing, done.

**MUTHU**
Bar closed?

**SEBASTIAN**
Not yet. There is time.

**MUTHU**
People have gone home early today. Only two tables occupied.

**SEBASTIAN**
Both couples. One looks newly married.

**MUTHU**
You know?

**SEBASTIAN**
I can tell. From the clothes they are wearing. Or not wearing.

**MUTHU**
And one couple really old.

**SEBASTIAN**
Must be at least fifty years married. They haven't looked at each other since they came in.

**MUTHU**
They were old members even when I came to the old club.

**SEBASTIAN**
Must be from the time of King George or Queen Victoria. Must have had dinner with that Churchill bugger.

**MUTHU**
Don't talk like that.

**SEBASTIAN**
Must have paid for that Churchill bugger's drinks. The old club, the old club! Now you'll start off on the good old days.

**MUTHU**
Don't! You don't know what you are saying. The old days were really the good days. The members were fine people then.

**SEBASTIAN**
They didn't give tips.

**MUTHU**
Not like the members you see today.

**SEBASTIAN**
I have no problem with them.

**MUTHU**
No problem? You are saying this? After all your...

**SEBASTIAN**
No problem. They go their way, I go mine. They know what they want from the club, I know what I want. No, that is not a problem.

**MUTHU**
What else, then?

**SEBASTIAN**
I have a problem with you – not you as you, but people like you.

**MUTHU**
Me? Have I hurt you in some way?

**SEBASTIAN**
See? That's the point. 'Have I hurt you in some way?' All feeling, no sense. All good intentions, no action.

**MUTHU**
I don't understand...

**SEBASTIAN**
Take this case of show cause notice and dismissal.

**MUTHU**
Jini miss and Jeevan sir?

**SEBASTIAN**
Yes, that. All you people from the 'good old days', what have you done about it?

**MUTHU**
What can we do? We are only club staff here.

**SEBASTIAN**
You wash your hands off. And all those others who keep sitting here, watching the tamasha – buzz buzz buzz buzz, giggling among themselves, not speaking up even once. What can we do? We are only members! Can you see how idiotic you look?

**MUTHU**
I know. You don't have to throw it on my face. I know I have weak knees and feet of clay. But what about you? What have you done about it?

**SEBASTIAN**
Very little so far. But I can't sit quietly and watch what is going on. I will do something. It will come to me.

**MUTHU**

Mani sir said you shouted at him.

**SEBASTIAN**

He has very tender ears. He has not heard me shouting yet.

**MUTHU**

What did you say to him?

**SEBASTIAN**

I told him to keep a mirror in front and practice talking courteously. He told me to shut up. I said, 'Now, right now you should look into a mirror.' He said he was warning me – I should mind my own business. I told him the President himself had said at the Club Day lunch meeting that all staff should help each other in improving performance. I said I would like to report that the honourable Executive Secretary was defying the President's order.

**MUTHU**

I still think you shouldn't...

**SEBASTIAN**

No, don't, you shouldn't, you must not, no, no, no! You talk just like my grandmother used to. You think you are talking to a six-year-old.

**MUTHU**

I was only saying...

**SEBASTIAN**

How about some yes for a change? Yes, go, you must, yes, yes. Get it up, yes. Go get it. Yes, some more, yes.

**MUTHU**

Sebastian! Shut up your filthy mouth or I'll...

*(Muthu goes up to Sebastian in anger. He realises that he is more shaken than angry. The older brother in him prevails. He looks apologetically at Sebastian.)*

I am sorry. I lost my head. It is not good to shout. I must not... You wind up here. I will go and lock up inside.

*(Muthu leaves. Sebastian watches him go. He looks in the direction of the last guests, acknowledging their departure.)*

**SEBASTIAN**

Good night, sir, good night, ma'am. Good night.

*(He bows mockingly, gestures comically, takes out a nip of rum from his pocket, seats himself at a table, pretends to pour drinks to a group like a club member, raises his imaginary glass in a toast, and then swigs from the bottle. He does not see Kevin Mascarenhas who has arrived and is watching with characteristic controlled amusement)*

**JUDGE**

What are we celebrating?

**SEBASTIAN** *(Collecting himself)*
Good evening, sir.

**JUDGE**
And a very good evening to you. So, is it Cricket? Has the Indian team succeeded in crossing one hundred in the first innings? Or is it a horse? What's the name? First Flight or Second Nature or Third Degree or something like that.

**SEBASTIAN**
Sir, no service.

**JUDGE**
Wrong.

**SEBASTIAN :**
Bar close 'leven o'clock, sir.

**JUDGE**
Wrong again. It will close at eleven, don't you worry. It is now three minutes to eleven. I have already placed the order. The barman wants you to collect the order and bring it here.

**SEBASTIAN**
Yes, sir. I go straight. Sir want snacks?

**JUDGE**
Just liquid refreshment, thank you.

**SEBASTIAN**
Yes, sir. Thank you, sir. I go, sir. *(He darts off)*

*(Kevin goes up to the table, examines it, re-lays the table with the cloth kept folded, adjusts two chairs at the table and sits down. He takes out a sheaf of papers and begins to study it. Sebastian comes in with a tray that has two standard and one small whiskeys poured into three separate glasses, a bottle of cold water, a pail of ice, and other accessories. He puts the service down before the Justice.)*

**SEBASTIAN**
Sir stock up very good. Water-ice sir?

**JUDGE**
Ice and water. Two cubes of ice first, please. *(Sebastian does the needful)* And what about you?

**SEBASTIAN** *(Looks up and grins)*
I wait that corner. Sir call, I come double fast.

**JUDGE**
Actually, I don't think I will need all of this. Just one should do for now. I'll tell you what – you sit there and have the other drink.

**SEBASTIAN**
Sir?

**JUDGE**
And you can pour the water in first if you like. Or have it on the rocks, or just neat – as you wish.

**SEBASTIAN**
Sir excuse me. Service staff not allowed...

**JUDGE**
Mr Sebastian, sir, it is now just past eleven. Which means you are off duty. The clearing up has been done already I can see. So I don't see why you can't join me for a drink.

**SEBASTIAN**
But still, sir, please... rules.

**JUDGE**
The rules say I can entertain a guest at the club. You are my guest this evening. So sit down and fix that drink for yourself. *(Sebastian sits obediently, does what he is told)*

Now, then, if we are going to drink together, we must make conversation, must we not? What shall we talk about, huh? Music? You want to talk about music? Let us make a quiz of this. You ask me a question and I'll ask you a question. Ready? Right, when was the last time a Regimental band played in the club? Don't know? Okay, when was the bandstand demolished to make way for the ice cream parlour? No? Right, try this. Which member of the club – no longer alive – had the largest record collection of classical music at home? *(Sebastian completely in a daze)*

All right, you ask me one.

**SEBASTIAN**
Sir, you sing song now?

**JUDGE**
And shatter the glass in all the windows of the lounge?

**SEBASTIAN**
All right, sir, I ask. How many club members sing God Save the King?

**JUDGE**
Queen. God Save the Queen.

**SEBASTIAN**
King, sir. One member. Only one left. Rest all dead.

**JUDGE**
I know who you mean. The only one left, ninety-four years old, and still marching on. You know the Committee Room, Sebastian?

**SEBASTIAN**
Yes, sir.

**JUDGE**

It was where they met on the first Sunday of every month. The Empire Loyalists Society. They played God Save the King just before they adjourned for dinner. Did you know any more of them?

**SEBASTIAN**

Only three sir. Now only one. Very fine gentlemen, ladies, sir. Strictly no tips.

**JUDGE**

The Society was the official Reception Committee for the visit of King George, I believe. Before my time, but I can well believe the stories.

**SEBASTIAN**

George five, George six, both King of India, sir?

**JUDGE**

Two Georges too many.

**SEBASTIAN**

They teach Indians, sir?

**JUDGE**

They taught my father to eat toast and marmalade at tea time. My father passed on the sacred text to me.

**SEBASTIAN**

King George shoot tigers, sir. Ten-twelve?

**JUDGE**

The pictures on the wall in the lounge – enough tigers to carpet the whole of Buckingham Palace.

**SEBASTIAN**

More than ten-twelve, sir?

**JUDGE**

We will never know the exact number, Sebastian. If we add up all the tigers slaughtered by all the royal visitors, and their viceroys, governors, collectors, commissioners, and the lot, not to forget their Indian bootlickers who pretended they were kings and princes themselves, if we add them all up, what do you think the total might be?

**SEBASTIAN**

Ohh – big number, sir. Hundreds! Maybe more.

**JUDGE**

Maybe a hundred times more than the total number of tigers alive today. It was all perfectly respectable. The law permitted it, encouraged it.

*(A pause. Sebastian stares at Kevin.)*

**SEBASTIAN**

Why people kill tiger, sir?

**JUDGE**

Hmmm. I have to think about that. Why, do you think?

**SEBASTIAN**

One reason I think, sir.

**JUDGE**

Fear? We kill from fear? Like we kill snakes – fear and ignorance. We kill earthworms because they look like snakes.

**SEBASTIAN**

Maybe, sir. But I think we kill tiger because jealousy, sir.

*(Another pause, as Kevin tries to absorb this one.)*

**JUDGE**

The tiger roars. We think we are afraid. We are taught to fear the tiger. But actually we are jealous of the tiger's roar. And all that it stands for. Sebastian, you son of a gun! I'll drink to that! *(Goes up to Sebastian)*

Too bad the bar is closed. We could have celebrated appropriately.

*(Going back to his seat)*

You know, Sebastian, I am going to take my shoes off. My shoes and my socks. Off. *(He does)*

**SEBASTIAN**

Sir, club rule...

**JUDGE**

The rule, dear boy, says that the dress must include shoes, with or without laces. It does not specify I must have them on. Ahh... that's good. I suggest you take off your shoes too. The grass is soft and cool. The club grounds are sacred. It is a mark of submission to take off shoes in holy places.

**SEBASTIAN**

Sir knows rule correct? *(He starts to take off his shoes)*

**JUDGE**

We should have done this with David Lean and company when they were here. Dress code printed on the invitation, 'Footwear off at the entrance please.' Did you see how many club members had their noses pressed flat for two months? Came from falling prostrate. The new visitation of the Empire. Yes, we should have done that at the reception.

**SEBASTIAN** *(Sebastian laughs tentatively)*

Secretary sir very strict.

**JUDGE**

Tell you what, Sebastian – you get me a copy of the club rules. I'll roll them up nice and tight. You then dip it into a big bowl of ketchup. Then I'll shove it up the Secretary's – you know – exhaust pipe.

*(They laugh, Sebastian a bit hesitatingly at first and then full-throatedly. Kevin extends his hand. Sebastian shakes it. They sit and look at each other.*

*Kevin sticks out his feet. So does Sebastian. They compare feet. Kevin offers his foot. Sebastian 'shakes it'. They laugh again.)*

**JUDGE**

A brief diversion before we return to the road with the dead end. You know, Sebastian, I think I've forgotten the nice feel of driving a car with bare feet. I think I'm going to drive home like this now.

*(He collects his shoes and socks and is ready to leave.)*

Maybe my brain will work better with the acupressure from the pedals.

**SEBASTIAN**

Sir is tired.

**JUDGE**

Not tired from doing something, Sebastian, but from not having done anything.

**SEBASTIAN**

I think sir is talking about...

**JUDGE**

Sir is talking about going home. Good night, Sebastian.

**SEBASTIAN**

Good night, sir.

**JUDGE**

Take care of your feet. If anybody asks you, say I ordered you to take them off. I wanted to inspect your socks. Inspected and found okay. The club service is safe with Sebastian. Good night.

*(He leaves. Sebastian watches him go.)*

**SEBASTIAN**

Good night, sir.

*(He sits down to put on his shoes. On second thought he carries them in his hand and goes out.)*

## SCENE 10

***The Club: indoor space***

*In the dark, the sound of sobbing. The light comes on to pick up Daisy and Shweta. Daisy is bent over, weeping. Shweta, in dark glasses, is seated next to her, trying to console her, but a bit distanced. After a while Jini walks into the area, surveys the scene, goes up to Daisy, and embraces her. Daisy responds by hugging her tightly and bursting into tears. Shweta watches with a hand on Daisy's shoulder.*

## SCENE 11

***The Club: the Secretary's office***

*Muthu is arranging papers at the desk. Sebastian enters whistling a tune, goes straight to the desk, sits on the secretary's chair, takes off his shoes, and puts up his feet on the desk. A shocked Muthu tries to unseat him.*

**SEBASTIAN**

Socks washed and clean. No holes.

**MUTHU**

Sebastian, you mad dog, what evil spirit has entered your head?

**SEBASTIAN**

Holy place. Mark of respect.

**MUTHU**

You will get dismissed. Punished and dismissed.

**SEBASTIAN**

You can dismiss an employee. How do you dismiss somebody who is not your employee?

**MUTHU**

What do you mean... ?

**SEBASTIAN**

White envelope on your right. The one with the picture of a rosebud. Drawn by my daughter. Yes, that one. Will you be a good fellow and put it on top in the tray, please?

**MUTHU**

This... you are... ?

**SEBASTIAN**

Yes, from me. I am leaving. No, I do not have relatives in Muscat. *(He puts his feet down and puts on his shoes)*

Actually, I don't know who my relatives really are and what it means to be a relative.

**MUTHU**

What will you do? Sebastian, I always knew you were a fool, a hot-headed fool. But this – you will end up in the gutter. *(Sebastian positions himself behind the Secretary's chair, puts on a pair of dark glasses, and stands like a security agent behind a VVIP.)*

**SEBASTIAN**

First I will learn to stand straight. If my mother were alive, she would be pleased. Straighten that back, she would say. I will stand straight.

**MUTHU**

Mad – you have gone completely mad.

**SEBASTIAN**

Then I will learn to speak straight. Simple. To the point.

**MUTHU**

You are playing with fire, Sebastian. They can hurt you. They will destroy you.

**SEBASTIAN**

And throw me in the gutter?

**MUTHU**

Yes, that is where you will end up. A hero in the gutter.

**SEBASTIAN**

So, what is the choice? A club sewer rat or a gutter hero?

**MUTHU**

It is not a laughing matter.

**SEBASTIAN**

You are right! We should be crying. But I found I have forgotten how to. We must go back to the circus and look at the clowns. Maybe it will come back.

**MUTHU**

I just don't understand you, Sebastian. I just cannot see the meaning of all this...

**SEBASTIAN**

Shhh! I hear the Chief Clown approaching. *(Mani enters. He regards the scene. Muthu mutters an apology to Mani, excuses himself, and starts to leave.)*

**MANI**

Wait! Don't go away, Muthu. You are still the supervisor of the bearer staff. There may be some explanation due from you. (*Mani walks up slowly to Sebastian, who remains standing rock still, feet apart, arms straight, hands clasped in front. Mani raises his hand, half testing, half intending to strike.)*

**SEBASTIAN**

Muthu, don't go yet. You may also be needed as a witness. *(Mani lowers his hand, controls himself, and sits at the desk.)*

**MANI**

All right, Muthu, you explain. We all know that street dogs show whimsical behaviour in the summer heat. But what is Sebastian's problem today?

**MUTHU**

Sir, what I can say? Sebastian come in just now. Very hot. He is asking...

**SEBASTIAN**

Audience. A five-minute audience in the durbar of the Chief... Ringmaster of the Club Circus.

**MUTHU**

Sebastian, you speak to Mani sir direct. I am out.

**MANI**

Sebastian, everybody knows what you are.

**SEBASTIAN**

Everybody, sir? Everybody knows?

**MANI**

Yes, a good-for-nothing loafer, thrown at the door step of the club ten years ago. Still, you behave as if you are doing the club a great favour by putting on your uniform and doing what you are paid to do.

**SEBASTIAN**

All that is the past, boss. I am now going straight. I will do everything in my power to make the club a clean and decent place where members will not be ashamed to bring their children. God's own club, boss. Muthu, that sounds like TV dialogue, no? You are liking?

**MANI**

Enough of your bud-bud. You better have something serious to discuss with me now, or I will have to make a file noting of your irresponsible behaviour. What do you want to say to me?

**SEBASTIAN**

Item one. I am leaving the club, boss. Quitting. Off. Full stop. Chutti.

**MANI**

You are... resigning?

**SEBASTIAN**

Ahh – that's the word. Resign. The letter on top in your tray.

**MANI**

Muthu, what is this? Do you have any... ?

**SEBASTIAN**

Happy, boss? Good news, no?

**MANI**

I hope you know what you are doing.

**SEBASTIAN**

Item two. On to item two, boss. I am resigning so that I can do item two.

**MANI**

Selling dirty pictures on the pavement on MG Road. Soon you will be selling your wife, then your daughter.

**SEBASTIAN**

Good guess, boss! Dirty pictures, yes. But not on MG Road. And not selling. I am giving away dirty pictures to people in the court.

**MANI**
The court...?

**SEBASTIAN**
All kinds of people in the pictures, boss. Big people, important people, some contractor people, some bank people. Big titles, boss – big offices. Item two, boss.

**MANI** *(To Muthu)*
How much does he know? Are all the files and papers... ?

**SEBASTIAN**
All safe, boss. In their proper place, in this room only. Only the Xerox machine is in another room, there.

**MANI**
Muthu, who else has this son of a bitch talked to?

**MUTHU**
Don't know, sir. He came, then you came. Don't know, sir.

**SEBASTIAN**
Don't worry, boss. You are safe. VIP security. I am there to protect you. Safe, boss.

## SCENE 12

***The home of Kevin Mascarenhas***
*In the dark, the sound of the weeping from Scene 10. The lights come on to reveal Jini, Jeevan, and Thelma.*

**JINI**
It was all so meaningless.

**THELMA**
I wouldn't say that, Jini.

**JINI**
There was nothing that came out of it, aunty. It made no sense. It was pointless.

**THELMA**
The disappointment I can understand, dear. The tone of despair is not called for. What do you say, Jeevan?

**JEEVAN**
We were prepared for difficult times, but not...

**JINI**
It was not mere disappointment, aunty. If you have high expectations and they are not realised, you are disappointed, and I suppose we can say you

asked for it. We did not have high expectations, really. We were prepared for the thickness of skin in the system. We would not be surprised by a verdict going against us.

**THELMA**

The point would be made. That is what I was saying too. It is wrong to call it pointless.

**JINI**

I'll take that back.

**THELMA**

People have sat up and taken notice. People are reading about it, talking about it.

**JINI**

I take that back. Maybe it was not pointless. But the price paid – the casualties on the battlefield... *(Pause)*

**THELMA**

I heard... I'm afraid I don't know all of it. What happened exactly?

*(Jini and Jeevan do not respond)*

It's all right, dear. You don't have to, if you'd rather not talk about it.

**JEEVAN**

It is difficult, aunty.

**JINI**

It is painful. But we must tell Thelma aunty some time or the other.

**JEEVAN**

You see, aunty, it is difficult also because we don't know if it is really connected to this whole business.

**JINI**

Let me tell her, Jeev. *(Jeevan nods)*

Let me make it short, aunty. Short, but not so sweet I'm afraid. Daisy is going to be divorced. Harish has practically given her notice to leave the house. And Shweta...she is beaten black and blue by Udit. An average of twice a week.

**JEEVAN**

They tried to maintain some little contact with Jini in the beginning. We sensed they were doing it – you know – at some risk. We urged them not to meet us. And not to feel bad about it. It didn't seem to have helped.

**JINI**

They stopped seeing us all right. It didn't seem to have helped in...

**THELMA**

Oh, my God! Oh, my dear, dear God...

**JINI**

Our best friends.

**JEEVAN**

Who knows how many other lives have been affected by our indiscretion.

**THELMA**

I am so, so sorry, Jini. Oh, my God. Please look down with kindness on your helpless children. Ohh...

**JEEVAN**

We really didn't want to...

**JINI**

But it had to be done some time.

**THELMA**

And you two? You have held together well, I hope.

**JINI**

Not without strains. But yes, aunty, we have survived.

**THELMA**

What have you decided to do? What next? I'm sure Kevin uncle will want to talk to you.

**JINI**

Oh, we will talk to him. Of course we will.

**THELMA**

Do, please do. You know he is most distressed about the course the whole case has taken.

**JEEVAN**

We will talk to him, aunty.

**THELMA**

Don't do anything till you've talked to him.

**JINI**

We've only... we have left the club.

**JEEVAN**

We could have continued on my membership, but we felt...

**JINI**

To put an end to the messy affair, getting messier and more complicated day by day, to put an end to it all – I offered to resign from the club on my own. I sent in a letter of resignation.

**JEEVAN**

Seeking gracious intervention from the Managing Committee to relieve her of the membership.

**THELMA**

Are you sure... ?

**JINI**

And separately, without waiting for their reply, the next day, Jeevan sent in his letter of resignation.

**THELMA**

And the Committee... have they replied?

**JINI**

They will, I'm sure. In good time. After the celebrations.

**THELMA**

Yes, of course.

**JEEVAN**

The news has spread, I believe.

**THELMA**

They couldn't conceal the rejoicing I suppose. Dear oh dear.

**JINI**

We must be leaving, aunty.

**THELMA**

What's the rush? Stay for dinner.

**JEEVAN**

We want to get home early.

**JINI**

For a change. I want to cook a proper meal. We want to eat together, and look at each other while we eat. It's been a long time.

**THELMA**

Good for you! I won't come in the way. But keep Sunday free for us. Join us at lunch.

**JEEVAN**

Thank you, aunty. We will look forward to that.

**JINI**

Funny how Sundays always meant brunch at the club.

**JEEVAN**

We'll come, aunty. Definitely. *(Jini and Jeevan leave. Thelma watches them go and starts to get the evening tea service ready. She then picks up a magazine, sits at her place, and starts to read. Kevin is heard approaching, singing. He enters, noticeably cheerful, tosses his jacket on a chair, settles into his own chair, and starts to take off his shoes and socks, the singing held.)*

**THELMA**

What on earth do you think... ? I hope this is not an announcement that you are being promoted to the Supreme Court.

**JUDGE**

Cold, cold. Three guesses.

**THELMA**

I'm not playing your silly guessing games.

**JUDGE**

But you loved them once.

**THELMA**

Over thirty years ago.

**JUDGE**

Ah, those lovely times – when we had minds of our own. Take off your shoes, Telly. You'll like the feel. Take them off. Come on.

**THELMA** *(Protesting and then giving in)*

No, no... You can do what you like... Why... All right, all right...

**JUDGE**

Do you remember how we played footsy under the table when your aunt Gabriella was around? *(Thelma gives in. They play games with their feet. There is a magical mood as they enjoy each other's company at evening tea.)*

**THELMA**

I have not heard you sing in a long, long time.

**JUDGE**

I have not felt a song in my heart in a long time.

**THELMA**

So... it is not a promotion.

**JUDGE**

Nah, that's nothing to sing about.

**THELMA**

What is it, then?

**JUDGE**

I just feel good. That's all. I noticed a pair of mynahs on the lawn as I came in. Haven't seen mynahs in donkey's years.

**THELMA**

They've always been there. You just haven't noticed.

**JUDGE**

I saw them today. They made such a lovely couple. They seemed to be so much in love.

**THELMA**

Kevin, is this some kind of elaborate ground preparation for... ?

**JUDGE**

And at the office – when I looked out of the window, I saw a pair of pigeons.

**THELMA**

They made such a lovely couple, they were so much in love.

**JUDGE**
And then the phone call.

**THELMA**
From the girl pigeon's angry father.

**JUDGE**
From Justice Desai's office. The club has dropped the case.

**THELMA**
The case?

**JUDGE**
Withdrawn. An application seeking leave to withdraw the case against our little Jini. Justice Desai called a meeting of all parties in his chambers. Settled out of court.

**THELMA**
You mean Jini...

**JUDGE**
Case withdrawn. Settled out of court.

**THELMA**
What about their resignations?

**JUDGE**
Redundant. But how do you know about their resignations?

**THELMA**
They were here – came to see both of us. You were tied up at the office. They waited a while and left.

**JUDGE**
Let's have them over for lunch on Sunday.

**THELMA**
Done.

**JUDGE**
I'll call them straight away.

**THELMA**
Redundant. I have already arranged it. *(Kevin smiles and relaxes. They sit back to enjoy the tea.)*

**JUDGE**
Much better for them to hear about it directly from the club.

**THELMA**
I should think so too.

**JUDGE**
Much better for them to call us.

**THELMA**
They will, I'm sure. As soon as they hear.

**JUDGE**
Much better for us to have tea time for ourselves.

**THELMA**
A pair of ageing mynahs on the patio.

**JUDGE**
If ever looks were deceptive! *(Thelma and Kevin sip their teas quietly, at peace with the world.)*

**JUDGE**
Telly, dear, do any of our friends need a good butler?

**THELMA**
A butler? Do they still have butlers?

**JUDGE**
You can give it another name, of course. In keeping with the times, he could be called the Principal Secretary or Chief of Mission or something like that.

**THELMA**
A rascal in gentleman clothes.

**JUDGE**
And underneath that, a boy scout in rascal's clothes.

**THELMA**
Maybe in a hotel.

**JUDGE**
Maybe a business of his own – training butlers.

**THELMA**
You have somebody in mind?

**JUDGE**
Do I? Yes, I think I do. (*Thelma and Kevin continue to have their tea quietly. As a slow fade out begins, the telephone rings inside. They continue with their tea. The fade out is complete.)*

***Close of play***

# Salt Licks

*An act in two plays. A play in two acts.*
***Vijay Padaki***

**FOR**
**GLYNN WOOD**

## INTRODUCTION

As Bugs says towards the end of the play, '... Can't be much of a song if it has to be explained!' Yet, it is customary for a play to be given an introduction, especially if it has to cross cultural boundaries for a fuller appreciation.

Years ago, I was invited to a meeting at the US Consulate office in Madras *(now Chennai)* for a discussion on a visiting American theatre production. The Officer's cabin overlooked Gemini Circle, with the flyover dominating the scene. The traffic on the flyover and below was at its peak at that time of day, but could not be heard inside. On the curved pavement below, there was a line of young people, mostly young men and women, forming an orderly queue hugging the wall of the Consulate premises. It was the season! I imagined the light disappearing all around the wall, the traffic thinning to a trickle, the street lamps coming on and the queue just beginning to form at 4 am. A play was born.

July is the student emigration season in most developing countries. Anybody who has stood in a queue for a visa at a US Consulate office in India will know what that means. Yes, the play does have something to do with the emigration of bright young people from India to silicon pastures. But, no, it is not meant to be a statement about 'brain drain' or some such phenomenon of great politicoeconomic significance. That task is left to others more adapted to it – perhaps the audience.

This play is content with the exploration of an idiom. Is that the word? Perhaps not. It cannot be so academically neat. Perhaps what is needed is to rescue natural imagery from the banishment it commonly receives. We might ask, for instance, what would happen if we allowed the business on stage to acquire a significance of its own, the words complying with the moves, rather than the other way about. We might then attend to the urgent task of rehabilitating our images, freeing ideation from the pressures of plot and structure. The performing group is advised to concentrate on the images to be created, move away from novelty, and arrive at an earnestness to play it.

The two parts of the play may be performed in any way chosen: as a two-act play, with the unity provided imaginatively by the performers; as a double bill; or even as two separate one-acters. The connecting links in the script between the two parts are kept few and tenuous. The writer's own preference is to view the two parts as integral in a single play. It should be no surprise if the audience – or the reader – does not continue after the first part.

The play is set in the late 'eighties or very early 'nineties. It is best to retain the period in a performance. 'Contemporising' the play may not help. The pre-liberalisation context for young people dreaming the American dream is important in the play. Getting there at any cost was the driving force. The future would take care of itself.

## Language Notes

### Item 20

*Bijoya Greetings:* Greetings on the occasion of Vijayadashami (Durga Puja). The Indian postal department has numbers for these greetings with standadised text for telegrams, popular 20 years ago.
*Lakh:* A hundred thousand
*Tirtha:* Holy water, the ritual of receiving it
*Arangetram:* Ceremonial first public performance of a trained dancer *(South Indian)*
*Basmati:* Aromatic rice used on special occasions
*Aap ki jaankari...Dhanyavad:* Airline announcement: For your kind information the outside temperature is 36 degrees Celsius. Passengers are requested to remain in their seats until the next announcement. Thank you.
*Kashi Yatra:* Pilgrimage to the holy city of Kashi

### Green Belt

*Garam masala:* Spice mix for hot curry
*Kumkum:* Vermillion mark on forehead and hair parting, symbol of married status
*Bindi:* Similar to above, a dot, not restricted to married women
*Touching feet:* Gesture of respect, usually to elders
*Chumma:* Just like that, for the heck of it
*Channapatna:* Town near Mysore famous for lacquerware and toys
*Tanjore:* Another South Indian town with tradition of wood and lacquer craft
*Kolam:* Rice flour designs on the floor of traditional homes, usually at entrance
*Rangoli:* Similar to above
*Celestial charioteer, archer:* Allusion to Krishna and Arjuna from the Mahabharata
*Ganapati stotram:* An invocation to Ganapati *(Ganesha)* sung/chanted before ceremonial occasions
*Pancha:* Prefix to mean penta or five
*Namak:* Salt, allusion to indebtedness – 'having eaten his salt'
*Dalit:* Term used by social activists for the lowest caste of disadvantaged communities
*Ekalavya:* Tribal youth in an episode in the Mahabharata
*Chor-police:* Cops and robbers
*Tirtha:* Holy water, the ritual of receiving it

# PART 1: ITEM 20

## CHARACTERS IN THE PLAY

ABU, JIM, BUGS, DJ .................. *Young men in their mid or early twenties*
SON ........................................................... *A slightly younger person*
MOTHER ............................................................................ *As stated*
GIRL .......................................................................... *In her early twenties*

*An almost bare stage. Only the essential plan and props are described here. The performing group is free to visualise their exact appearance, sizes, and positions. Additions to the bare essentials are also permissible, but it may be best to keep these to the minimum.*

*A lamp post. Or is it a bus stop? A receptacle attached to it that says USE ME. The slightest separation of two levels, suggesting a pavement and a road. An entrance-exit Left, another on the Right.*

*The emphasis in the narrative is on action. Although it might be tempting to pigeon-hole the content of the play into some predetermined category of dramatic form or the other, that something-or-other quality is probably better conveyed through things the actors do, rather than through sets and visual cues bordering on the surreal. Some hand/personal props are essentials. Other props and costuming – to be thought about, but within the general ground rules adopted.*

*The play opens with a dimly lit stage, showing Abu sitting all by himself on the kerb. He has a rucksack. Projecting out of the bag are several chart-like rolls of paper. Abu is sitting still. Over the sound system is heard the dingdongding that precedes an announcement. Abu sits erect, expectantly. Offstage, the bulb horn of an auto rickshaw makes a strident statement. Abu relaxes. The dingdongding on the sound system is heard again. Abu sits erect. Offstage, the agitated voice of the Mother is heard.*

**MOTHER** *(Off)*

Find the head. Go find the head. Here. Put it down here. There. There's a tree there. Go to the tree there. Behind the tree. Go behind the tree there. I'll be here. There, there, there.

*(Abu relaxes. The dingdongding on the sound system comes on again. Abu looks offstage. A woman's voice begins an announcement in a velvety smooth formula manner over the system.)*

**WOMAN'S VOICE**

Namaskar. For the gracious people, a new international pack may shower steel-belted radials on the young complexion in four flavours for the one that satisfies, to touch, to feel, while flights of angels sing to rest the extra mile with the goodness of almonds.

*(There is a crackly interruption by a brusque male voice on the system.)*

**MAN'S VOICE**

Cabin crew to close and arm all doors. Close and arm all doors.

*(The stage brightens. A short pause. Abu moves downstage to one side, takes out a scroll, examines the contents, sets it down, takes out a piece of chalk, and begins to draw a diagram on the road. Through a good part of the play, Abu will be preoccupied with his drawing task – beginning with a square, adding more squares, culminating in an 'aeroplane' hopscotch court. He does this with much concentration and method, referring occasionally to one or more of the scrolls as thought necessary.*

*Jim enters. He carries a shoulder bag, which contains a prominently visible abacus. He comes up to Abu, stands behind him, paying no particular attention to the drawing. Abu, intent on the drawing, shifts his position. So does Jim, staying behind him.*

*The mother enters. She is short and plump, but energetic. She is leading the Son, who is holding her hand. He carries a holdall with an umbrella tucked under the belts. He is considerably taller than the mother. The mother's gait matches her speech in agitation as she marches across the stage with the son in tow.)*

**MOTHER**

Where's the head? Which way? Which way is the head?

*(The son tries to stop behind Jim, but is pulled away by her)*

Look sharp. We've got to find the head. Where's the head?

*(They exit. Bugs enters. He wears an extraordinarily thick pair of glasses and carries an elaborate cutlery set in what looks like a leatherbound executive briefcase. He regards Jim and Abu from some distance and prefers to sit on the kerb under the post, carefully resting the case against it.)*

**JIM**

Eighteen.

**ABU**

Heartiest Bijoya greetings.

**JIM**

Nineteen.

**ABU**

Heaven's choicest blessings on the showering couple.

**JIM**

Twenty.

**ABU**

Speedy recovery from new arrival.

**JIM**

My plate's empty. *(Bugs open the case, takes out two knives, a spoon, and a fork, and places them before himself on the road as at a dining table. He stands to attention and sings)*

**BUGS** *(Singing)*

'... From sea to shining sea.' *(He holds the last note for a few beats, stops abruptly, and sits down again.)*

**JIM**

So Abu stuck?

**ABU**

Abhimanyu was not my choice.

**JIM**

So Abu stuck.

**ABU**

Not anybody's choice but grandfather's. Mother, no vote. Father, no voice. He couldn't spell Abhimanyu in the school admission form.

**JIM**

So Abu stuck. Could have been Abhi.

**ABU**

Abhishek on the left. Abhijit on the right.

**JIM**

I had a dog.

**ABU**

His name was Abu.

**JIM**

Yeah. No, his name was Chatrapati Gaurang Bahadur.

**ABU**

Grandfather was stubborn.

**JIM**

In the record book.

**ABU**

He could be meanly stubborn.

**JIM**

He sired the Bahadur line. You've heard of...

**ABU**

He was mean.

**JIM**

But we called him Abu.

**ABU**

Better than Daboo.

**JIM**

He taught me to count.

**ABU**

Dabloo on the left, Babloo on the right.

**JIM**

He taught me everything – principles of ballistics, carbon dating in palaeontology, orthodontia in midlife endogenous depression. But first and last he taught me to count.

**ABU**

He had gold-capped canines.

**JIM**

Count Abu I called him.

**ABU**

His bite was worse than his bark.

**JIM**

He was mean?

**ABU**

He bit the postmaster's generals.

**JIM**

The mean is squared.

**ABU**

He bit off the doctor's orders.

**JIM**

The square is hypertensive.

**ABU**

He bit off father's marbles.

**JIM**

Hypertension is a sign of angularity in the rectum. *(Abu has finished the first of the squares by now. He stands in the middle of the square and 'tests' it by jumping a few times within the square – east-south-west-north. As Abu bends to take another scroll from his bag, Jim places his abacus on his backside, reels off a quick computation.)*

**JIM**

Twenty-six overs, twenty-six maidens, twenty-six runs, one pimple.

**ABU**

Hot cross buns.

**JIM**

Nine months old. *(Jim hands Abu the abacus, who in turn presents the scroll to Jim. Abu sits inside the square with the abacus pressed against his temple and proceeds to 'tune' it to a reference note produced by himself. Jim walks across to Bugs and sits facing him, spreading the scroll in front of himself.)*

**ABU**

Ping... ping... ping... PONG! *(Jim and Bugs spring up and stand to attention.)*

**BUGS** *(Singing)*

'... But his soul goes marching on.' *(Bugs holds the last note for several beats, stops abruptly. He and Jim exchange places in a change of guards drill. They stand to attention in the changed places.)*

**ABU**

Pong... pong... pong... DARJEELING! *(Jim and Bugs relax. They strike up a conversation as they pick up the cutlery and scroll before them respectively and move to the post. Abu takes out another scroll and starts on the second square.)*

**BUGS** *(Chattily, as he makes a cone out of the scroll)*

Monochromatically speaking, the aftermath of the interlude was verily the upshot of preambles.

**JIM**

Merry gentlemen.

**BUGS**

The ointment stitch in time was to toddler Tara what taxi meters were to troublewithnamesstartingwithheff.

**JIM**

Fungus *(He starts placing items of cutlery in Bugs' cone)*

**BUGS**

And haitch. As in Utchinson's itch.

**JIM**

Humus.

**BUGS**

And jay. As in Jailor Jumboolingam.

**JIM**

Jim Venkatapathy, how do you do.

**BUGS**

Same as you.

**JIM**

I don't!

**BUGS**

Same to you.

**JIM**

Same to same.

**BUGS**

Point to point.

**JIM**

Appa's service. Love forty, and Connors in the dressing room. The Pomeranian was Bimbo. Amma's chit fund. 22 carats in Carter's peanut sack. Home crushed. Two balls beating as one court.

**BUGS**

Dust to dust.

**JIM**

V Janakiraman. *(Extending his hand)*

First class first. *(By now the cone-cutlery bouquet is complete.)*

**BUGS** *(Handing him the bouquet)*

First to last.

**JIM** *(Handing him the bouquet)*

Last to leave.

**BUGS** *(Handing him the bouquet)*

Leave of absence.

**JIM**

Granted.

*(They jointly place the bouquet in the receptacle on the post and kneel reverentially before it. DJ enters. The clothes he wears contain many pockets, all of them bulging with a seemingly inexhaustible supply of paper clips (Uclips). He walks in slow, halting steps, leading a chain of paper clips, the end of which we shall never see. He keeps adding to the chain from any and every pocket, but paying no particular attention to it. He positions himself centrally and works by himself. The mother and son rush on.)*

**MOTHER** *(To DJ)*

The head, the head. Which way? Which way the head? *(She notices the chain going offstage and rushes off in that direction, pulling the son along.)*

**DJ**

Aimmm... *(He holds the note briefly. Bugs and Jim rise.)*

Eemmm... *(He holds the note briefly. Bugs recovers the bouquet from the receptacle and hands it to Jim, who takes out the cutlery and hands the items in a bunch to Bugs.)*

I'mmm... *(He holds the note.)*

**JIM** *(Joining, cone in hand)*

Ohmmm... *(He holds the note.)*

**BUGS** *(Joining, cutlery in hand)*

Yoommm... *(He holds the note. All three stop together.)*

**ABU**

Two-and-a-half lakhs. That's what he said. Two-lakhs-and-a-half. Breakfast, lunch, dinner, morning, noon, night. Two-and-a-half lakhs. Two-lakhs-and-a-half. *(Abu has now finished the second square. Jim goes to Abu, steps into the square, and tests it – jumping north-east-south-west. He rolls up the second scroll with the first, while Abu takes out a third. They start work together on the third square. Bugs goes up to DJ.)*

**BUGS**

Why?

**DJ**

Mmmm...

**BUGS**

Whymmm?

**DJ**

It's all in the head.

**BUGS**

Kishandas Gurcharandas, MP. My father. MP, Kishandas Gurcharandas. Season Ticket.

**DJ**

In the eye of the beholder.

**BUGS**

Myself Bhagwandas Kishandas. Son of Kishandas Gurcharandas, MP.

**DJ**

Diversity and or university vis-a-vis largest technical manpower united in third degree.

**BUGS**

Bugs. Yes? *(Extends hand as for 'tirtha'.)*

**DJ** *(Giving him a clip)*
Yesterday.

**BUGS** *(Tossing it over his head, extending hand again)*
I had buck teeth till age ten.

**DJ** *(Giving him a clip)*
Today.

**BUGS** *(Tossing it over his head, extending his hand again)*
I had braces till age fourteen.

**DJ** *(Giving him a clip)*
Chips for all by twenty-first century fox.

**BUGS** *(Tossing it over his head, standing to attention.)*
Carrots for breakfast farsightedness. *(He collects his cutlery set, stands it in front of DJ)*
Hit and run case.

**DJ**
If I miss?

**BUGS**
Open and shut.

**DJ**
I take this?

**BUGS**
In the event of a sudden collapse in middle order batting you can always take a horse to water.

**DJ**
Singularly first person possessive.

**BUGS**
So kind of you.
*(He takes the end of the chain from DJ's hands and leads it ever so carefully in the direction of Jim and Abu. He positions himself before the two of them just as the third square is completed. They stand aside.)*

**BUGS** *(Continuing)*
In the name of the son's capitals. *(He undoes one clip and drops it in the first square.)* Father's full blockhead. *(He undoes another clip and drops it in the second square. He takes out a third clip, holds it against the light.)*
Twice born. *(He drops it into the third square, now complete.)*

**ABU**
Into the valley.

**JIM**
With bells on her toes.

**DJ**

Follow the yellow brick road.

*(They kneel as if in prayer at their respective places – on two sides of the three squares drawn. The mother and son enter, survey the scene, and go up to Abu. He points in the opposite direction, off. They go to Jim. He points in the same direction. They go to DJ. He points in the same direction. They go to Bugs.)*

**BUGS** *(Singing)*

'... Such a lovely face.'

*(He holds the last note briefly, stops abruptly, and points in the same direction. The mother moves off, notices the son kneeling next to Bugs, returns to pull him away, but stops to look at the three squares drawn. Sensing an imminent intrusion, the four others pick up their individual props and step back cautiously. In a quick move, the mother picks up the chalk, draws the next two squares [forming the T with the first 3 squares], hops through the squares drawn so far, picks up the son, and rushes out.*

*Bugs returns to DJ with the end of the chain, while Jim and Abu resume work on the squares – a new scroll, some fresh computations.)*

**BUGS**

So kind of you.

**JIM**

Ceteris paribus.

**BUGS**

We are all so, so different, but then we are in spite of and notwithstanding.

**ABU**

Mutatis Mutandis.

**BUGS**

It's the distant effort, the view from the hillocks, to get above from where you're at.

**JIM**

Modus operandi.

**BUGS**

You will, then?

**ABU**

Raison d'etre sine qua non post hoc reductio ad libidinum.

*(DJ accepts the end of the chain. Bugs picks up his cutlery set and leads DJ to the other two.)*

**BUGS**

Dhananjaya of wealthy mind, healthy body.

**ABU**

On my left, weighing in at 150, four times gold-fingered.

**DJ**

Best of my abilities.

**BUGS**

Dear John mightier than sword.

**JIM**

Dhanana Janana baker's man.

**DJ**

Last but not least

**BUGS**

DJ, by the long shorts.

**DJ**

I remain, yours obediently.

**BUGS** *(Pointing to the squares)*

In!

*(They kneel on two sides of the squares already drawn. Adding the sixth square assumes the proportion of a group project. Through the following passage, DJ handles his chain rather like prayer beads, but also adding clips to it now and then. The others often look to DJ for direction. The actual speech among the four, through the passage, is left for the performing group to improvise, within the important guidelines:*

*Stick to the rhythm-pattern struck so far for the four characters.*

*Avoid overdoing the gibberish.*

*Attempt earnestness; avoid caricature.*

*If in doubt, the entire passage may be done without speech.*

*The group combines speech (if needed) and business for a rapid handling of the scene which requires:*

*– drawing a square between the first and second, on one side;*

*– realising error, erasing it, starting again;*

*– drawing a square between the second and third, on the other side;*

*– realising error, erasing it, starting again;*

*– drawing a square between the fourth and fifth, correctly;*

*– being plunged into doubt about the rightness of the drawing.*

*The four of them resume their kneeling position and put their heads down in meditation. The Girl enters. She is dressed in a backless choli and a low slung widewhirl skirt. She is very slim waisted. Seen from behind, her waist forms the neck of a woman's face painted on her back, beaming, inviting. The top of the skirt forms the top of a sleeveless gown for the figure at the back. Yes, there is the hint of a cleavage too. Chain anklets on bare feet would be quite in order. She carries an army canteen water bottle with a strap and a screw-on cup. The girl talks to nobody in particular, but does appear to be addressing the four men, referring occasionally to the squares and, perhaps, to their 'instruments'.)*

**GIRL**

Hi! I'm Linda. No, that's not my real name, of course not. But what the hell – you can't live all your life with the name given to you by somebody you don't know, you don't see. So, why not, I say. Linda's okay, I guess. Lily aunty called me that. She heard me singing in the school concert and said she loved my voice. It reminded her of Linda someone. Big name, she said. Lily aunty thought I should take singing seriously. Yeah, I was in great demand and all that, but what the hell – you can't just – do you remember the jingle for Cosmo club sodas? 'You can count on... ' Lily aunty just dragged me to this guy who was looking for a new voice – well actually a new face – oh, it was nothing much really. I did about eight or ten such spots and said enough is enough. I've got to concentrate on my dancing. I told Lily aunty that. That's not her real name, of course not. I told her I was going straight to the lawyer's office and getting my name changed officially to Linda. You won't believe it, but in the arangetram, the programme had my name printed the old way, and the compere kept referring to me as Linda. Baby Linda. I was thirteen then. The first thirteen-year-old in an arangetram, the compere said. At least in a long while, the Governor said. A full three-and-a-half-hour show it was. No shortcuts. Hard work it was. Hard work and discipline. Hard work and discipline and complete surrender. People ask, how I manage, where I get the stamina from. Performances, professional engagements, travel – and to still manage studies, exams. You can't just get away with a first class now. Who'll look at you? Who'll give you aid? I hardly had time for any serious swotting, but what the hell – ninety-five-point-six is not too bad I guess. I really must make up my mind soon. A. Here or there. If here, B. What next? If so, C. Where? If not here, and if there, D. What then? You know what I mean? Hey, I don't know your names. I'm Linda. That's not my real name, of course not. But what the hell – you can't live all your life...
*(She stops. A short pause. She moves swiftly to stage centre and positions herself facing upstage. She pours a cup of water for herself. The mother and son enter. She goes up to the girl. The son goes to the face at her back.)*

**MOTHER**

The Head. Where's the head. We've got to find the head.
*(The girl gargles loudly with the water from the cup and points off.)*

It's in the letter. The head at sunrise. The tail piece to the letter says it. The head. Quite clearly it says the head. *(The girl gargles again, points off again.)*

The head before the sun peeps through the cracks in the flyover. Before the tailenders wag the barking trees.

**GIRL** *(Squirts elegantly in the direction she is pointing)*

Kashi yatra!

*(The boy zips the umbrella out from the holdall and hands it to the mother, who grasps it and strides out. The boy is about to ask her a question. The girl snaps her finger and points in the direction of the group.)*

Sunny side up!

*(The boy does not move. She turns to face him, points to the group again, and smiles.)*

You can count on Marlboro Valley for the very finest...

*(The boy moves in the direction of the group, obediently, cautiously. He pauses, wondering how exactly to join them. The group springs up and forms a tight semicircle above the boy. They sing a jingle.)*

**ABU**

A, you've licked the aftertaste.

**JIM**

B, there's no more body odour.

**DJ**

C, the cholesterol's gone.

**BUGS**

It's as simple as ABC! The complete cigarette, the complete chocolate. C-in-C – the chocolate filtered cigarette for complete satisfaction.

**ALL FOUR TOGETHER**

It's as simple as ABC, Always buy C-in-C!

*(The boy rushes out. From now on, the men talk to only the backside of the girl, even trying to catch the attention of the face there. The girl's speech maintains the tempo till the very end, but her face takes many drastic turns, contrasted to the face on the back. The men go up to the girl, who turns to face upstage again.)*

**DJ**

Comprehensive proof of the spherical contour of any surface may be either via in situ systems or from remote sensing methodologies.

*(She turns to him, interested. Jim moves swiftly.)*

**JIM**

The orthogonality of multiple linear dimensions in a composite topographical space may be likened to a cyclical equation of rotational parameters. *(She turns to him.)*

**BUGS**

The paradigm shift calls for a reticular homeostatic functional device monitoring the interactive dissipative transfer losses on a real time basis. *(She turns to him.)*

**ABU**

In accordance with the law of parsimony, the sandcastle theory of structural attenuation posits the warp and woof of convex surfaces as returning full circle to a flat earth single helix. *(She turns to him. All four of them are pleased. They revert to the jingle.)*

**ALL FOUR TOGETHER**

It's as simple as ABC. Always Buy CinC. *(The girl turns upstage, pours some more water into the cup. The Group tries again.)*

Old Mother Hubbard is in ecstasy, the cat's in the cupboard but the dog don't see. *(The girl giggles loud, stops, replaces the cap, walks over to the receptacle, and squirts elegantly into it. She then faces the group.)*

**GIRL**

Drain plug. *(The girl walks over to the drawing and settles into it. The men scramble for the receptacle.*

*There are two parallel scenes now. The girl examines the four sets of instruments, and with or without their help proceeds to complete the aeroplane. The receptacle, now yanked off the post, is fought for by the four, changing hands frequently. When the girl has finished with the drawing, she claps her hands in glee. The men stop, drop the receptacle, and stare at the aeroplane. The girl demonstrates the hopscotch, tossing and picking up an imaginary chip in the process. She then comes up to the men.*

*There are two parallel streams in the following passage, the Girl speaking together with any of the men. The streams begin gently, but build up to a competitive level in volume.)*

## STREAM 1

**GIRL**

Super economy without compromising international standards in safety, luxury, and inflight comfort. Children and dogs allowed. For first timers, the ability to distinguish hog from hen might be an added qualification. For while Lily aunty's supply of phenobarbitone was the fish out of water, the loaves of bread formed a human chain against the great pretender. Whack! Wart-n-all. Bingo! Dart-n-mouse. Zing! Ton-o-washing at the flick of a button. Frankly, my dear, I care a great deal more than a Dane for his father's ghost. Aerobics apart, the sheer dragnet of cultural lag is a surrender to the sensual nuts and bolts. Foot down, that's my instant coffee. Feet first and last, that's the bearded spiritual in Bermudas. I am. Therefore I want. I wanna wanna wanna wanna wanna wanna wanna to the power of wanna.

## STREAM 2

**ABU**
Callipers this side up.

**JIM**
Fragile and handpicked.

**DJ**
Export orders against imposters.

**BUGS**
Alligators in the bath.

**DJ**
Atrocious green slipped into silken lace.

**BUGS**
The greening of valleys in god's playpen is uncensored.

**JIM**
Ethnic chic long ago in contemporary blister.

**ABU**
Bluster.

**JIM**
All in all, blistering bluster.

**ABU**
Californicacious spacious.

**DJ and BUGS** *(Together)*
Chartbusters tandem sprocket.

**ABU and JIM** *(Together)*
Before it melts into lava, double quick.

**DJ**
Hark! *(They all press their watches against their ears)*
Come in Roger...

**JIM**
Incoming Roger...

**ABU**
Over and out.

**BUGS** *(Singing)*
'... Glory to the new-born king!' *(He holds the last note briefly, stops abruptly, and moves to the girl. The others follow.)*
Out and out.

**ABU**
Rent a cabbage.

**JIM**

Tipperrary red canary.

**DJ**

Ohmmm...

**ALL**

Anties in her panties!

*(While the Girl continues her monologue in Stream 1, we have voices in unison in Stream 2 from this point onwards)*

## STREAM 1

**GIRL**

Get thee to a puppery! To a puppery, git! Tally ho! Daylight come and I wanna. Come rain, come midsummer knocks, the doormat holds the secret kinky. Two and one score the filly fancy free fully pipped the post box. Foot, foot, foot! Heavy handed. Even handed down to the minutest seconds. Far from being shopkeeper's duty for the price of free samples, the politico-socio-economico-historico chocochips fallout would make the most neurotic froggie croak a hysterical anthem.

## STREAM 2

**DJ and BUGS** *(Together)*

**DJ**

Take the A train. North by northwest. Eighty days to sail the wind out of the jackpot. Apocalyptic leaps and bounds on quantum wheel chairs presuming Dr Livingstone's onion soup. St Nicholas surely had a hand in it.

**BUGS**

The origin of the practice of sending messages of greeting on a pictorial card utilising the services of the postal department is attributed to the promotional strategy of an unregistered factory manufacturing playing cards.

**JIM and ABU** *(Together)*

**JIM**

Price elasticity following Young's modulus clearly points to the tag on a pair of Levis as a function of the magnetic field in Basmati rice vis-a-vis eleven sticks and a butt as a fitting reply. In conclusion, buy now, fly later. Tomorrow is last week's leftovers.

**ABU**

Grandfather rode a horse to work. Banned automobiles to a ring of kite thread. Father smoked his Austin Six behind the barbershop. Grain by grain. Custom made prescription. *(Pause. Looks at Jim)* Can you hear me out there? I swear I don't. *(They stop. All four stare at the girl, still continuing.)*

**GIRL**

Albeit whatsoever, Lily aunty's garden is nonetheless. No promise without smoke. No problem children. Foot-n-mouth!

*(She pauses. She takes her water jug and tosses parts of it to them, the plebeians in the arena – the cap, the strap, the plug. Pause.*

*The four men now speak together in unison.)*

**ABU**

If I weren't a gunner, I wouldn't be here. Number Four gun – fire!

**JIM**

Terra firma to the point of order but not one inch more!

**DJ**

They called it a calling, the call of the molly-coddled cobbler.

**BUGS**

Passing the duck stops the here and now web silence. *(A pause)*

**ALL FOUR TOGETHER**

Nostradamus! *(The mother and son have entered. They sense the tension in the scene. The mother moves towards the girl, hesitates, and whispers to the boy.)*

**MOTHER**

The tail, the tail.

*(The boy points in the opposite direction. The mother leaves. The girl tosses the jug to the boy with a tired smile. He catches it. The girl turns her back immediately. The boy passes the jug quietly to one of the four and slips out.*

*The three others move swiftly to reassemble the jug. They offer it to the girl, who walks away to the aeroplane. They hang it on the post in the receptacle's place.)*

*The girl starts tidying up the area. She places one scroll neatly in each of the squares – taping them down if necessary. She places cutlery correctly at four places around the aeroplane. She uses the chain of clips to make a decorative border on three sides of the aeroplane. She places the abacus at the head of the setting. She takes her time on these chores, ending at the foot of the first square, ready to start on the hopscotch.*

*Meanwhile, the men regard the receptacle on the ground. They take turns picking it up and tossing it to hit the post. After a few hits and misses, they close in on it on the ground. The boy enters, sits on the holdall and watches. The men first toe the receptacle around a few times between them. Gradually the kicking gets more vigorous, more frenzied, and more vicious. There is one final allout kick towards the post. The boy has remained still, watching. One of the four walks up to the boy. The three others follow. They form a semicircle around him.)*

**ABU**

Give a dog a funny bone.

**JIM**

Prime ribs on tenterhooks.

**DJ**

Pass the salt licks to the wounded.

**BUGS**

Pass.

*(They go over to the girl, who darts into one of the squares for safety. Moving strictly outside the hopscotch perimeter, they handle the girl inside, at first gently but firmly, passing her on like a fragile parcel, gradually getting more forceful, even rough, managing finally to push her out of the aeroplane on the entry side. The girl is immediately helpless, in fright and immobilised. The men pick her up together and bring her into the hopscotch, rigid and horizontal. They lay her spread-eagled against the aeroplane pattern, face up. They regard her in this position briefly and then sit around her in the places laid by the cutlery. The boy goes up to the receptacle, picks it up carefully with the end of the umbrella, and places it at the foot of the post, under the hanging water jug. He then positions himself next to the post. The men pick up a knife and fork each and freeze with the cutlery in their hands. The velvety smooth voice of the woman on the sound system comes on again.)*

**WOMAN'S VOICE**

Aap ki jaankari ke liye, bahar ka taapmaan chhatees degree Celsius hai. Yatriyon se nivedan hai ki vey aglee soochna tak apne jagah par hi baithen rahen. Dhanyavad.

*(The girl starts on her opening monologue again: 'Hi! I'm Linda... ' By the time she's at 'Lily aunty thought I should take singing... ', the mother has entered. She goes up to the girl at the head and speaks over her monologue.)*

**MOTHER**

They told me to come back tomorrow. Try tomorrow, they said. It's too long. It's too long already, they said. The tail is well past the flyover, and the sun has passed the cracks hours ago. Crackers to the early worm. You take care of yourself now.

*(She exits, pulling the son away with her. The girl is continuing with her monologue as the lights begin a slow fade out.)*

***Close of play***

# PART 2: GREEN BELT

## CHARACTERS IN THE PLAY

ABU, JIM, BUGS, DJ ........ *Young men in their late twenties or early thirties*
SWAMI (SON) .................................*A bit younger than the other men*
AMMA (MOTHER) .................... *The fifties have closed in, but who cares*
LEENA (GIRL) ............................................*About the same as Swami*

Leena calls Swami's mother Ammu. The others say Amma.

Although this play may be performed independently, a reading of the companion piece *Item 20* should help.

*The interior of Swami's one-room apartment. The limited space is evident not so much by the number of things on stage, as by what they are. For Swami is an artist, a rather catholic one. Among other things, we see a prominently placed easel with a painting. It is a picture of a part of a lamp post (or is it a bus stop?) with a receptacle attached to it that says USE ME, looking rather like a graphic view of the city at night, from a window. Another prominent display is a long and wide banner of computer paper with the bold printout that says CONGRATULATIONS JIM. A single exit on one side of the room suggests a kitchen on one side of it and a shower and toilet on the other. The entrance to the apartment is on the opposite side, from a passage. The door is not visible on stage, although heard opening and closing to the accompaniment of 'Yankee Doodle', electronically piped. The location, we discover presently, is American, but the gestalt is not particularly explicit.*

*Abu, in a smart but sober suit, is wondering if he should sit and, if so, where. Leena is commuting between a recipe book propped up in the room and a half-done dish in the kitchen. With her attention still on the recipe, she tries to make Abu comfortable. In the process, she begins to attend to the room, arranging things, putting things in place. Abu joins. Soon he is making trips to the kitchen.*

**LEENA**

It's mostly done. Another minute or so and you can add the garam masala. It's all mixed, and ground, and kept ready. In the coffee mug on the right – the white coffee mug with the LA Olympics on it.

**ABU**

I still think we could all have met at a restaurant.

**LEENA**

God, it must be the only surviving LA Olympics coffee mug in the whole of LA.

**ABU**

Or met here and gone over, all together.

**LEENA**

The only one in this whole country maybe.

**ABU**

An Indian restaurant too. If that's what everybody wants.

**LEENA**

Certainly the only LA Olympics mug in the whole world with garam masala in it.

**ABU**

There are Indian restaurants here, you know. Lots of them. You can get anything you want.

**LEENA**

There's nothing you can't get here. All within the routine shopping. No out-of-the-way trips. No fancy prices either.

**ABU**

If that's what you all want, that is.

**LEENA**

Just stir it a bit if you could, please.

**ABU**

There's a place they call Madras. You know how it's pronounced here – Mad-rus.

**LEENA:**

Okay, you can put it in now. All of it. Stir it nicely. Put it on simmer and cover it, please.

**ABU**

It's actually Pakistani. Run by a Paki family. It's called Madras though.

**LEENA**

You sure you don't want to sit for a while? There's not much to do now.

**ABU**

They even serve Kingfisher beer there. Did you know that?

**LEENA**

I'm sorry, I can't offer you a drink or something. I'm not sure I know where Swami keeps these things.

**ABU**

They should be in soon, you said. We can wait.

**LEENA**

Besides, we could wait for Jim at least.

**ABU**

Yeah, Jim...

**LEENA**

Swami's mom brought in a great big load of stuff when she came. Frying stuff, chutneys...

**ABU**

When was it announced?

**LEENA**

She had written six months ago that she...

**ABU**

Jim. When was it?

**LEENA**

Jim. Jim's green card. Oh, just about a week ago. Yes, about a week. I remember Ammu had just returned from her Disneyland package and was telling us all about the wine and cheese evening at some place or the other, and Bugs came in with the news.

**ABU**

And Jim himself?

**LEENA**

Oh, we didn't see him till after the weekend. He was busy, he said. Busy working on a paper for some conference in Boston.

**ABU**

Swami's mother... Does she... ?

**LEENA**

Ammu! She's into haff and laff already. Real fast. She's sweet. She's made herself quite at home here, you know. Bugs drops in at least...

**ABU**

Does she know about Bugs? *(Pause. Leena goes over to Abu and adjusts his tie.)* Topic change time.

**LEENA**

That he was the first to make it past the post? That his work permit is actually yellowing?

**ABU**

First with a work permit.

**LEENA**

What if she doesn't know?

**ABU**

First to be upwardly mobile.

**LEENA**

Then, again, what if she does know? *(She breaks off)*

**ABU**

From Services Section in the Department Store to Floor Operations at the airport. A senior janitor supervising a junior staff of two other janitors.

*(Leena now improvises in the limited space, freshening up, removing her apron, changing a part of her dress, doing her hair, and so on.)*

**LEENA**

What she'll find a bit difficult to understand is the difference. Bugs is different. He's done so many things since he came here.

**ABU**

Like dropping out. Ditching the MD surgery programme.

**LEENA**

Like designing a reversible coat. One that he could wear at medical school by day and at the cafe by evening.

**ABU**

As a waiter. Well, he swapped that for a pair of overalls some time ago.

**LEENA**

What Ammu and most of us won't understand – you included, Abu – is that Bugs is different. His world is different. The colour of the card means nothing to him. The work permit is just a formality – just a step in the direction. Even full citizenship, when it does come, will be just that – a mere formality.

**ABU**

What direction? Where is he headed?

**LEENA**

Have you tried asking him?

**ABU**

Have you?

**LEENA**

I have tried. I can't say I understand fully, but I think I've learned to... what's the word...

**ABU**

Respect...

**LEENA**
No, not that. Yes, respect, but something more.

**ABU**
Sympathise...

**LEENA**
Not sympathise... that's too close to pity.

**ABU**
Appreciate...

**LEENA**
Forget it! You see what I mean? We can't see things as different or unique. We can't accept it. Everything must be reduced to a single word.

**ABU**
You could have a regular column in India Abroad, you know. Heart-to-Heart with Leena. Or Linda. Or your full name, if you think that might work better.

**LEENA**
Which one? Leena Vasanth? Or Leena Simpson? Or Leena Vasanth Simpson? Or Leena Vasanth Simpson Vasanth?

**ABU**
I'm sorry, I didn't mean to...

**LEENA**
Just Leena should be fine.

**ABU**
I'm really sorry. I shouldn't have...

**LEENA**
But not Linda.

**ABU**
That's the name we first knew you by.

**LEENA**
Linda is over.

**ABU**
If you were wearing a tie, I'd try to adjust it.

**LEENA**
Topic change time.

**ABU**
Where are the others?

**LEENA**
They'll be in by and by. Ammu went out with Swami after we got the Biryani done. I said, I could handle the curry. You'll never guess where they've gone.

**ABU**

Okay, shock me.

**LEENA**

Boy, you're in that kind of mood today.

**ABU**

You have a prescription?

**LEENA**

Taking off your jacket and tie might help. Helping out with arrangements might help.

**ABU**

Going out for cigarettes might help?

**LEENA**

Giving up cigarettes might help. You know Swami and Jim don't...

**ABU**

Yeah, I know. Funny things this country does to some people.

*(Abu has taken his jacket off and draped it carefully over whatever prop appears most suitable. He is about to take his tie off when the musical door chime goes off. He quickly restores the tie in place. Leena goes to the door. Abu does too. They stop, each politely insisting on the other staying back. There is a minor scuffle. Abu pulls Leena to the middle of the room and holds her in place tightly, then embraces her. She waits. When Abu loosens his hold to get more intimate she pushes him hard, and he lands on the floor. She laughs, picks up his jacket, and tosses it to him. Meanwhile the door chime has run a few times. The mother's voice is heard.)*

**AMMA** *(Off)*

Leena! Leena, it's us. We didn't take the key. We can't let ourselves in.

*(Leena produces a cake, still in its packaging. She keeps it before Abu, smiles, and gives him a pat or pinch, on the cheek.)*

**LEENA**

A reward. But it is customary in this sport for losers to return the prize to the management for charitable use.

*(She goes to the door. Abu remains seated on the floor with the cake before him. He takes out a pack of cigarettes from his jacket, takes a cigarette, places it in his mouth, and stops. Ammu enters, followed by Swami and Leena. Ammu has short hair, a large pair of rings on her ears, and a distinctly contemporary make-up, striking but unobtrusive. She wears a T-shirt and bolero with pants, looking just a bit large, but largely comfortable. She enters with a girlish beam, pirouettes, and strikes a pose from a mail order catalogue next to Abu but not noticing him.)*

**AMMA**

Well, what do you think? *(Leena and Swami clap)*

**LEENA**

Bee-yoo-tiful. I didn't think you'd cut it so short. But it's really nice. You look great!

**SWAMI**

Hi, Abu.

*(Amma turns slowly and notices Abu, who claps methodically thrice. She takes a deep bow in acknowledgement.)*

**AMMA**

If I bend any lower, I won't be able to straighten up again. What's that you have before you?

**ABU**

Oh, something for the charity bazaar. From one who has...

**LEENA**

His contribution. A cake to go with the wine. Or the coffee. Or whatever.

**ABU**

I don't believe it.

**AMMA**

I don't either. It's Abhimanyu. Abhi. Abu.

**ABU**

You've cut your hair.

**AMMA**

You've brought a cake.

**ABU**

Your clothes, your... you're wearing...

**AMMA**

You are sitting on the floor.

**ABU**

Your kumkum...

*(Amma straightens. She moves towards the kitchen, stops. She returns.)*

**AMMA**

Wait a minute. I'm not needed in the kitchen.

*(An awkward pause. Leena, Swami, and Abu move simultaneously. Leena tidies the cushions and seats. Abu places the cake carefully at a table. Swami does his bit. Ammu stands still, watching the clumsiness with some delight.)*

**AMMA**

Halt! *(They do)* All right, since you've been such good children on the whole, I'll tell you. The kumkum went. It was going anyway. It remained because of Swami's insistence. But when the stick-on bindi came on, the kumkum powder had actually gone already. Red stick-on bindi, yellow stick-on bindi, white stick-on bindi. No bindi. Going, going, went!

Manju – the older one – she grumbled a bit. But Swami insisted. Manju grumbled just a bit, dutifully echoing what her in-laws might have said. Then the baby arrived, and all was forgotten. Yes, I married early, had my two children early, had my one grandchild early. Early retirement plan too. So – is that all clear now? *(She goes up to Abu and takes his hands in hers. He bends to touch her feet. She raises him, then picks up his jacket, and gives it to him.)*

Here, you better keep it on. You look so smart in jacket and tie. *(Abu puts it on.)*

**LEENA**

Glamorous grandma Ammu! *(Leena comes up and hugs Amma. Swami joins them. Abu watches for a while. Leena extends the circle and takes Abu in. DJ enters. He has a prominent beard, which he carries with ease. His clothes are an assortment of garments imported from third world countries. His speech is campus American. He carries a bottle of wine with a ribbon on it.)*

**DJ** *(Entering)*

Hey, don't you guys know better than to keep the door open in this part of...

*(He sees the tableau)* A group photograph? I can join, can't I?

**AMMA**

Ah, Mr Dhananjaya, KB of transcendental fame. Do come in.

**SWAMI**

Yes, do. Over here.

*(They strike a pose, as for a group photograph. Through the passage below, they improvise short exchanges in the grouping.)*

**DJ**

What's this for?

**LEENA**

Chumma.

**DJ**

Greeting number 21. Wishing the function every success.

**AMMA**

Can't it be my birthday?

**SWAMI**

Amma's rebirthday.

**DJ**

Number 5. Many happy rebirths of the day.

**ABU**

Get the photographer to hurry.

**LEENA**

It's his coffee break. We've got to wait.

**AMMA**

If I hold this any longer, my dentures will fall off.

**LEENA**

What if they keep grinning on the floor?

**ABU**

What if they hop across the floor grinning?

**SWAMI**

Exit grinning.

**DJ**

The case of the vanishing cheese.

**AMMA**

Oh god, dear god, please shorten coffee breaks in your next five-year plan.

*(Jim enters. He is modestly dressed, nondescript in appearance, generally five years behind current fashions. He is rather attached to a cloth shoulder bag that has seen much service. He speaks as he enters.)*

**JIM**

It's simply not safe to leave the front door... *(He stops)* Oh, god...

**AMMA**

Dear god, thank you for listening.

**ALL**

Congratulations!

*(They surround Jim. Abu breaks off. DJ gives Jim the wine, who gives it to Swami, who gives it to Amma, who gives it to Leena – who takes charge.)*

**ABU**

I'd better see to the door *(He goes out)*

**LEENA**

You're not slipping out for cigarettes, I hope.

**AMMA**

And you're not going to smoke this evening away, I hope.

**SWAMI**

It's all right, Amma. *(Abu re-enters)*

**ABU**

As a matter of fact, an occasion like this calls for cigars. You know that, I guess. Here, *(He takes out a set.)* One each and one to spare. Unless Leena and Amma want one each too. Then I'll have to really go out and...

*(There are protests and admonitions from the group, notably from Leena and Swami. The others object, but laugh it off.)*

**JIM**

Just a minute. *(They quieten)* It is true that four out of the six in this room do not smoke. But whoever said you must smoke the cigar when you are offered one? It is just the gesture, the custom. Right, Abu?

**SWAMI**

You don't offer something you know is out of place. Not to people close to you.

**JIM**

We don't send Christmas cards to each other? To a hundred others like ourselves?

**LEENA**

Jim, this evening is for you. Will you cut out the seminar stuff for a change, and let us take care of you?

**JIM**

All right, all right. It is just the spirit of the thing that I was trying to...

**LEENA**

And Abu, this evening is Jim's. It is being held at Swami's. And Swami has his mother over. So you will be sweet, won't you, and keep the tobacco lobby out of the party?

**ABU**

Sure. Sure thing. I'll save them for DJ's birthday.

**DJ**

At your place? So it's fixed?!

**ABU**

But for now, we must remember that we are the mongrels in this exclusive set.

**LEENA**

And that it's Jim's day.

**SWAMI**

And that it's Leena's party.

**LEENA**

So...

**ABU**

So, we behave.

**DJ**

Every mongrel will have his day.

**JIM**

Oh, by the way, I picked up something. Here.

*(He takes out a small bouquet of flowers from the bag and gives it to Leena.)*

**LEENA**
For me?

**JIM**
Well...

**AMMA**
Very sweet.

**LEENA**
Yes, so sweet.

**AMMA**
So, what is Assistant Professor J Venkatapathy working on nowadays?

**JIM**
Oh, a paper for a conference in...

**DJ**
In Boston. We heard about that.

**ABU**
What's the target for the tenure track?

**JIM**
I don't know. You can't put numbers on these things.

**AMMA**
Anyway, what are you working on?

**JIM**
Dolls.

**LEENA and AMMA** *(Together)*
» Dolls?
» Did you say dolls?

**JIM**
Yes, on Channapatna dolls. It is a sort of economic modelling based on – you know – a doll within a doll within a doll, and so on.

**LEENA**
The Matryoshka dolls of Russia.

**SWAMI**
From the Semyonov region, North-East of Moscow.

**JIM**
The same as the dolls from Channapatna, South-West of Bangalore.

**SWAMI**
Tell us about it, Jim.

**DJ**
In English, if possible.

**JIM**

All right. Let's say you had an old camera that you want to replace with a fancy new model. You decide to give it away as a sort of gift. You give it to, say, your driver. We did that in Bangalore. He is very happy, of course, with your generosity. Only it takes him a couple of months to realise that using the camera costs a lot of money. And his pattern of income and expenses simply can't – well – can't afford it.

**LEENA**

Where do the dolls come in?

**JIM**

Well, it happens to the bigger doll too. Your employer offers you a car at the book value in the office. Why not, you say. Soon your lifestyle changes, making all kinds of new demands on your time and money, simply because you have the car. The car didn't follow changes in your lifestyle, you see. It preceded it, caused it. You are forced to run faster and faster.

**AMMA**

And that is progress?

**JIM**

That is one kind of economic development.

**ABU**

And so on up the line, to the bigger and bigger dolls.

**JIM**

That's right. Even entire nations. For instance, this country doesn't want to produce some chemicals anymore. Whatever the reason – too bothersome, too energy intensive, bored with the toy, whatever. They take the whole plant, clean it up a bit, put a ribbon on it, and present it to a smaller, poorer country. Wow – a bargain! Then they're stuck with it.

**LEENA**

What happens to the biggest doll? The outermost one?

**JIM**

That is precisely where our work is concentrated at the moment. We believe that, over time, the giver doll will have to carry the weight of all the receiver dolls within itself. And the largest, outermost doll will be the most severely strained.

**DJ**

And you're figuring out the form and extent of that strain.

**JIM**

In a mathematical language, yes.

**LEENA**

You actually get paid to put some numbers on these dolls within dolls?

**JIM**

You'll be surprised how much money there is in this kind of research. And where that money comes from.

**AMMA**

What about Tanjore dolls? Anything in that? It used to be such fun watching their balancing acts, dancing and smiling softly at us all the time.

**JIM** *(Laughing and patting Amma)*

It's not exactly child's play. But it can sometimes be as much fun.

**LEENA**

Here, Ammu. You take charge of this. *(Gives her the flowers.)*

I'll look into the curry topping. *(She goes out, taking the wine with her.)*

**SWAMI**

What this place does not have is a vase.

**DJ**

A chandelier.

**ABU**

An ash tray.

**AMMA**

A shortage of pundits.

**JIM**

A flower vase? Maybe we can...

**AMMA**

Yes, maybe we can. With a good old party game. *(She drops into a chair with the flowers held in front of her.)*

The Queen of Sheba wannnts... something to hold her flowers! Go! *(Abu, DJ, Swami, and Jim rush around the room looking for something, anything that might do, not without some disruption to the tidying up just done. An idea occurs to all of them at about the same time. The bathroom! The kitchen! They rush in that direction. Leena appears with an oven mitten on her hand.)*

**LEENA**

Ammu, where do you think you might have kept... ?

**AMMA**

And the winner is Leena!

*(Amma goes up to Leena, takes the mitten off her hand, puts the bunch of flowers into it, and holds it up like a Wimbledon trophy. The group applauds. Amma wonders where and how to stand the ensemble. She then decides to empty the mitten. She presents one flower to each in the group around her, talking pleasantly as she does so.)*

**AMMA** *(Continuing)*

It was gracious of you to have responded so readily to our invitation. Do convey our warmest regards to your charming family. Yes, it has been such a long time, really. The last we saw them, they were that high, were they not? Have they really? What on earth are they going to do in that great wide arena outside the institution walls? With a ban, too, on the export of the species for laboratory experiments in other lands... Oh dear, oh dear, there are still two left in here.

*(Leena takes out another flower and hands it to Amma herself.)*

Thank you so much, my child. The wonderful things they teach them in laboratories nowadays... Oh dear, oh dear, there is one more.

**SWAMI**

I suppose that is the cue for Bugs to ring the doorbell.

*(The others all lean expectantly towards the door.)*

But Bugs is going to be a bit late, so we will have to find a better way to work with flowers.

*(Swami hangs the mitten with the lone flower in it on a hook on the easel with the painting.)*

**JIM**

An inspiration.

**ABU:**

An archetypal image.

**DJ**

A distinctly new genre.

**AMMA:**

A new political party!

**LEENA**

Okay, Swami, what's this about Bugs coming in late. Did he speak to you?

**SWAMI**

Yes, he has to work the afternoon shift today. And he said he has to drop April home and then get here.

**ALL**

» Drop whom?

» April?

» Who does he have to drop?

Etc. *(Pause)*

**SWAMI**

April.

**AMMA**

It's a girl?

**SWAMI**

Yes, April. The second of three sisters – March, April, and May.

**DJ**

Could June be far behind?

**ABU**
Wait a minute. You know who picks names like that?

**SWAMI**
Yes, she is black.

**JIM**
She... Bugs is... I mean do you think...? When did Bugs tell you?

**SWAMI**
Tell me about what? About being late today? Just yesterday.

**ABU**
And about April?

**LEENA** *(Who has remained silent so far)*
What about April?

**DJ**
What do we know about her?

**LEENA**
We? Who's we?

**DJ**
Whose side are you on, anyway?

**ABU**
Look, all of us here, we've known each other for – what – over seven years now...

**JIM**
Eight. Eight years from the time we got our first student visas together.

**DJ**
In the same queue too. The same Consulate office.

**SWAMI**
How can we ever forget that ant's nest at Gemini Circle?

**ABU**
Eight years. And we've remained good friends, close friends, over all this time, right?

**JIM**
Not without our differences.

**ABU**
Whatever. The fact is we have stuck together.

**LEENA**
Don't you think that has been possible only because of the differences?

**SWAMI**
Unity in diversity and all that.

**DJ**

The great Hindu all-embracing stranglehold.

**LEENA**

Yes, but look where it has led you.

**AMMA**

You've done rather well for yourselves I can see. I mean not just you, but all of us.

**LEENA**

By what standards?

**ABU**

By any standards I should think.

**LEENA**

What do you say, Ammu? You've come down only recently. Your impressions are fresh.

**AMMA**

Swami, some rice flour.

**SWAMI**

Rice flour?

**LEENA**

I don't think there's any in the kitchen.

**AMMA**

Chalk.

**LEENA**

Chalk? Here in... ?

**AMMA:**

Salt. I saw an unopened packet of table salt. Open it. *(Swami leaves to fetch it.)*

**LEENA**

Ammu, dear, what on earth are you up to now?

**AMMA**

Your Mussoorie public school enunciation is rather well preserved. How come you haven't picked up an accent yet?

**LEENA**

Have I not?

**AMMA:**

Not a trace. 'Have I not?' when you should be saying Haven't I?

**LEENA**

Well, thanks. It takes some effort. I have to work at it – to keep the accent out, that is. I am happy to learn that it shows. *(Swami returns with the packet of salt.)*

**JIM**

Actually, it is not just the accent or diction. The vocabulary too. And the construction, and the figures of speech. We stand out, because we are – you know...

**LEENA**

Superior?

**SWAMI**

I don't think he meant that. Not Jim, of all people.

**AMMA:**

'Oh, you speak such good English!' Do you hear people saying that?

**ABU**

All the time!

**AMMA**

I've heard it half a dozen times already.

**SWAMI**

Mr Halpern upstairs was the first, wasn't he?

**AMMA**

But what next? Do you get any closer?

**DJ**

What's that supposed to mean, Amma?

**AMMA**

Is the drawbridge lowered? Is the tower gate opened?

**ABU**

So, who's to blame?

*(Amma takes the opened pack of salt from Swami. Through the next passage, she proceeds to draw an elaborate 'kolam' in the space just before the passage to the door. She does this with great élan – positioning herself carefully, spreading her legs, bending down fully from the waist [not squatting], rising now and then to check the geometric accuracy, but without shifting her feet.)*

**AMMA**

As school kids we went to great lengths to get the frontmost seats in the cinema hall... Can you do one on twenty-four points Leena? You put the points down first like this... Do you remember? Get there early and grab the front seats. Then you grow up and want to go further and further back... The trick is to begin at the centre and work outwards... Further and further back. You actually pay good money to go further back... Do you see how the curves come out? Better balanced – you can't go wrong when you start from the centre... You want to go up front again, of course. And let yourself go, and really enjoy yourself, the way you did before. But you can't... You mustn't take too much of the rice flour at one time. Just enough. Like this. Open the fingers just so, and gently push it through with the thumb... You think you can't. Something tells you it's wrong to think you can. And then you think it's right to think you can't. And then... When in doubt about the loop, remember the rule, 'Odd numbers, cross over. Even numbers, loop back...' And then you think you can't. And then you can't.

*(She is up, checking progress so far. She continues.)*

Okay, Leena, you want to try?

**LEENA** *(Positioning herself just like Amma, opposite her)*

You should ask Jim, really.

**AMMA**

Jim!

**LEENA**

They used to have an annual rangoli contest in National College at Dussehra time, and Jim's team always won.

**JIM** *(Positioning himself on one side)*

What about Swami?

**AMMA**

Swami!

**SWAMI** *(Positioning himself on the fourth side)*

I can manage the simpler designs. The more complicated ones are beyond me.

**ABU**

What you need are stencils. You know, a template.

**DJ**

Or transfers. Just stick and peel. Done in twenty seconds.

**AMMA**

The President of Du Pont might be interested in that idea... Shall we extend it to forty points? Here, I'll set the points. *(The four of them now busy themselves on the pattern, bending and rising at different times, sharing the packet of salt, talking as they work.)*

Each of us can take one end... Good marketable idea, DJ. India alone presents such a vast market. Then on to Bangladesh, Sri Lanka, Thailand.

**ABU**

DJ doesn't need stickers and transfers. He has the most marketable product of all here.

**LEENA**

Eastern philosophical wonders in convenient after dinner packs.

**DJ**

Rich chocolate wrapping, and the choicest liqueurs inside.

**SWAMI**

Ecstatic.

**JIM**

Esoteric.

**LEENA**

Exotic.

**AMMA**

Erotic.

**ABU**

Thrown in as the bonus is DJ himself. At no extra cost.

**DJ**

That's what the audience wants anyway.

**LEENA**

And unto the gigglers shall be delivered the giggles, said the celestial charioteer to the disconsolate archer.

**ABU**

DJ doesn't have to market any dream product here from any distant land. He is the most marketable product himself.

**JIM**

Tell us DJ, how have you managed to remain unscathed? Unentangled?

**SWAMI**

Defying the laws of probability and chance?

**DJ**

Well, I've been lucky, I guess.

**LEENA**

You're being modest, I guess.

**ABU**

It's simple. We come here. We work hard. We do well. We earn our just rewards. It attracts attention, draws admiration. Envy too. Some envy and some resentment. That's a great balancing force. You are attractive and at the same time unattractive.

**LEENA**

Close enough from a safe distance.

**AMMA**

So they respond in the expected manner when you are the gracious host, wide-eyed wonder and all, but somehow manage to misplace your telephone number, so they don't know how to call you, to have you over in return.

**JIM**

Blacks too?

**ABU**

You can't include blacks! *(Amma laughs to herself)*

**JIM**

Maybe you didn't mean it that way, Abu, but that's the way it sounded.

**AMMA**

No, I wasn't laughing at blacks. But you are right too. They can't be included, can they?

**ABU**

They are different.

**LEENA**

And we are different.

**ABU**

Yes, we are.

**LEENA**

Although not exactly peaches and cream ourselves.

**DJ**

No need to be so patronising, Leena. In one lifetime, a black doesn't achieve what one of us can in five years.

**LEENA**

When did you find that out, DJ?

**JIM**

When he left the country, which couldn't achieve in forty years what others had in four hundred years.

**SWAMI**

Anyway, Bugs is changing all the rules.

**AMMA**

I wonder how it would be if Mr Halpern upstairs was a black. *(She rises)* Done! Bhagwandas Kishandasji, please don't keep your mortal subjects waiting too long. *(The four of them move out to reveal the completed kolam, which looks grand in its alien surroundings, although simple in construction. An idea. Leena and Amma place their flowers at two points of the Kolam. The men follow, and make a pleasant pattern of it. The group experiences a oneness standing in a semicircle around the pattern on the floor.)*

**AMMA**

Congratulations, Jim. May the part of you that is theirs strengthen the part that is ours.

**JIM**

Can anybody recite a Ganapati stotram? *(The door chime goes off, running the full length of Yankee Doodle. The group disperses. Swami and Leena move to a corner. Jim, Abu, and DJ are by themselves. Amma goes to the mitten on the painting, takes out the flower, and moves to the door with it. She returns hastily.)*

**AMMA**

It's Mr Halpern. He wants to know if there's going to be a party here this evening.

**LEENA** *(Rushing to her)*

Tell him it's a small get-together – just five or six of us.

**AMMA**

If he asks what about?

**LEENA**

Tell him about Jim. Tell him he's welcome. *(Amma goes out. Swami and Jim rush forward. Jim picks up the flowers from the floor. Swami tries to erase the kolam, but seeing it only spread more, rushes off to get a pan and brush from the kitchen area. Before his return, Jim gathers all the white dust into one small heap using his hands. Swami sweeps up and dashes off. They all resume their places. Amma returns.)*

**AMMA**

He says he can't come just now, but will be delighted to drop in later.

*(She is delighted too. Then she notices the cleaned-up floor. Her expression changes as she goes to where the bunch of flowers is kept.)*

He says the smell of the curry wafting up the hallway is just divine.

*(She picks up the flowers, drops them, picks up the mitten, and wears it.)*

Bugs is on his way. I saw him cross the street talking to Mr Halpern.

*(Amma goes to where the kolam was and waits, hand extended. Bugs enters. He is casually dressed, more convincingly American in appearance than the others, and carries himself with a gentle elegance. He holds a gift-wrapped parcel in his hands. He pauses at the entrance.)*

**BUGS**

Greetings. I'm sorry I had to... *(He sees Amma, shakes her hand, and then gives her a warm hug. The others come forward and greet Bugs.)*

Congratulations, Jim. Here, I brought a little something for the occasion. I hope you like it. *(He gives the gift to Jim, who moves to put it away. Leena joins Swami.)*

**LEENA**

Why don't you open it, Jim?

**OTHERS**

» Yes, why don't you?

» Let's see what it is.

» C'mon, open it now... *(Etc. As Jim opens the gift)*

**JIM**

Why, it's a – what do they call it – it's a potpourri. Isn't that what it is?

**LEENA**

Po-purri. It's pronounced po-purri.

**SWAMI**
How thoughtful of you, Bugs.

**AMMA**
How sweet, how original.

**ABU**
How American.

**DJ**
How symbolic. Herbs and spices from the East to grace a shack in the West.

**JIM**
What do we do with the plastic wrapper? Should we take it out?

**BUGS**
Let it remain inside. The plastic pack has tiny holes to let out the fragrance.

**SWAMI**
Mmmm. You can smell it in the air already.

**LEENA**
Over the curry and biryani!

**AMMA**
It's just like it was in the home of your Professor, Swami. It's just like that.

**JIM**
Thanks, Bugs. It is very nice.

**BUGS** *(Giving Jim a hug)*
All the very best in all you do, Jim.

**SWAMI**
How long does it last? The fragrance?

**BUGS**
Oh, I don't know. About a year, I guess.

**LEENA**
The brass pot is pretty too.

**DJ**
They seem to all come in brass holders.

**LEENA**
Look, it says 'Made in India' here. This brass holder is from back home.
*(Short pause.)*
Come on, DJ, say something appropriate for that.

**DJ**
Herbs is East, the pot is East, and the twain shall meet out West.

**AMMA**
Bugs, before you came in...

**LEENA**

There was a little discussion going on here. About you.

**BUGS**

Oh?

**JIM**

Behind your back you might say, but well meant.

**AMMA** *(Quickly)*

Not just you. All of you. We were wondering...

**JIM**

What makes this group so special? At least that's what it is to me.

**AMMA**

We were wondering how a bunch of such different nuts could come into the same cookie? Is the metaphor okay, Leena?

**LEENA** *(In an American accent)*

Pretty good going, Ammu dear.

**SWAMI**

It's a family, Amma.

**BUGS**

Oh, it's more than that. We are like brothers. We belong. *(There is a noticeable awkwardness)*

**ABU**

A more disparate fraternity you're not likely to see.

**DJ**

Desparate, did you say?

**AMMA**

Why should they all be the same?

**JIM**

Factory made and guaranteed...

**AMMA**

Pancha-Pandava. That's what you are. You are like the five Pandava brothers.

**SWAMI**

That is some elevation, Amma. Only you can think of such...

**ABU**

In exile – is that what you mean?

**DJ**

Wow! And we have with us a Draupadi too. *(Leena, momentarily embarrassed, steps away from Swami.)*

**AMMA**

Well, not in a literal sense. But Leena does look after you boys rather well, doesn't she? She certainly puts up with a lot of epic chauvinism in this – in this – what do you call this apartment?

**DJ**

Pandava pad.

**AMMA**

Pandava pen you could call it.

**SWAMI**

Over here it means a prison, Amma. From penitentiary.

**ABU**

Does she by any chance have a favourite Pandava warrior?

**LEENA** *(Recovering, moving back to Swami)*

That's allowed, isn't it?

**ABU**

Topic change time.

**SWAMI**

I told them about your being late, on account of...

**BUGS**

On account of?

**DJ**

Straight to the point, then. What's this business about you being wrapped up in the pages of a calendar?

**BUGS**

Come September and it will be April in my apartment – pad – pen.

**ABU**

Who is she? What do we know about her?

**BUGS**

About April? It's from April showers. *(Half in tune)*
They bring the flowers
That bloom in May.
You won't know that one. It was before our time. Her aunt told me about it.

**JIM**

So we begin with her birthday.

**BUGS**

January 28. That's her birthday. No, not in April. The girls and the brother were named after important events in the past – events and dates in the lives of the parents. April was when her old man got a full-time job after a year's layoff. March was when her parents saw the movie that moved them so. Christopher Columbus – starring Fredric March.

**DJ**

There's a brother too.

**BUGS**

Yeah, August. The month in which the parents patched up after a violent quarrel, a near split.

**AMMA:**

Tell us how you got to know April, Bugs.

**BUGS**

She plays the drums. And a mean reed flute in between if she gets in the mood.

**JIM**

She's part of your band!

**BUGS**

What would we do without her!

**ABU**

How's it going, Bugs? Are you breaking even now?

**BUGS**

It's not bad. We're doing all right, I'd say. Three evenings a week now.

**DJ**

And your songwriting?

**BUGS**

That's picked up too. Mainly because of April.

**DJ**

Ohh... sounds like a movie script already.

**BUGS**

No, no, you didn't get that right. It's because of April I realised I was writing such bad stuff earlier. I needed to stop everything, switch off, and listen to the sounds around me for a while. Just shut up and listen. I realised how tattered my lyrics really were – third-hand renditions of second-hand sounds.

**LEENA**

And then you started afresh?

**BUGS**

Yeah, it was April who showed me that good lyrics come from not being ashamed of your own feelings – putting them in your own words. No imitations.

**SWAMI**

And it worked?

**BUGS**
And it worked.

**JIM**
No imitations.

**BUGS**
No imitations. Just my own self.

**SWAMI**
It can work only in this country.

**JIM**
It is extraordinary, isn't it? In surroundings with the highest pressures to conform, you can also strike out calmly in your own direction, and it is quite all right, quite acceptable.

**LEENA**
I remember the title of a report in a women's magazine. I must have been in my tenth then. It said America Goes Dry. It was about...

**AMMA**
I remember that one. It was actually an excerpt of a report from a British magazine, reproduced in our own weekly. America Goes Dry. Yes.

**LEENA**
It said that American homes had stopped wetting their toothbrushes before applying the toothpaste on it. Some piece of research...

**AMMA**
And it urged British homes to go the same way.

**LEENA**
We don't know what it did to British families, but the Vasanth home in India certainly went dry immediately afterwards.

**AMMA**
And the homes of hundreds of other readers, I'm sure.

**DJ** *(To Leena)*
Was that about the time you switched from Bata canvas shoes to Nikes?

**LEENA**
About the time I switched from oh gosh to oh shit.

**BUGS***(Laughing softly)*
You felt so red-blooded, right, when you first heard yourself saying it? The easy American sound of shit.

**DJ**
Lots of fibre to it.

**ABU**
I don't know about wet and dry brushes, but there was a time I was brushing my teeth four times a day.

**AMMA**
You had a Colgate scholarship...

**ABU**
Then it came down to three. Then to two.

**DJ**
And now, fully grown and mature, he has settled down to once every three days.

**ABU**
My grandfather always said, if you must brush only once, make it after dinner. Not first thing in the morning.

**SWAMI**
If you want your razor blade to last longer, shave after a bath.

**JIM**
If you want a really neat haircut, get it after you have washed your hair.

**BUGS**
All very scientific, huh?

**DJ**
Sound engineering principles.

**BUGS**
Leena?

**LEENA**
Present.

**BUGS**
What did your grandparents tell you?

**LEENA**
Well – if you must boil and filter your water, do it the other way around. Filter first, then boil. They also said little girls should be seen and not heard. Solid scientific basis for that, they said.

**AMMA** *(To Bugs)*
Your turn. *(She punches him affectionately with her gloved hand.)*

**BUGS**
From his deathbed my grandfather sent a message to his favourite target practice grandchild – to be translated into convent school English by his doting mother. She came personally to pick me up from school, in the only chauffer-driven Studebaker still on the roads, and transmitted the message, 'Go West, young man, to rediscover the East. And don't be in a hurry to get back.'

**AMMA**
And then?

**BUGS**
And then he died. My mother said I simply had to discharge the old man's dying wish.

**LEENA**
And did you?

**BUGS**
Discharge his dying wish?

**LEENA**
Rediscover the East.

**BUGS**
I certainly discovered what the West was not.

**DJ**
Like it was not all white.

**BUGS**
Far from it. And it's not all black either.

**ABU**
If we know what you mean.

**BUGS**
You know what I mean.

**JIM**
The thing is, we are all inventing histories all the time. All according to our own fantasies. While they are busy inventing India, we are busy inventing an America too.

**SWAMI**
A god's own garden of a country which has only apple trees.

**LEENA**
And about one hundred million clones of the original Eve.

**ABU**
Most of them bite harder than they bark.

**BUGS**
I'd like to believe you were only joking.

**ABU**
You mean it's not true?

**BUGS**
A crude joke, but still only a joke.

**DJ**
God, you've changed Bugs.

**BUGS** *(He has picked up the packet of salt and is examining it.)*
Packed in USA. Namak. Sealed and delivered in the US of America.

**DJ**

You really have changed.

**AMMA**

So have you all. Have you not?

**SWAMI**

The trouble is we have fixed notions of people from some moment of time in the past. And it surprises us that what we see today doesn't exactly tally with that sepia-toned photo in one corner of the mind.

**LEENA**

And to think we played marbles together!

**ABU**

It happens in the business world all the time. Look at this character in the three-piece suit, we say. He started as a delivery boy in that departmental store down the road.

**AMMA**

Almost as if... as if there is some regret that they haven't remained the same.

**LEENA**

So that our own change may feel more real?

**JIM**

Look at DJ. He was a student activist with a Dalit group back home. What was it called, DJ?

**ABU**

Ekalavya. What else?

**DJ**

There were many things unoriginal about us.

**JIM**

And where is he now? What happened to his left orientations?

**DJ**

Well, my granddad said, if you turn left three times, you'll be facing right.

**ABU**

And you will have seen the world in the process.

**DJ**

He also said that in a round world there can be no straight lines.

**LEENA**

What a lot we have learned from our grandparents!

**AMMA**

You could put together an Encyclopaedia Geriatrica.

**LEENA**

Grandfathers all. No place for grandmothers?

**AMMA**

One of these days my grandson is going to tell me, 'Little grandmothers must be seen, and not heard.'

*(Bugs, who has been listening but not taking part in the discussion is softly tapping a beat on the packet of salt. He notices that they are watching him. He keeps the packet down on the table, draws himself to his full height, steps slowly to the entrance, stops. The others catch on. They slip into the schoolboy game of 'draw'. Bugs turns around slowly and waits. It is Main Street now, four gunmen ranged against Bugs. In a flash the guns are out, and there is much stylish shooting all round. Pause. They all laugh. The game continues. Jim picks up the pack and places it on Swami's head. Bang, bang, bang. The pack drops. Swami steps forward grinning. Abu picks up the pack and tosses it up. Bang, bang, bang. It livens up. DJ tosses the pack to Bugs, who catches it deftly and tosses it to another. It is caught and tossed and caught several times. Amma tries a catch with her mitten, baseball style. She drops it. Scramble. They kick it around the floor a while. Jim retrieves the pack and tosses it fast to Abu, who misses, and it hits Swami's painting. They stop abruptly.)*

**AMMA**

Time to eat.

**LEENA**

Why don't you guys come and help?

*(Leena and Amma go to the kitchen, followed by Jim, Abu, and DJ. Swami and Bugs shift things to make some floor space. Bugs picks up the salt pack. He taps the beat again and starts humming with it. Swami takes down the picture from the easel, puts it on the floor in the cleared space, face down.)*

**SWAMI**

Is that the new song? *(Bugs nods yes)*

The one with the repeat requests. What's it about?

*(Bugs and Swami talk as they ready the space for the meal, keeping plates on the floor, around the picture board, paper napkins at each place, and a set of wine glasses.)*

**BUGS**

What's it about? *(He smiles)*

Can't be much of a song if it has to be explained!

**SWAMI**

I'm sorry. I guess if you can't explain a poem or a play, you can't explain a song.

**BUGS**

Or a picture in a frame. I can tell you what it's like, not what it's about... It's like the opposite of the moment of truth.

**SWAMI**

The opposite... like knowing that you don't know?

**BUGS**

Something like that. Like a negative Zen. Like a sad discovery of a void. But not exactly unexpected. Sudden, but easy in passage, like a slow freight train.

**SWAMI**

Will you sing it for us? Probably not.

**BUGS**

For you – why not? Is there anything else we can do here?

**SWAMI**

I don't suppose so.

*(Bugs resumes his tapping and humming. He slips into his song gradually, beginning with a scat rendition of what might be the band's prologue on an electric guitar. He continues to exchange a couple of remarks with Swami before getting into the song proper. Meanwhile, he has taken off his shoes, found a place for himself on the floor, and sat down, rather like a classical vocalist from India. Swami moves quietly to pick up a fresh frame from a corner, mount it on the easel, staying there, listening to Bugs.*

*The song by Bugs is crooned softly, but with some intensity. It is best not choreographed with moves, not 'staged', and not full throated in delivery. The song is to be set to tune by the performing group. Minor changes may be made in the wording if absolutely necessary for convenience of meter, retaining the substance of the lyrics.*

*Bugs sings the song softly.)*

**SONG BY BUGS**

Soft floating ladders curved
before my eyes suspended
slippery
they race ahead
unfixed untrapped
by the lecherous stare

Peals of laughter yet unread
in the pages of her almanac
silvery
they coat the lead
blueing browning
stardust into desert sands

Concert in the park with words stillborn
Swallow dive to pool waters gone

A song from the choir of rosebuds strained

in unison ribbon bound
glory
in modest red
shifting lifting
thorny vapours in the air

Sprinting legs plaster cast above
match point van out from forty love

Clockwork set for tomorrow
woke up yesterday
raintree
of words unsaid
soothing smoothing
we learn to love again

*(Bugs stops, and puts his head down. When he looks up, Swami is by his side, his hand on Bugs' shoulder. They smile)*

**BUGS**

That's it. It sounds different with the band, of course.

**SWAMI**

I'm sure it does.

**BUGS**

Did you... ? Could you see anything in it?

**SWAMI**

I saw a wire fence, tightly woven, barbed, electric. It was dissolved by an uprising of sweet peas enclosing the barbs, affirming their love – her love in deed, mine in steely theory.

*(The group from the kitchen enters carrying things – biryani, curry, raita, bread, cake and wine. They chatter among themselves as they put it all down in the middle, move to the entrance, take their shoes off, and find places on either side of Bugs.)*

**AMMA**

What about Chor-Police? You never played Chor-Police?

**DJ**

Cowboys-Indians was much more fun.

**LEENA**

Always a big argument about who should be the Sheriff.

**ABU**

Do you remember the time the cops were really after DJ, and he went into hiding?

**JIM**

A whole week. For a whole week we spoke to DJ only on the phone.

**AMMA**

Was that when he hit the neighbour's cat with his air gun?

**LEENA**

No, that was a mere border skirmish.

**ABU**

This one was the case of a pair of creative geniuses far ahead of their times.

**AMMA**

There were two?

**ABU**

Jim! Who else? You wouldn't guess looking at him now.

**LEENA**

The two of them went to the newly constructed commercial complex in Indira Nagar. None of the shops was occupied. They all had their shutters down with the big bold letters saying TO LET. In one swift manoeuvre, Jim and DJ covered eighteen shops, just adding the letter 'I' between the two words.

**JIM**

Of course, with the rep he had, everybody thought it was DJ, and DJ alone.

**AMMA**

And look at you know. An emeritus professor already. *(They sit)*
Swami, joining us?

*(Swami goes to the entrance, takes his shoes off, and goes to his place to sit. He notices the wine, picks up the bottle, pours some in each person's glass, and then takes his place. They pick up their glasses.)*

**LEENA**

It's your place, Swami. Go on.

**SWAMI**

Congratulations, Jim!

*(With the others still holding their glasses, Swami switches hands, cups his right hand, and takes three quick sips of the wine like 'tirtha', pouring from the wine glass into the cupped hand each time and tossing the last drops over his head. He stops, switches hands again, and waits.)*

**LEENA**

Ammu? You want to... ?

**AMMA**

Dinner is served, Mr Halpern!

*Fade out*
***Close of play***

# Gold And Silver

*A coupe on the Grand Trunk Express*

***Vijay Padaki***

FOR
**ESTHER AND GORDON MUIRHEAD**

## CHARACTERS IN THE PLAY

ALICE TAYLOR ................................ *A retired school teacher from India, now living in England*
JEETENDRA MUKHERJEE ............... *A former student, now visiting her*
MAVIS ............................................................. *Alice Taylor's help*

## SCENES

**Place:** Alice Taylor's home, in a suburban township
**Time:** At the start of the twenty-first century

## INTRODUCTION

The play draws on images in a memory bank from the Railway townships in pre-independence British India. It stops there. The content of the play is not meant to be autobiographical, although it must be admitted that separating memories from personal experience in telling a tale is not an easy task. Equally, it must be clear that Miss Taylor is largely a fictitious person, but inspired by memories of a real-life person all the same.

It could be said that the play was in the making somewhere in the back of the head for a very long time. It was first written as a short piece at the time of India's Golden Jubilee of Independence in 1997 as a little gift for friends in the Royal National Theatre in London. Bangalore Little Theatre had an exchange programme with the National to celebrate the Golden Jubilee. The rah-rah of fifty years of Indian Independence served as an interesting but incidental backdrop.

The reconnection with the friends ten years later, coinciding with the Diamond Jubilee, served as a stimulus for a fresh version, but remained only an idea. The bits and pieces began to fall together quickly into a longish one-act gestalt.

What emerged in the foreground was rather like a short section on a long train ride. It was clear from the beginning that the compartment must have only two occupants, whatever the difficulty in sustaining the contact, with so much to talk about before the next station, with so little time, not knowing where to start, where to head next.

No detailed description of the two characters seems necessary. It must be evident that Alice Taylor is approaching ninety, ageing on some counts, and defying age on others. Jeet Mukherjee is in his sixties, but cannot quite remember his exact age when he is on a train ride.

While Miss Taylor's home is certainly in old England, no special effort seems required to convince us of the locale.

In a double-bill production, the play should go well with *Action Stations*, written much earlier. The two plays can be performed in both stage and radio versions.

The play has a duration of about 45 minutes. There is a shorter version of the play of about 35 minutes.

## FIRST PERFORMED

First read at the National Theatre, London as part of the collaborative project with Bangalore Little Theatre celebrating 50 years of India's independence, 1997.

First performed in full by The Red Curtain, Kolkata, November 2014

*Alice Taylor* .................... ZARIN CHAUDHURI
*Jeet Mukherjee* .................... PRADIP MITRA
*Production Design* .................... KATY LAI ROY
*Production Manager* .................... NAUREEN SHAH
*Stage Management* .................... MEET TYAGI, ANKITA PANDEY, CHIRAG VYAS, DANA ROY
*Special Props* .................... RAHUL I SIRCAR
*Light Design* .................... TOM LAI
*Sound* .................... SUBHAGATHA RIVU SINGHA
*Publicity, Front of House* .................... BAISALI CHATTERJEE DUTT
*Producer* .................... SUMIT LAI ROY
*Directed by* .................... SWARAN CHAUDHRY

## OPENER OPTION – 1

*With Mavis*

*The play opens in the dark. We hear the sound of a Viennese waltz from an old gramophone record. Presently we hear a car driving up and stopping... the door opening and closing... footsteps... knocks on the door... a door opening... voices.*

**MAVIS**

Good afternoon. You must be...

**JEET**

Mukherjee, Jeetendra Mukherjee.

**MAVIS**

Ah, welcome. I am Mavis. Did you find the place easily?

**JEET**

Your directions were perfect. Is she in?

**MAVIS**

Yes, of course. She's in. She doesn't go out anywhere. Just the monthly outing to the village.

**JEET**

I'm glad she is in.

**MAVIS**

First the doctor, then the dentist, then to say hello to her friend, Mrs Singleton. Her golden retriever, actually, not Mrs Singleton.

**JEET**

And the church?

**MAVIS**

No, not the church. The bridge club, yes.

**JEET**

I hope you haven't told her about...

**MAVIS**

She doesn't know. In fact nobody does. I've kept it a secret, as you asked me to. Well, come on in! You can go up to her room right away. Shall we... ?

**JEET**

Thank you.

Door closing... footsteps... A spot comes on Down-right on Mavis and Jeet.

**JEET**

I really don't know what I am going to say when I see her.

**MAVIS**

It's been what, fifty years?

**JEET**

Much more actually. Jamalpur in the fifties... the Railway School. I still remember the living room in her cottage...

**MAVIS**

Was it as crowded as it is here, I wonder. Furniture and knick-knacks from all over British India? *(The lights come on to reveal Alice Taylor's living room. On a single seat sofa, which has known better times, is Alice, head bent, asleep. She might have a cat on her lap, also a senior citizen.)*

**JEET**

Lamps, photo frames, a dozen tables covered with laced cloth, books, magazines, papers, books and more books... much of the wall space covered with magical things from so many faraway lands... much of the floor space too.

**MAVIS**

It's the same still. Her room in there is the room from India, every piece in place. You should feel at home! There, on the right side of the passage.

**JEET**

I can't believe it.

**MAVIS**

The things on the floor... you'll find lots of record covers, some records too. She can't put them back by herself, and she won't let me touch them. I have to do it when she is out.

**JEET**

And her parrot.

**MAVIS**

There are two of them in there. And a cat, usually snoozing on her lap.

**JEET**

It was such a long time ago...

**MAVIS**

There is also the Railway field telephone next to her! Yes, the one with the crank handle on the side. That's our intercom. If she gets to like you, she will call me to serve tea.

**JEET**

With toast and marmalade.

**MAVIS**

With toast and marmalade. Right, go on in. *(The sound from the gramophone once more... The music ends, but the turntable keeps on, the stylus in the last groove. The record is unattended. Mavis exits. Jeet approaches the room from Up-right. Alice takes her time waking up, but remains on the sofa. Jeet knocks. Alice responds by turning to the station telephone and giving the handle a few hard cranks, and then picking up the receiver. Go to start of play)*

## OPENER OPTION - 2

*Without Mavis*

*The play opens with the sound of a Viennese waltz from an old gramophone record in the dark. Presently the lights come on to reveal the living room of Miss Alice Taylor. It is a room crowded with pieces of old furniture, knick-knacks, lamps, photo-frames, laced tablecloths, books, magazines, papers, and more books. Much of the floor space is occupied with things not put back in their places. There are at least two bird cages. On a single piece sofa, which has known better times, is Alice, head bent, asleep. She might have a cat on her lap, also a senior citizen. On a small table, next to her, is an old station telephone with a calling crank handle. The music ends, but the turntable keeps on, the stylus in the last groove. The sound of a doorbell that has gone hoarse. There is a second attempt. No response. The caller tries knocking. Alice takes her time waking up, but remains on the sofa. To the second round of knocking, she responds by turning to the station telephone, and giving the handle a few hard cranks, and then picking up the receiver.*

*Go to start of play*

## START OF PLAY

**ALICE**

Mavis, am I expecting anybody? No? Who do you think is at the door, then? You don't? Well, then, the rule book says you should find out. No, it can't be the postman. He only knocks once. *(A snort that might be a half laugh. We recognize this as a characteristic throughout the play)*

And not quite so rudely. No, it is definitely not the postman. He taps the door, never knocks. I know his tapping. It goes tap-tut-tut-tap. This one was dugga-dugga-dugga-dugga. Yes, please do. *(She puts the receiver down. Almost immediately she cranks the handle again and picks up the receiver.)*

Mavis, are you still there? You were going to? Good. Was I going to say something? No, you know what to do, I'm sure. Oh, yes, one more thing... Mavis, are you there? You are? You should be at the door! We are keeping somebody waiting. Yes, please do. *(She puts the receiver down)*

She must ask if there is an appointment. She always forgets. She must ask, 'Is Miss Taylor expecting you? Do you have an appointment?' She forgets. A visitor at this time in the afternoon! Not another pest! Oh dear, oh dear, I must look dreadful. A ghost from the Bengal swamps.

*(The telephone rings again. She picks up the receiver)*

Alice Taylor, Good evening. Afternoon, you say? Mavis, it's you again? You did? Did you ask if he had... ? Oh, he did? The colour of his jacket? Shoes? They match. He should be all right. Age? Safe. Can't have men under sixty dropping in on a single woman at this hour. You don't? Well, let me tell you, you'll live and learn. Yes, you will, and then you'll come running to me and say... He has what in his hand? A bouquet? A bouquet of roses? *(A half song)* 'One for every time you broke my heart...' Do you think he might be a journalist? A journalist – I cannot meet this evening. He could be a journalist disguised as a salesman. Then, again, he could be a salesman disguised as a journalist. *(Noticing Jeet, whispers into the phone)* Wait a minute. No, it won't be necessary, Mavis. Mr Sheep in wolf clothing has found his way in. No, no cause for alarm. I can see the bobbing tail underneath the jacket. Tea? Not just now, thank you. Three long rings if we decide to have tea. Yes, please do stand by. Thank you, Mavis. *(She puts the receiver down)*

Hmmm... *(A long pause.)* You blinked first!

**JEET**

Good morning, Miss Taylor.

**ALICE**

Your hat, held against your heart to shield it from stray small arms fire, you may put it on the lamp there. No, it's not dusty.

**JEET**

Thank you. And I will just... *(He puts the gramophone off.)*

**ALICE**

Good evening, Mr...

**JEET**

Mukherjee.

**ALICE**

Mukherjee. Good evening. And to what do I...

**JEET**

Jeetendra Mukherjee...

**ALICE**

Mukherjee.

**JEET**

Jeetendra Mukherjee.

**ALICE**

Mr Mukherjee, let me not keep you standing. Unless your business is to take a minute or less. Is it?

**JEET**

I'm all right, thank you.

**ALICE**

Then it will be a minute or less. And this bouquet... I suppose it is for the lady of the manor?

**JEET**
Miss Taylor, I came...

**ALICE**
You're not a journalist, are you?

**JEET**
You don't like journalists.

**ALICE**
Are you?

**JEET**
Not after last Sunday's write up.

**ALICE**
I simply will not have... You read the Sunday piece?

**JEET**
The Sunday column by Bob Martin. He got it all wrong.

**ALICE**
I shall never again, never ever again – yes, he got it all mucking wrong.

**JEET**
I know.

**ALICE**
You do?

**JEET**
I think I do. I'm sure I do.

**ALICE**
Imagine bringing poor old Motu into it.

**JEET**
You have two parrots. Which one is Motu?

**ALICE**
That's him on your left. You might as well give him his green pepper while you're there. It's in the tray below.

**JEET**
And that's Mumtaz there?

**ALICE**
That's Mumu, yes. One for her, too, please.

**JEET**
Not many have seen an Indian parrot in this part of the world.

**ALICE**
Not ones from Rawalpindi, I'm afraid. The parrots in the court of Akbar the Great were Rawalpindi stock. Did you know that?

**JEET**

And when he asked the wise Birbal how many parrots there were in Delhi, he replied...

**ALICE and JEET** *(Together)*

Four thousand three hundred and twenty-one.

**ALICE**

That's right. You know that story?

**JEET**

If there are any more, they have come in from outside Delhi. And, on the other hand, if there are...

**ALICE**

If there are any less... You know the story.

**JEET**

I should. I learned it from you. *(Pause)*

**ALICE**

Hmmm... Come here, let me look at you. *(Jeet steps forward)*
Who are you?

**JEET**

I had to see you.

**ALICE**

Mukherjee, you said.

**JEET**

Jeetendra Mukherjee.

**ALICE**

Am I supposed to know who that is? My, my, my, Jeetendra Mukherjee from the Furs and Feathers pet shop on Kingston Street. How nice of you to drop in on your way back from the waterhole. And how many parrots have flown in from Delhi this afternoon? Is that what I am supposed to say?

**JEET**

You called me Jeet.

**ALICE**

Jeet. That means victory.

**JEET**

That's what you said. Jeet, the victor. Always the victor, you said. A winner. You said you'd call me Jeet. It suited me, you said.

**ALICE**

Goodness! You sound like a stuck record.

**JEET**

Jamalpur.

**ALICE**
What do you know about Jamalpur?

**JEET**
The prettiest railway township of all.

**ALICE**
As long as the East Indian Railway was there.

**JEET**
And the loveliest school of all in all the railway towns.

**ALICE**
Wait! I'm not saying anything more. Which newspaper is it this time?

**JEET**
And easily the most lovely schoolteacher.

**ALICE**
I told you – no more journalists, no more interviews.

**JEET**
Bob Martin got it all wrong.

**ALICE**
Wrong? He can't tell a beet from a banana.

**JEET**
He couldn't care.

**ALICE**
He kept digging. Furiously at it. I couldn't stop him. Like a dog gone mad, he was digging. He kept putting words into my mouth. Before I could utter a word in protest, he would start digging again.

**JEET**
Sixty years of independence torn up by a mad dog.

**ALICE**
It was like taking out the most precious pictures from a family album and tossing them out of the window.

**JEET**
It was a vicious column.

**ALICE**
Blown away. *(Pause)* It wasn't like that at all. They were beautiful times. They are making us look like a taxidermist's shop display.

**JEET**
It's probably what people here want to see. They want to see what they want to believe.

**ALICE**
That's all there is everywhere – on the tube, in the papers. It's sixty years of Empire cock-and-bull all around.

**JEET**

I am sorry they did that to you.

**ALICE**

They did it at fifty. They are doing it all over again now at sixty. All the tamasha, all the noise – all the ignorant noisemakers.

**JEET**

A country's golden jubilee comes only once.

**ALICE**

The tarnished gold must be studded with fake diamonds. *(Pause)* All right, then, you are not a journalist.

**JEET**

Not a taxidermist neither.

**ALICE**

Either.

**JEET**

Either.

**ALICE**

Quaint American mannerisms of speech. Neither here nor there.

**JEET**

I am sorry.

**ALICE**

Imported freely into the country now, I suppose.

**JEET**

Well, with the economy opening up some time in...

**ALICE**

The thin edge was in! Who knows what else will follow... *(Pause)* So, who is Mr Mukherjee?

**JEET**

Jeet.

**ALICE**

Jeetendra, did you say? So, Mr J for Jeetendra Mukherjee, What can I... ?

**JEET**

Wait let me show you. I'll take my jacket off...

**ALICE**

Mr Mukherjee!

**JEET**

And my shirt and vest... No, I don't need to take them off, just lift them up a bit... like this... Let me sit next to you and show you.

**ALICE**

Mr Mukherjee, stop! This is not the house you think you are in!!

**JEET**

I half imagined it would be like this. How would you know? How could I expect you to? After all these many years. Over fifty years!

**ALICE**

Stop, I said! Stop this instant, or I will do something I can't be held responsible for!

**JEET**

There! Under the right shoulder blade, spreading to the middle. *(Pause)*

**ALICE**

Mukherjee?

**JEET**

The shape of a walnut.

**ALICE**

The son of...

**JEET**

RK Mukherjee. Ratin Kumar Mukherjee.

**ALICE**

RK... Muckerji they called him in the club. Or just Muck. Ratin Kumar Muckerji. The head of rolling stock at the workshop. Or Rats! Rat Muck sometimes.

**JEET**

1948-1953 *(The telephone rings. Alice picks up the receiver.)*

**ALICE**

Yes, Mavis? No, Mavis, nothing untoward at all. Whatever gave you the idea? A salesman and a gentleman. Oh, walnut. Not furniture, the nut. No, thank you, Mavis. I will call when we think we could do with some tea. Yes, three long rings. *(She keeps the receiver down)*

Jeet Mukherjee from Jamalpur Railway School, 1948-53. Well, well, well!

**JEET**

I had to see you. May I now... ?

**ALICE**

Yes, you may tuck your shirt in now. No, you don't have to leave the room. Hmmm... How nice of you to drop in. On your way back from where?

**JEET**

I happened to be in the country, attending a technical conference in Manchester. I saw the Sunday column...

**ALICE**

And you remembered.

**JEET**
I have never forgotten.

**ALICE**
You can keep your jacket and tie off, if you wish to.

**JEET**
I think, I will, thank you.

**ALICE**
More like home?

**JEET**
Less binding.

**ALICE**
The Raj as a state of mind. Wasn't that his line?

**JEET**
He was trying to ridicule something.

**ALICE**
If he was trying to be ridiculous, he succeeded admirably. When will this generation ever learn to grasp the wholes beyond the parts?

**JEET**
It was trash. But it helped me find you.

**ALICE**
And learn to wash their socks? *(She softens)* Come and sit next to me. You can draw up the chair there. Just put the pile of records somewhere else. Put them on the floor.

**JEET**
I'll put the cushion from the chair on the floor, if you don't mind. Here, next to you. I'll sit on the floor next to you. May I? *(Pause)* Just as we did after the lunch break. *(Pause)* And you'd stretch out your palm... and I would put my hand in it...

**ALICE**
And I am to pat your hand in my palm, I suppose...

**JEET**
Four times.

**ALICE**
Did you believe what it said? The Sunday column?

**JEET**
About you and the school and...

**ALICE**
About my family.

**JEET**
There was something in it about...

**ALICE**

You didn't know, did you? I have no idea where he got all that from. It wasn't from me.

**JEET**

It seemed a needless diversion in his account of the East Indian Railway.

**ALICE**

Nobody knew about my father. Nobody except my mother. And I, later, in little bits. I was determined to go to India and find out for myself what actually had happened, and why my father had...

**JEET**

There's no need to... I understand.

**ALICE**

The East Indian Railway office in London took me on. They had schools that needed us. My passage to India was assured.

**JEET**

To Jamalpur. Was that your first posting?

**ALICE**

The first and the last in the Railways. I stayed on until the Company pulled out of the schools completely. That was a good five years after the British wound up.

**JEET**

Our gain. We'd never have had you if you'd left immediately.

**ALICE**

I did find out... about him... about myself...

**JEET**

It's all right. You don't have to... we'll just let the past rest in the past. *(Pause)*

**ALICE**

Yes, I remember now, you sat next to me like this.

**JEET**

Do you remember the time... ?

**ALICE**

You had a fight! It was a bigger boy, a strapping Anglo-Indian lad, I think it was. A good two years older and a good two inches taller. It was about a girl, wasn't it?

**JEET**

Yes, it was. She was new in the school.

**ALICE**

A fight to the finish, the boys called it! Behind the carpentry, under the neem tree. What chivalry! A nine-year-old locked in battle with an eleven-year-old over the hand of a dimpled Punjabi lass on transfer from Cawnpore.

**JEET**

She couldn't make conversation in English when she came to Jamalpur.

**ALICE**

She spoke with her eyes, did she?

**JEET**

I was hurt badly. I don't remember much else.

**ALICE**

The Railway doctor was rushed to the school. He gave you some stitches and a dressing on the head, and then gave you both a dressing down.

**JEET**

I must have looked quite stupid.

**ALICE**

Before he left, the good doctor gave you both a compliment – but he spoke in private to us in the Headmistress' room. He said you were growing up to be fine young men!

**JEET**

The boys all loved him, but from a safe distance.

**ALICE**

He also advised us not to make anything more of it. Especially with the parents.

**JEET**

His parting shot to us, I remember well – that the Railway Institute Boxing Club was where we should be.

**ALICE**

Did you join up!

**JEET**

Only for two seasons. It didn't seem to be my line at all.

**ALICE**

Distinctly non-vegetarian. *(Pause)* And there you were after lunch, sitting just like this, and trying to say so many things, all at one time, without opening your mouth once.

**JEET**

Wondering how to show myself at home in the evening.

**ALICE**

You learned a very important lesson in life that day.

**JEET**

It was banged into my head after all.

**ALICE**

Your parents told me. Not that day, but six months later, at the school concert. I don't recall the exact words they used, but it was about the way you had faced up to things.

**JEET**

Why don't parents tell their children such things themselves?

**ALICE**

They were proud of you.

**JEET**

I suppose they were. I'm sure they were, now. I think I missed knowing that for sure at that time.

**ALICE**

It was the way things were done then.

**JEET**

I'm sure it was. *(Pause)*

**ALICE**

I was very proud of you too.

**JEET**

I think I knew. I felt it.

**ALICE**

Seated like this? When the battle was done and the wounds licked?

**JEET**

I didn't speak a word, you said.

**ALICE**

I didn't say much either. I couldn't. Another part of the code of those times.

**JEET**

On that day, I wanted my own Miss Taylor, more than any Punjabi lass, in any part of this planet. All I wanted was to put my head on your lap... like this.

*(Pause. The telephone rings. Alice picks up the receiver; she listens for a while.)*

**ALICE**

Hmmm... Iodine. In a hundred years of medical research, they haven't come up with anything as effective as iodine. No, he's not a medical salesman. He just happens to know a lot about iodine. It hurts, of course it does. But it's the surest sign that you are alive and well. More so if you're kicking. No, thank you, Mavis, not yet. Three long rings, yes. *(Pause)*

**JEET and ALICE** *(Together)*
What did you do after you left the school?

**JEET**
I asked first.

**ALICE**
I thought I did.

**JEET**
If you insist...

**ALICE**
I don't have any such authority anymore. Not over anybody.

**JEET**
You never got us to do things by authority.

**ALICE**
You complied anyway.

**JEET**
Yours obediently, but yours sincerely. Shall I?

**ALICE**
If you insist!

**JEET**
Let me work backwards from now. I am an engineer. I specialise in installation in start-up operations. Should I explain that?

**ALICE**
You stand firmly with your feet well apart, bend, get a good grip on the starting handle, and crank vigorously till the engine fires. I'm sure that's not what it is, but go on

**JEET**
Well, in a way, yes, that is what I'm required to do.

**ALICE**
But from a nice office in front with cushy furniture and a pretty secretary who wears heels that go click, click, click, click. You have lots of others doing the cranking for you at the back.

**JEET**
I wish we could afford secretaries. Pretty or plain, who cares?

**ALICE**
Do you crack a whip, a cat o' nine tails? Like a boatswain in a slave ship, getting them all to keep time? In–out–in–out...

**JEET**
With the crew you get on board nowadays, we end up doing a lot of the rowing ourselves.

**ALICE**

When did you get into this line? I thought you'd become a scientist in a lab or an astronomer or something like that. Who do you work for? Is it a big company? Do they look after you well? What's your family like? You have a wife? Or two? Where are you located? There's a Friday afternoon test for you! That's just the first set of questions.

**JEET**

Can I do them in any order?

**ALICE**

No assurance I'll remember everything on Monday morning, but go ahead. Yes, any order.

**JEET**

Married, after I got my second job. Late by my family's standards. Two children, a boy and a girl. I keep a picture in my pocket diary. Here, let me get my jacket, I'll show you.

**ALICE**

One plus one making two. Very good. Very neat.

**JEET**

That's the wife, Anita.

**ALICE**

Railway family?

**JEET**

No, I'm afraid the line ends with me.

**ALICE**

What a good looking family! You must have crossed your silver wedding.

**JEET**

*(Hesitant)* It was... some time ago.

**ALICE**

When was it, then?

**JEET**

This photo was taken...

**ALICE**

Not the photograph! But, all right, if you'd rather not...

**JEET**

It was taken nearly two years ago.

**ALICE**

Right, this photo was. Tell me about the children. Didn't you play choo-choo train with them? Will they give the Railways a look?

**JEET**

They have their own ideas, their own plans. That's Rishi on the left. There's very little he doesn't know about computers.

**ALICE**

And I suppose the girl wants to join Amnesty International.

**JEET**

Not quite that, but...

**ALICE**

What do you call her?

**JEET**

Nomita. We call her Noni.

**ALICE**

She's sweet. No, she shouldn't spend her life tracking down democratically elected dictators. *(She puts the photo away.)*

**JEET**

She is training to become a nutritionist.

**ALICE**

Once there were policemen in uniform on the streets, you could go up to for help. They went about as plainclothesmen sometimes. The rules have all changed. Plain criminals can be expected now to go about in uniforms.

**JEET**

Yes, times have changed.

**ALICE**

That's all I hear everybody saying. Times have changed! It's another world now, Miss Taylor. Times have changed! Tinker, tailor, soldier, sailor, all make way for the master thief.

**JEET**

It's all so...

**ALICE**

Overpowering. Is that the word?

**JEET**

More. Much more than that.

**ALICE**

I wonder, Jeet, do people out there ever see how dangerous life is. Do they have time to see? Do they know how vulnerable they really are? And how helpless we are in the midst of all the crossfire? There is no safety in your own home.

**JEET**

It is no different in...

**ALICE**

Even the chirpy reporter from a Sunday paper can be an agent of Attila the Hun.

**JEET**

An Englishman's home is his castle, isn't it?

**ALICE**

It doesn't say anything about the poor old lonely English woman. I have rambled. I am sorry, I let myself go like that. Thank God, I can still tell when I am rambling. Your daughter, Noni, she was learning to cook, you said.

**JEET**

Not cooking itself, but what should go into it. She is studying nutrition.

**ALICE**

What's the point in knowing what sorts of things to put into the pot if you're not going to put it on the fire yourself?

**JEET**

She has to learn that too. But the study of nutrition is much more than...

**ALICE**

Oh, I know what nutritionists do! You think I am an ignoramus from the lower house of Parliament?

**JEET**

Yours or mine?

**ALICE**

Ours, I believe. Two lost civilisations rediscovering each other in this their sixtieth year of divorce.

**JEET**

Is there hope?

**ALICE**

But, Noni will do very well as a nutritionist I am sure. I wish there was some way to let her loose on Mavis there in the kitchen.

**JEET**

How long has she been with you?

**ALICE**

Ever since I moved in here.

**JEET**

Which was?

**ALICE**

My turn, I suppose.

**JEET**

Anita, my wife...

**ALICE**
She has been a wonderful mother, homemaker, and companion, has she not? And she works too?

**JEET**
She is a paediatrician.

**ALICE**
Now, let me see, that isn't the person who plays with your feet.

**JEET**
You know it is not.

**ALICE**
She is the one with the surgery in the nursery. Still playing Doctor, Doctor.

**JEET**
That's her.

**ALICE**
Good for you! A proper double-income, two-car, two-phone family, then?

**JEET**
Well, yes and no.

**ALICE**
That sounds more like a no.

**JEET** *(Pause)*
It is not so easy for two professionals – husband and wife. There can be strains – stresses and strains you are not quite prepared for. *(Pause)* Anita...

**ALICE**
But life goes on, does it not?

**JEET**
It does. It must.

**ALICE**
It has, in your home? You've managed all right? That nod would be called tentative, but it looked like a yes. Can we take that to be a yes?

**JEET**
I should think so, yes.

**ALICE**
Glad to be of some service, sir!

**JEET**
Miss Taylor, I must...

**ALICE**
Down, boy! Sit! That's better. No excitement after sunset is the rule, you remember. Bad for the digestive juices. *(Pause)* The fact is that we can all do with a bit of this sometimes. Having somebody by your side. The truth is we can all do without turning somebody into a crutch.

**JEET**

I understand...

**ALICE**

Wait! I think the phone is going to ring! Hmmm... behaving silly today. Let me see. *(Picks up the receiver)* Thank you, Mavis, for not ringing. No, Mavis. Yes, Mavis. Thank you, Mavis. *(She puts the receiver down and turns to Jeet)* Where do you wish I begin?

**JEET**

From the time you left Jamalpur.

**ALICE**

I was all set to return to England. Return to what, I asked myself. My mother had died, and there wasn't much of a family that I could turn to.

**JEET**

She must have been less than fifty then. How did she... ?

**ALICE**

Pneumonia, they said. It was the favourite malady of Brits in India. They embraced it wildly. She was terribly emaciated, they said. There were other explanations. But most agree that she had simply stopped thinking about living. She had switched off the mains up there.

**JEET**

You didn't get to see her.

**ALICE**

It wasn't to be. The first available boat would take me at least forty days to get here.

**JEET**

Is this where your mother... ?

**ALICE**

Yes, this was my mother's home the last twelve years of her life. It was kept locked up till I returned, with the caretaker agreeing to live in the pantry annexe. Just as I was winding up in Jamalpur, there was an announcement of a new school being opened near Mussoorie. They were going to offer the Junior and Senior Cambridge certificates, and a message arrived that they would like to have me over.

**JEET**

You couldn't say no.

**ALICE**

It wasn't easy believe me. It was the most difficult decision in my life.

**JEET**

I cannot picture you in any setting other than the Jamalpur school.

**ALICE**
It was a pretty little schoolhouse, wasn't it?

**JEET**
I can still see you cycling in every morning through the front gate, a single flower in your hair, the big, bright prints on your skirt making waves with your pedalling.

**ALICE**
Wait! I must know – was it you that painted the big sunflower on my bicycle seat?

**JEET**
It wasn't me I swear it.

**ALICE**
Right, carry on.

**JEET**
You loved zinnias, didn't you? It was often a large zinnia in your hair. And a bunch of flowers in the wicker basket attached to the front of the bike. All of us rushing up to greet you – and the first one to reach you had the privilege of carrying the basket in for you.

**ALICE**
And the dogs.

**JEET**
And the dogs! It was the only school where the dogs from our homes were allowed. That was so, so much like you.

**ALICE**
A school-going child is a dog's best friend.

**JEET**
You had two of them at home, didn't you? The house on Regent Street?

**ALICE**
Three, as I remember it.

**JEET**
And four cats.

**ALICE**
Peaceful coexistence.

**JEET**
And parrots and mynahs and guinea pigs, and even a mongoose I remember.

**ALICE**
A litchi tree in the back garden.

**JEET**

The litchi tree! How could I forget that? The juiciest litchis that side of Muzaffarpur.

**ALICE**

Do you remember Mastan?

**JEET**

The cockatoo! He was a great favourite with all of us.

**ALICE**

He came to Mussoorie with me. Almost made it here to England. The restrictions were rather severe.

**JEET**

There must have been some way you could...

**ALICE**

The only way, they said, was to stuff him. It was not the Britain I wanted to return to.

**JEET**

It might have been easier soon after Jamalpur. Before Mussoorie.

**ALICE**

But I stayed on.

**JEET**

Yes, you said the decision was very...

**ALICE**

I had to. *(Pause)* I had to make amends. I was entering a mission of atonement. Can I tell you about it?

**JEET**

You know you can.

**ALICE**

Will you believe me if I tell you that I have not talked about this to anybody till now?

**JEET**

I don't know what to...

**ALICE**

Anybody, ever.

**JEET**

I am honoured.

**ALICE**

You have done this to me. Let me look at your eyes. Hmmm... glassy. I will know only tomorrow whether I should hate you for this or give you a bar of chocolate.

**JEET**

From the wicker basket.

**ALICE**

There was a turning point. There are turning points in our lives all the time. We miss most of them. We go on as if things are unchanged all around us. I don't know if you remember the last day of January in 1948.

**JEET**

The thirty-first of... the day after the death...

**ALICE**

That's right. He was no more. When the news broke out over the radio, the evening before, I only knew that a great man, perhaps a really great man, had passed away. It was no more than that. For Miss Alice Taylor of the Railway School in Jamalpur, it was a certain Mr MK Gandhi that had expired. She had not known the Mahatma the world had lost. The next day they announced a prayer meeting.

**JEET**

Under the giant peepal tree in the maidan. I remember that very clearly.

**ALICE**

We were all there. I sat at a distance, not knowing how to join in...

**JEET**

There were bhajans, Christian hymns, recitations from Kabir, and Rahim, and Tulsidas, some of them also turned into bhajans.

**ALICE**

Wanting to be part of it, not knowing how. And then there was a group song composed specially for the occasion. It admitted shame that we had betrayed the father, and wondered if we would ever be able to redeem ourselves. I never quite remembered the word used.

**JEET**

Pashchyataap.

**ALICE**

I was disturbed.

**JEET**

It was a time of great sadness.

**ALICE**

That is what I did not understand. Why the sadness? Why was I not feeling sad? I did not realise it then, I did not realise it till years later, when I was in Mussoorie, that the prayer meeting had been a turning point. Come here a moment. Help me get to that book case. *(He does)* Look at this. Do you recognise this?

**JEET**

It looks like the books we had in school. Is it by any chance... ?

**ALICE**

A Text Book of History. Volume 1, English history. Volume 2, Indian history. Do you remember any of it?

**JEET**

English history or Indian?

**ALICE**

Any of the stuff and nonsense? About the bravery of the demigod called Robert Clive, and the treachery of Shivaji, the mountain rat?

**JEET**

There was a label for every one of them, wasn't there? An epithet – the palace builder, the pleasure seeker, the noble, the evil.

**ALICE**

It was all black and white. The purity of the white, the rottenness of everything else. We taught you things that would serve no purpose whatsoever. About William the Conqueror, the procreative dispensations of the Normans, and Charlemagne and Aix-la-Chapelle, and all the rest of it. You had Michaelmas holidays at the time of Dussehra. There was a Guy Fawkes Day!

**JEET**

We knew we had to get the pronunciation right.

**ALICE**

And Saladin. Saladin and his sword. Saladin and his swordsmanship. Do you remember that?

**JEET**

It's coming back.

**ALICE**

Using up a lot of space in your brains, not allowing other more useful things to get in.

**JEET**

It wasn't all useless. We have made something of our lives, haven't we?

**ALICE**

Have you? It's not just the Moslems in the subcontinent who turn West in reverence five times a day. *(Pause)* Yes, you have done well.

**JEET**

We are all wogs, aren't we? Some greater, some less, but wogs nonetheless.

**ALICE**

And we made you so. I made you so.

**JEET**

You can't take the blame all on yourself. You were one small part of a larger – what do you call it – a whole history.

**ALICE**

A small part that was completely avoidable. We owe you an apology.

**JEET**

Oh, come on, Miss Taylor...

**ALICE**

This supercilious island nation owes an unconditional apology to the whole of the subcontinent for at least one of its sins of commission.

**JEET**

It's all in the past. It's forgotten.

**ALICE**

You can forgive and forget the wars and the massacres and the looting of the land. All of these will be made up. But you can never forgive the permanent damage done to the mind. It is not buried with you when you die. It is passed on. It will stick for generations. Ask Rishi and Noni.

**JEET**

You connected us to the rest of the world. You gave us...

**ALICE**

Ask Rishi and Noni.

**JEET**

Science and technology.

**ALICE**

We gave you science?

**JEET**

A scientific temper...

**ALICE**

You had a five-thousand-year-old civilisation without science? What exactly do you mean by scientific temper?

**JEET**

A method – a discipline. To seek verification of ideas, not mere beliefs.

**ALICE**

To test a hypothesis before accepting it as belief.

**JEET**

Yes!

**ALICE**

'I do not believe what I see until it is proved true.'

**JEET**

In essence, yes.

**ALICE**

Is that the only way? What about, 'I do not disbelieve what I see until it is proved untrue'?

**JEET**

It could easily be a superstition.

**ALICE**

Oh, yes, indeed. You could have a sort of superstitious science... and of course you could also have scientific superstition.

**JEET**

You gave us the English language. You gave us a language to speak to the world, and English literature, and Shakespeare, and...

**ALICE**

That velvet-tongued opportunist? What do you say in Urdu for that? Matlabi, I think.

**JEET**

William Shakespeare, matlabi!

**ALICE**

The philanderer, who oiled his way into the London aristocracy and charmed them with his verbosity to finance his pet projects, his adolescent fantasies.

**JEET**

The loquacious charm translated into a hundred languages around the world!

**ALICE**

Think about it, Jeet, would the name Shakespeare mean anything, anywhere, if it was not for the Empire?

**JEET**

It is great literature nevertheless.

**ALICE**

Because we taught you to believe that – that it is great. Did you know, Jeet, that English literature was never a subject for schooling before the Empire? Physics and mathematics and geography, yes, they were subjects that could be taught. And studied. Literature was something you did. You didn't teach it or study it. It was entirely in the interests of the Empire that English literature was brought in as a course of study.

**JEET**

Was it his fault that he stood out in history as a great writer?

**ALICE**

Is it their fault that hundreds like him, in every land, every bit the same in creative energy, never got to be known by the rest of the world?

**JEET**

Coming from you, there must be something in that. But I have to confess I don't know anything about the...

**ALICE**

He who knows not and knows... I must sit down. *(Pause)* You are not a child anymore. I cannot teach you.

**JEET**

You are still Miss Taylor to me.

**ALICE**

I was in Delhi for a few days before I shifted to Mussoorie. I was a guest one evening at the home of a wealthy Delhi family. They were going to have a private recital by a singer, the legendary Rasoolan Bai. Do you know who she was?

**JEET**

I'm afraid not.

**ALICE**

You would not. No matter. You'd know the name Billie Holiday though. They had many things in common, Rasoolan Bai and Billie Holiday. Exceptional talent, unconventional singing styles, stubbornly individualistic, and paying the price for it. Exploited by the self-appointed patrons, dying penniless. There she was, at one end of the chandeliered drawing room, Rasoolan Bai herself, weather-beaten, frail, but in full control of her composure. She must have known that at the end of the concert, after the encomiums and the nine-course meal, her hosts would leave her out in the cold night. Her deep, raspy voice was not the least bit feminine, and her songs were mostly about the many disguises in which pain enters our lives. I knew at last what I had to do in Mussoorie.

**JEET**

You didn't teach English history, starting with William the Conqueror.

**ALICE**

And Saladin had run out of feather cushions.

**JEET**

Music? You didn't give up music, did you?

**ALICE**

That was what the official appointment expected of me. I was to teach English language and music.

**JEET**

But!

**ALICE**

But... It was a new school. There weren't enough teachers. The children were already there. And we simply had to get on with it.

**JEET**

And so you took on other subjects. What else did you teach?

**ALICE**

Football. Football and hockey, both. Carpentry. Then pottery, and soon the whole crafts programme. I was asked to take charge of the scouts and girl guides, and I could take them trekking at least twice a month. Of course I had no idea of these responsibilities before I reached the school.

**JEET**

Just English language and music it was to be.

**ALICE**

I had also no idea of the state of mind of the Principal. I had to simply play along. It was very much the Barmecide's feast the first month or two. But the playing along paid off.

**JEET**

The Barmecide's feast...

**ALICE**

The reality of illusions. You learn to believe in seeing what's not visible.

**JEET**

It was the play in our annual concert, The Barmecide's Feast.

**ALICE**

Here, let me show you how it goes.

**JEET**

No need, Miss Taylor, I think...

**ALICE**

Absolutely charming tale. I want you to play something on the gramophone. There, look into that pile next to the terracotta elephant head. You'll find a record called Arabian Fantasy. Got it?

**JEET**

This one?

**ALICE**

Right, put it on. *(He does. It is an old tune from a western orchestra braving oriental sounds...)* Turn it down a bit. There on the radio. The pick-up is connected to the radio. Turn it down at the radio. *(The music is softer)* Bless the inventor of the pick-up. I can actually adjust the volume listening to music.

**JEET**

You listen to a lot of music still?

**ALICE**

Vitamin M.

**JEET**

You obviously have a healthy level in your system.

**ALICE**

Keeps all the other vitamins working in step. But we are digressing. Where were we? Oh, yes... come back here and sit down. On the carpet would be better, just as you were, a minute ago. Can you sit cross-legged with your shoes on? Good...

Now, watch carefully. I have nothing on the table in front of me. In fact, there is no table in front of me. I signal with my right hand, like this... Along comes a servant from the royal kitchen, carrying a large tray with an ornate silver dome. He lifts the dome... the tray is empty... he sets it down... and I say... Ah, thank you, my dear fellow. What a magnificent dish of roast lamb... My kitchen staff are the very best, really.

**JEET**

They must be I am sure.

**ALICE**

Mmmm, the wonderful aroma of the wine it was marinated in... my, look at the toppings... almonds and figs, and honeyed potato, all laid on a bed of fresh salad... As I keep admiring the dish, I am carving myself a helping. Then I pass the tray to you and invite you to help yourself.

**JEET**

I am puzzled at first. But I decide to go along. I carve out a piece for myself... pretend to take a bite... then make the right noises, praising the dish... and complimenting the kitchen staff while at it.

**ALICE**

Very good. You've got the hang of it. You know who you are, of course.

**JEET**

Miss Taylor, it was a wonderful play. I remember it quite clearly. I was in the play myself.

**ALICE**

It was a beautiful play, wasn't it? And you were in it...

**JEET**

I was the beggar boy who learned to believe.

**ALICE**

That was you! Ohhoho, of course, my goodness, it's all coming back.

**JEET**

I can't believe you didn't remember straight away. You made me sit cross-legged in the play just like this.

**ALICE**

And you did, you did. *(Pause)* You were very good too. You seemed to really believe there was the magnificent dish on the empty tray. *(Pause)* I was a bit worried about you. Yes, it's all coming back.

**JEET**

Miss Alice, may I ask you a rather silly question?

**ALICE**

Hmmm. Your right, I suppose. Go ahead.

**JEET**

Do you have a credit card?

**ALICE**

No.

**JEET**

You know what a credit card is, I suppose.

**ALICE**

Yes.

**JEET**

Some call it the greatest invention since merchant banking was conceived by the Italian grain merchants.

**ALICE**

In the Middle Ages, it is said. The Italians had it right then.

**JEET**

Well, thanks to the card, we don't need to actually see money in our hands anymore. We buy things and sell things and pay actual prices for things without ever having to handle the money ourselves.

**ALICE**

But there must be real money somewhere, in some royal palace kitchen.

**JEET**

Of course, there must be.

**ALICE**

Have you ever seen it? Has anybody seen it?

**JEET**

You don't have to.

**ALICE**

I used to think that being prosperous depended on working hard to earn the means to prosperity. The rules have changed, haven't they? It is now all about the right to borrow money before actually earning it.

**JEET**

I suppose you could put it that way. *(Pause)*

**ALICE**

You may turn off the music now. *(The record is turned off.)*

**JEET**

We were talking about the new school in Mussoorie.

**ALICE**

Yes, the new school in Mussoorie.

**JEET**

You thought you were to teach English and music, but found yourself very soon taking on...

**ALICE**

Yes, learning to play along – and learning as you play along.

**JEET**

And the reward?

**ALICE**

The supreme satisfaction of rediscovering the land, the extraordinary beauty in its simplicity. The joy of being able to do so much with so little.

**JEET**

The students – what were they like?

**ALICE**

They were like the fresh saplings in any garden – full of hidden strength, but vulnerable until they took root.

**JEET**

The parents must have had great faith in the gardeners.

**ALICE**

The parents... they knew not what they wished, they wished not what they wanted. They talked of a brave new nation with their public faces. In private they wanted things to remain exactly as they had been from the days of the East India Company.

**JEET**

I remember the times. We were all confused.

**ALICE**

They were confusing times.

**JEET**

It took a good twenty years for me to know who I really was, to tell the wants from the wishes.

**ALICE**

And not hate your father for it?

**JEET**

And still love him for it.

**ALICE**

It was forbidding. Supposing we'd made a mistake? Supposing we failed?

**JEET**

Failed?

**ALICE**

In the garden. In talking to the tiny flower buds as we tended them, getting them to open their eyes, and to see for themselves that they were not some imaginary daffodils or tulips, those two-dimensional blotches of colour they'd see only in our picture books, but that they were the most gorgeous marigold and gulmohar, full bodied and real.

**JEET**

You succeeded, didn't you? You didn't fail?

**ALICE**

We thought we succeeded. I think we did.

**JEET**

It could not have been without the teacher from Jamalpur.

**ALICE**

Hired to teach English language and music.

**JEET**

Did you teach music after all?

**ALICE**

I did, indeed. Not the up and down SATB thing. A little bit of that, yes, but lots and lots of other things.

**JEET**

It used to be so grand at the morning assembly – the hymnary on Monday mornings, military marches on Fridays!

**ALICE**

Two hours, twice a week in the classroom. Much more outside. We were learning music all through the year in Mussoorie.

**JEET**

Did they have a piano? Like the one in our assembly?

**ALICE**

They didn't. And that was a great boon, as I was soon to find out. We started by learning the folk songs of the people all around us, on the mountain ranges and in the foothills. I discovered for the first time the joy of learning music through my ears, rather than from my eyes.

**JEET**

Bach and Beethoven, Gilbert and Sullivan, were they all consigned to...

**ALICE**

Nothing of the sort. We had them all, and the children loved them all. In music alone can all the anger of history be dissolved. Their understanding was deep, but unpretentious. They could feel and touch and play with the music, and make it a part of their everyday life, not having to parrot answers to please a music teacher. They could connect easily to a pastoral symphony because they had already discovered the sacredness of the hills through the cowherd's evening song. *(Pause)*

**JEET**

It must have been a wonderful experience... mission accomplished, the garden in full bloom. When did you... ?

**ALICE**

Hmmm... The Grand Trunk Express had run its course. It was time to rest the old steam engines.

**JEET**

What are the students from this school doing? Have they kept in touch with you?

**ALICE**

Have they? None that I can remember. I do read about one or the other, now and then. No, they have not kept in touch, as you put it. It could be a good sign – that I am not needed.

**JEET**

Some migrated.

**ALICE**

Some did, yes. Some to England, I know.

**JEET**

There was a Lal. His father was Head of Mechanical Engineering. A very bright student, always into prizes.

**ALICE**

Yes, Lal.

**JEET**

His father had a British passport, didn't he? The family moved to England soon after he left school. Do you know about him here?

**ALICE**

Yes and no.

**JEET**

And that means... ?

**ALICE**

No, I am not in touch. Yes, I know about him.

**JEET**

You do?

**ALICE**

Unfortunately.

**JEET**

Oh...

**ALICE**

He is more Brit than the Brits themselves. He is showing distinct signs of becoming – what's the word... ?

**JEET**

Racist?

**ALICE**

No, not quite. That's too simple. In Britain he wouldn't qualify if he was not a Brit in the first place. Let's say it has something to do with the embarrassment of once belonging to a six-thousand-year-old civilisation. He joined the army, changed his name from Krishenkant Lal to Kris Kent. Married a girl from Liverpool, divorced her two years later, reportedly because of her pursuit of a research career. It was in Asian Studies, I think.

**JEET**

Miss Taylor...

**ALICE**

Quite a contrast to other first generation immigrants – you know, Indians who try so hard to be more Indian here than the Indians back home. *(Pause. Jeet rises.)* You have to go? It was more than a minute, wasn't it?

**JEET**

It was an intrusion, I am afraid. I came without letting you know, but I am ever so grateful that you let me see you.

**ALICE**

Can I ask a service of you before you leave?

**JEET**

Certainly.

**ALICE**

On your way out, would you please turn on the gramophone again?

**JEET**

I'll do it straightaway. *(He goes to the gramophone)* This record... it is the music you played to teach us dancing. You insisted that we should all learn to dance.

**ALICE**

You were shy.

**JEET**

Music and dancing had to go together, you said.

**ALICE**

Very shy.

*(Jeet gets the record playing. It is the Viennese waltz. He listens for a while. He goes up to Alice.)*

**JEET**

May I?

**ALICE**

My privilege, but your pleasure entirely.

**JEET**

I take your right hand like this, and with my right hand...

**ALICE**

With your right hand you first straighten the bend in my back. That's better. It's the sofa that does this one. You can tell from the bend in my back which chair I've been sitting on. Different strokes for different cricks from different chairs. Ah... much better.

**JEET**

Shall we...

**ALICE**

What do you think we are waiting for – the night watchman's whistle? *(They dance. The Viennese waltz builds up)*

**JEET**

Miss Alice Taylor, I presume. My, but what a pleasant surprise meeting you here... allow me to... shall we move to the library, then? Yes, please... no, thank you... not no, please, yes, thank you... Thank you, Miss Taylor, thank you... Miss Taylor, you are... are you awake Miss Taylor? Oh dear, Miss Taylor, you are falling asleep. Here, Miss Taylor, let me help you into your sofa... right here... eeeasy now... there you go... that's it, Miss Taylor, go to sleep now... Here, I will cover you with this shawl.

*(He picks up a shawl lying next to the sofa and covers her. The telephone rings. He picks it up.)* Mavis? Yes, it's me... Yes, she wanted the music... No, she didn't... She has decided to rest a bit. Just a little nap, I think. Yes, please, in about ten minutes. That should be fine. Thank you, Mavis.

*(He puts the receiver down and moves to pick up his hat, and jacket. He watches her from the entrance.)*

*A slow fade out.*

***Close of play***

# Head Start

*A romp in the garden*
***Vijay Padaki***

**FOR**
**DAVID AND DOREEN HORSBURGH**

## CHARACTERS IN THE PLAY

### In the Snips

PAVI ........................................ *A mother*
SUSHI ........................................ *A friend*
ABHI ........................................ *A little son*
MUNNI ........................................ *A little daughter*
FATHER ........................................ *A missionary priest teacher, school principal*
SISTER ........................................ *A nun teacher, school principal*

### In the Snaps

RAMAKRISHNAN ................ *A young man getting to college (Ramki/RK)*
APPA ........................................ *His father*
AMMA ........................................ *His mother*

Pavi and others in the Snips need not have continuity in storyline. They need only be identifiable as characters. Ramki and his parents are getting somewhere in their Snaps.

## INTRODUCTION

Head Start is a confluence of two streams of discussion with friends in the theatre over several years. The first had its origins in the question, 'Is it really possible for a play to be relevant – however one might choose to define the term – and still be simple and uncomplicated in both content and narration?' The question first occurred at a time when my professional work involved an exploration of the organic links between changing institutional structures in society and changing societal value systems. I started writing a series of short plays as reflections of those changes in society, part real-life, part fictional. Head Start was one such dramatisation, attempting to encapsulate the changing perceptions of education over three generations, but in as un-academic a way as possible. The second stream had in it some experiments in form and style in writing. More specifically, I had been playing with a modular structure in which the first part of the play could be a one-acter, quite complete in itself, and with the addition of the second part we would have a full-length play. Head Start is the second of such 2-in-1 plays. As with the first one, Salt Licks, also included in this volume, people in the Theatre have preferred the whole over the parts.

The play runs its course in two parallel streams. The Snips peep into the lives of Pavi and her two primary school kids, Abhi and Munni. The Snaps take us into the home of Ramki, a graduate engineer in the making. There is a brief confluence of the streams towards the end.

Ten years after the remarkable David Horsburgh left us, there were signs of a fresh appreciation of his seminal contributions in development education. We remembered him constantly through the production of this play. The play is, in some way, about education, about three generations of experience with education in India. It was most fitting that the opening performances were for CRY.

The play has a running time of 40 to 45 minutes in Act I and 45 to 50 minutes in Act II. The exact duration will be determined by the 'business' put into the scenes by the performers. Act II should be played in one stretch without a second intermission. The play is constructed for performance with the least technical facility, but with a great deal of imagination.

The play is set in the early 'nineties. It is advisable to retain the period in performing the play. The action of the play is in four locations: the school premises, Ramki's room at home, a park, and Abhi-Munni's room at home.

### Language Notes

*Beta:* Literally, son – used affectionately for any child
*Mogra:* Jasmine flower
*Dabba:* Box, container
*Yennaiah:* Roughly – What, man!

*Ramaiyya Vastavaiyya:* From film song of the late 50s (still popular)
*Sakhhat:* Terrific
*Uttarayan:* A January festival
*Sarathy:* Pilot – allusion to Arjuna, the charioteer for Krishna
*Gharana:* School – of music / dance tradition
*Aur kuch bolo na:* Why don't you sing something else?
*Suno beta:* Listen dear
*Hai na bete:* Isn't that so, dear?
*Itna samajhdar hai woh:* He is so wise
*Achhi:* Nice
*Yeh aunty nahin hai bhoot hai:* This isn't an aunty – it is a spook
*Jig-nuts:* Peanuts
*Mastan:* Epithet usually for wizard
*Garuda:* Eagle
*Suvarna:* Gold
*Bhima:* Strong, powerful – as Bhima of the Pandavas
*Thair-satham:* Curds-rice – Simple home meal
*Hundi:* Collection box
*Googly:* Tricky spin bowling in cricket
*Thata:* Grandpa
*Lakh:* One hundred thousand
*Rasam:* Thin soup-like dish, eaten with rice or drunk plain – South Indian
*Arangetram:* Ceremonial first public performance of trained dancer (South Indian)
*Rangapravesam:* Debut on stage – used in same way as arangetram
*Nakshatra:* Star
*Shastra:* Treatise, body of knowledge with theory and practice – often sanctified
*Toofan Mail:* Name of legendary fast train – a song of the forties

## FIRST PRODUCED

First produced by Bangalore Little Theatre with shows dedicated to CRY (Child Rights and You) at Bangalore and Madras, January 1996

### In the Snips

*Father Principal* .......... VIJAY PADAKI
*Pavi* .......... MEERA PRASANNA
*Sushi* .......... NANDITA KAIKINI
*Abhi* .......... VAIBHAV PRASANNA
*Munni* .......... VIBHA PRASANNA
*Sister Principal* .......... YVETTE MONTEIRO

### In the Snaps

*Ramki* .......... DEEPAK THIMAYA
*Appa* .......... S SEETHARAM or UK JAYADEV
*Amma* .......... VEDAVALLI SEETHARAM or POORNIMA VYASULU
*Set design* .......... RV MATHEW
*Assisted by* .......... ABHAY TOSHNIWAL
*Lighting* .......... PRAKASH BELAWADI
*Assisted by* .......... PRADEEP BELAWADI
*Property* .......... KC SEKHAR
*Costumes* .......... YVETTE MONTEIRO
*Tour Manager* .......... KC SEKHAR
*Designed and directed by* .......... VIJAY PADAKI

# ACT I

## SNIP ONE

*The missionary Principal in the annual drill of interviewing children for admission. Pavitra (Pavi), her son Abhishek (Abhi), and her friend Sushila (Sushi) are waiting for Abhishek's turn. They are standing in an imaginary queue.*

**MISSIONARY FATHER**

Next! *(The queue moves. After a while...)* Next! *(It moves again)*

**PAVI**

Keep practising, beta. Your turn will come soon. Names of flowers...

**ABHI**

Rose... sunflower... lily...

**PAVI**

And what grows in Sushi aunty's garden?

**ABHI**

Mogra.

**PAVI**

Jasmine! It's called jasmine. Now, you remember fruits? Names of fruits? And then colours – how many colours? *(To Sushi)* The trouble with these admission interviews is the waiting. Getting here before seven in the morning – no place to sit even...

**FATHER**

Next!

**SUSHI**

Do you want a biscuit, Abloo?

**ABHI**

No thank you, aunty.

**PAVI** *(Helping herself to one)*

Have, beta. You haven't had a proper breakfast. You want a banana instead? *(Abhi makes a face)* You got the colours?

**SUSHI**

There's cold lime juice in this flask. Whenever you feel...

**FATHER**

Next! *(The queue moves)*

**PAVI**

Today of all days Rosy has taken off. I've told her hundreds of times – tell us in advance, tell us the previous day. But no, just like that she bunks the day. I had to go get the milk, wash a whole pile of dishes, fix Jaggu's lunch dabba, get Abloo ready, coach him a bit – poor boy, he couldn't sleep early even last night, with the birthday party at the Chopras.

**SUSHI**

They always have at least fifty kids running riot at Bunty's birthday party.

**PAVI**

And their parents...

**FATHER**

Next! *(Pavi and Abhi step up. Father Principal looks down.)* What is your name?

**ABHI**

Orange...

**FATHER**

Next!

## SNAP ONE

*Ramakrishnan's room. Lots of business before the first word is spoken. Sound of American FM program – an ad followed by RJ's voice, followed by pop song, unrecognisable, but only too familiar. Scene opens with a 2-in-1 all by itself. Presently Ramakrishnan enters with a brown-paper laundry package. He is in trendy pants and shirt. He keeps the package down carefully, looks at himself in a mirror that might be there, takes out a comb and resets his hair, looks pleased with the result, and begins to undress. Shoes, socks, pants... He looks again at the mirror and shares his appreciation with himself. He turns the 2-in-1 down low. A long whistle at the figure he sees in the mirror and addresses.*

**RAMKI**

RK, RK, you gorgeous hunk, what the shit are you doing wasting your time here? You should be there – where the real action is. *(He breaks into song, transformed into an American rock star, probably of British origin.)*

And you gotta be there
When it's time to be there
And you gotta be there with your lo-huh-ver
Ohoohoh, you gotta, you gotta be
You gotta be there

*(Satisfied with the salutation, he takes a bow and proceeds to open the laundry pack as he turns up the 2-in-1 again. Very carefully he takes out a*

*dhoti and a silk kurta. From his pants, he takes out a slip of paper, reads it as if revising for a term paper, puts it down, picks up the dhoti, and unfolds it. Amma's voice is heard.)*

**AMMA** *(Offstage)*

Ramki! Are you there?

**RAMKI**

I'm here, Amma. *(Turns the 2-in-1 down)*

**AMMA**

In your room? Now? When did you get back?

**RAMKI**

Just now. I'm getting dressed.

**AMMA**

Dressed? At 6:30?

**RAMKI**

We're going out, Amma – to the Jasraj concert.

**AMMA**

Oh... Pandit Jasraj. Tonight? Isn't it after dinner?

**RAMKI**

Yah, yah – we're eating out and then going.

**AMMA**

You'll be here when Appa comes? He gets in early today.

**RAMKI**

Yah, yah, yah... *(To himself again)* First-a-meetah. Thenna-bite-ah. Thenna-little-ride-ah. Ooowah! Three chikkichikkichicks led by three top campus cats. No, three handsome German Shepherds. Correction, two German Shepherd types and, in the lead, ladies and gentlemen, yes, it's him, there's no doubt at all, it's him, you can see for yourself, it's him – the magnificent stud, the Great Dane, Garudachar Ramakrishnan of Fourth Year Electrical! *(He takes a bow)* Oh, RK, RK, look at yourself. I mean, really, just look at you – all that gorgeous brute power wasted. Whatta goddamn waste on local chicks. A Great Dane like that deserves a great big... Oh, what the hell – it's only another six months...

*(He turns up the 2-in-1 and tackles the dhoti – step by step as put down in the slip of paper. He halves it, wraps it round himself, adjusts the halves, tentatively anchors one side, and then carefully takes his shirt off. He drapes his shirt on a chair [or any other prop], looks at himself in the mirror again, whistles, and continues. The draping is slow, awkward, but not slapstick. Appa enters, unseen, and stands watching. He is in office clothes, a loosened tie, maybe a jacket, not quite the current cut.)*

**APPA**

Use a ten-paise coin.

**RAMKI**

What? Oh, when did you come?

**APPA**

Here, let me show you. Actually, you can make a little bulb with your forefinger and tuck it in before rolling it.

**RAMKI**

It's okay, Appa, I think I've got it.

**APPA**

But the tenpaise coin is the simplest and safest. Let me see if I have one.

**RAMKI**

No, no, it's not necessary. See, it's in place.

**APPA**

Yes, but by the time you climb downstairs it will be down four inches.

**RAMKI**

I'll do it again. Okay, I'll use a coin. No, don't bother, I have one, I think in my pants – here...

**APPA**

The trick is to pull your tummy in, just a little, before fixing the right side – that's right – now, put the coin there...

**RAMKI**

I'll do it, Appa. I can do it.

**APPA**

Don't wear it so low. It's not like your swim trunks. Above the paunch – here – so it won't slip off with bending and stretching.

**RAMKI**

Is this high enough?

**APPA**

Fine. Now, turn it a few times down with the coin inside. That's it. That's fine. How does it feel?

**RAMKI**

Yeah! Cool... It feels all right, Appa.

**AMMA** *(Off)*

Ramki, I think Appa is here.

**RAMKI**

He's here.

**APPA**

He's here.

**AMMA**

Oh, shall I keep your buttermilk on the table?

**APPA**

I'll come down in a minute.

**AMMA**

What are you doing there? Ramki said...

**APPA**

I was just showing him... I was telling him about the car.

**AMMA**

The starting problem this morning?

**APPA**

Yes, that.

**AMMA**

And Gangamma and me pushing it up and down the driveway. What a show! Anyway, come down quickly.

**APPA** *(Turning to Ramki, mimicking him)*

Cool, gentleman, cool!

**RAMKI**

The car – it's not...

**APPA**

It's there.

**RAMKI**

But the starting trouble...

**APPA**

I had the battery changed. No choice. It had to be replaced.

*(Ramki, relieved, lets out a long whistle. He decides to continue with the dhoti. He manages without much help from Appa now on, but with some help from the slip of paper.)*

**RAMKI**

I'm sorry, I couldn't take it to the garage last week. I hope there's nothing more to the starting problem.

**APPA**

You are the engineer in the house! *(Pause)* Yes sir, it cost us fifteen hundred all told, but the job is done. No sir, there will be no more pushstarting – not for another couple of years, I hope. *(Pause)* Yennaiah, what is the occasion? Some wedding reception?

**RAMKI**

No, no wedding. We are going to a music concert.

**APPA**

Who's we? Your motorbike gang?

**RAMKI**

Please, Appa, it's not... no, not that group. Not all from that group. Some from there and some others...

**APPA**

Don't keep the pleats so narrow. They'll bulge. Keep them wide – use your whole hand for that.

**RAMKI**

Okay, I'll redo it. This much?

**APPA**

Concert – dhoti-kurta – new group – car. No motorbikes. Nice, nice. A tribute to Pandit Jasraj. I hope he sings well tonight.

**RAMKI**

Sing? I thought he played the sitar...

**APPA**

Maybe he does, privately in his bath, but he's never made it known.

**RAMKI**

Shit, a vocal concert!

**APPA**

Watch it now, watch the language. It may be okay out there with your gang, but I don't want droppings all over the house.

**RAMKI**

I'm sorry, Appa. It's just that... a classical vocal concert is not – you know – but I'm glad I found out now, here, before...

**APPA**

In our kind of music, the more you listen, the deeper will be your appreciation of vocal music. The singer's voice – it is the humblest of musical instruments, but capable of the most intricate musical patterns – when properly broken in and tuned.

**RAMKI**

I never thought about it that way.

**APPA**

Something to think about. *(Pause)* What do you know about Hindustani classical music? I didn't know you had taken an interest. *(Ramki is fully attired in dhoti and kurta by now. He is touching up.)*

**RAMKI**

Oh, it's only recent. I don't know much, but I'll learn slowly. I mean, I learned today that Pandit Jasraj is a singer.

**APPA**

What do you know about Carnatic music? *(Pause)* Amma plays the veenai on Sundays you know.

**RAMKI**

I know, I know. We are afloat in a great big stream of rich tradition and yet we are as insensitive as fletsa and jotsa.

**APPA**

Flotsam and jetsam. Quite different from fauna and flora.

**RAMKI**

Or Laurel and Hardy. I'm sorry, Appa. I didn't mean to... you know I mean no disrespect for tradition.

**APPA**

Who said anything about disrespect? Look at yourself – you look really nice in that. Now, I didn't ask you to wear that. I didn't even know you were going to a Jasraj sitar concert. It just happened by itself, didn't it.

**RAMKI**

Well, yes... it just happened...

**APPA**

All right, who is she?

**RAMKI**

What?

**APPA**

The question is, what is the mysterious force that reduces a full-grown son of mine to a confused heap... still, a handsome brute, as he is led in ceremonial attire to his sacrificial... shhettak! *(Gesturing a decapitation)* In other words, who is she?

**AMMA** *(Off)*

Ramki! There is a call for you.

**RAMKI**

Coming!

**AMMA**

It's Anand. Shall I ask him to call later?

**RAMKI**

No need. Just tell him I'm on my way. *(Pause)* Do you really think it looks all right?

**APPA**

It looks fine.

**RAMKI**

Thanks, Appa.

**APPA**

Hey – Ramaiyya vastavaiyya – let me look at you properly. Yes... saved by the bell, but a hell of a lot of fight left in him yet. Oho – you are looking sakhhat.

**RAMKI** *(With some effort, holding back tears)*

Appa... I'll take good care of the car.

*(Amma enters. She sees the two of them together.)*

**AMMA**

My, my, my! I prayed for a son and the gods sent me a prince. I wish my mother was alive to see this Uttarayan gift from the heavens.

**RAMKI** *(Embarrassed)*

Amma, it's just...

**APPA**

It's just a music concert. Ramki is going with... friends.

**AMMA:**

You mean Anand and...

**APPA**

Yes, Anand and... the others. You see they have just recently stumbled upon the Great Indian Cultural Attic. And our Ramki has to play the role of sarathy and guide tonight in their rummaging. *(He squeezes Ramki's hand)* Oy, just peep into the record cabinet in the living room, on your way out. There is an album of Jasraj there. Read the liner notes at the back. Something about his gharana pedigree, about the Sanand princely state in Gujarat that patronised him in his youth, his famous Darbari Kanada rendition – you know, little titbits to stoke the conversation... at the right moments.

**RAMKI**

I have to go. *(He exits quickly. Then from offstage)*

I'm taking the front door key. I can let myself in.

*(Amma and Appa are looking off after Ramki. A door slams. A pause. Amma turns to Appa.)*

**AMMA**

You know, when I came in, my heart missed a couple of beats. I thought he looked so much like you did twenty-five years ago.

## SNIP TWO

*Sister Principal in her habit in the annual drill of admission interviews. Pavitra, daughter Munni, and friend Sushi await Munni's turn in an imaginary queue*

**MISSIONARY SISTER**

Next! *(The queue moves)* Next! *(It moves again)*

**PAVI**

And what will you sing if you are asked?

**MUNNI**

I want to sing sing-a-songa-sispenna-pockafulla-rai. *(She swings into tune)* Fouratenty blagerds bakini pai...

**PAVI**

Shhh. Not so loud. Only when your turn comes.

**SUSHI**

So sweet! Beta, don't forget to say good morning.

**PAVI**

Sing a song you learned when you were a baby. Aur kuch bolo na – Mama's taught you so many new poetries.

**MUNNI**

I know! That one – about the tiger.
Whuttimotta handarai
Koofemda feefool simmetrai

**SUSHI**

Symmet-ree beta, not symmet-rai

**MUNNI**

Aunty, handarai se rhyme nahin hota

**PAVI**

Okay, you like doe-a-deer, no? Will you sing that one?

**MUNNI**

Thoo! It's too easy – so boring. *(Mocking, in fast-forward mode)*
Doe-a-deer-a-female-deer-ray-a-droppa goldersun
Me-a-name-I call-myself-nana-nanananana
So-da-deedageedapoo
La-da-peedapeeda goo...

**SUSHI** *(Controlling her laughter)*

Suno beta, you sing whatever comes to your mind.

**PAVI**

She's the limit, Sushi. God knows what she'll do when her number comes.

**SUSHI**

She'll be fine, Pavi. She's a clever girl – hai na beta? Sing for yourself, not for anyone else.

**MUNNI**

Aunty, that one! Sing, sing a song!

**SUSHI**

Good idea! You like that very much na?

**MUNNI** *(Starts off)*
Sing, sing a song...

**PAVI**
Oh no! Sushi, she doesn't know the second verse – she gets stuck.

**SUSHI**
It's okay, Pavi. She sings it so well. And she likes the song. That's nice, Munni. Now just close your eyes, sing the song to yourself, so you'll know all the lines. Okay beta?

**PAVI**
She's such a nut. Insists on having her way. Insists, insists. Even if its abs clear she can't do it, she must...

**SUSHI**
She'll be all right.

**PAVI**
So different from Abhi. Itna samajhdar hai woh. Learns so quickly. He listens, you see. This one drives me up the wall. I'm so glad you came along. I don't know how I'd have managed without you.

**SISTER**
Next!
*(The three of them step up. Pavi guides Munni up front. Sister is still looking into her papers. Presently she looks up.)*

**SISTER**
Good morning. *(Pavi and Sushi mumble a response. Munni is silent. Pavi notices, prods Munni. No response.)* And this is your daughter, Mrs...

**PAVI**
Yes, Sister.

**SISTER**
Come here, my child. *(Munni doesn't move)*
Come, come. *(Munni takes a step forward, on Pavi's prod)*
What is your name? *(No response)*
I'm sure Mummy and Daddy have given you a nice name – all for yourself. *(No response. Pavi looks at Sushi, desperate)*
You must tell me your name, child, so we can talk.

**SUSHI** *(Stepping in)*
Your name, beta. Aunty is asking you. Achchi Aunty hai – she wants to make friends with you.

**MUNNI** *(to Sushi)*
Yeh aunty nahin hai. Bhoot hai.

## SNAP TWO

*A park or any other public place. Amma is seated on what might be a stone seat. Appa joins her, carrying a pack of branded potato chips.*

**APPA**
No sign of him.

**AMMA**
Maybe he's fallen ill.

**APPA**
Never on a Sunday. He can fall ill any time in the week. He'd never do that on a Sunday.

**AMMA**
Your own Sunday is incomplete, you mean!

**APPA**
You could say that, I suppose. What's a Sunday stroll, down to this place, without jignuts from Mastan.

**AMMA**
And Badshah at the coffee house cycle stand.

**APPA**
And Badshah at the cycle stand.

**AMMA**
And Pinto at the magazine stand, Bhaskaran at the bakery.

**APPA**
The fellow at the fancy snack bar said he hadn't seen anybody selling jignuts the last two or three days.

**AMMA**
He wouldn't know, he wouldn't notice.

**APPA**
He said he had jignuts too – same company, same kind of pack as these chips. Twelve rupees, he said.

**AMMA**
He might have gone to his village or something. *(Pause)*

**APPA**
'The venom of scorpions, serpents, and centipedes turned to honey.'

**AMMA**
What's that?

**APPA** *(Laughs softly)*
That's how he got the name Mastan. *(In the vernacular)*
'You are bitten by scorpions, serpents, and centipedes.

What do you do? What can you do in this cruel world?
Here comes Mastan with a talisman most delightful!'
That's how he sold his jigjuts in the old days. Mastan and his jignuts – freshly roasted, freshly salted.

**AMMA**
He was a lovely fellow.

**APPA**
All nice fellows.

**AMMA**
They could make a movie on him.

**APPA**
Nah! Movies are about complicated people.

**AMMA**
People put into complicated situations.

**APPA**
Who wants stories about simple people?

**AMMA**
He was a lovely fellow. *(Pause)*

**APPA** *(Looks at her)*
Do you think so too? He won't come back? *(Begins to open the pack of chips, reads)* 'Made from choicest farm-fresh potato, grown specially for the company in best conditions. Permitted flavouring under licence. Nett weight 50 gms. Date of mfg – blank. Rec. retail price, blank... '

**AMMA**
Have they found someone?

**APPA**
Twenty-two bloody rupees for a packet of blanks.

**AMMA**
Have they? Last week they were supposed to...

**APPA**
No! *(Back to the chips)*
Costs more than double, and what do we get? A fancy bloody packet filled with fancy bloody hot air to make it bulge and look full.

**AMMA**
Come on! It's not like you at all to get worked up like this. Things will work out. They always do – you've always said that.

**APPA**
And people actually pay that much to eat this dung... I'm sorry... I shouldn't have said that. *(Pause)*

**AMMA**

It's all right. Actually, it can't be so bad. It's made by the same Brahmin bakery people near Balaji Lodge. They are just – you know – I suppose they are keeping up with...

**APPA**

Yes, I know. *(Pause)*

No, they haven't found someone yet. 'The right mix of qualifications and experience,' they said – they haven't found one like that.

**AMMA**

You know you have friends in the company. Many in the main office admire you.

**APPA**

Yes, but there are less and less every year.

**AMMA**

After all, you were chosen to hold the additional charge – okay, temporarily they said, until a final decision – but it meant the company recognised you were capable of handling the job.

**APPA**

Yes, for six months. Then extended twice on paper for six months at a time. And then? Not even the formality of proper extension. I've been in this ridiculous extension state for two and a half years now. Almost permanently a temporary Divisional Manager.

**AMMA**

The job is a difficult one – an important one.

**APPA**

How simple-minded can you get! One thing is sure, you won't be selected as a manager in the company.

**AMMA**

Yes, I come from a finishing school in Switzerland, you see! What do I know of the world of commerce and business? I can only qualify as Prime Minister of a third world country.

**APPA**

If there was a job like Minister for Morale & Cheerful Platitudes, you'd get it with zero competition.

**AMMA**

And you? Don't forget you are a Garudachar! You can fly up there and zoom freely in any direction you wish, from any commanding height you choose.

**APPA** *(Laughs softly)*

You know the joke they used to crack about our names in school – my cousins Suvarna and Bhima were in the same school. They used to sing *(In the vernacular if possible)*:

'Wingless, featherless, Garudachar.
Moneyless, penniless, Suvarnachar
Powerless, toothless, Bhimachar.
Hail the Achar trinity! Magnificent non-entity!'

**AMMA**

You never told me that one before. It's fun!

**APPA**

Of course, it was all in fun. We were actually all quite good in our own ways – hockey, cricket, scouting, volleyball. Pretty good in studies too. Lots of boys actually envied us, I think, for what we could do. *(Pause)*

**AMMA**

I think I'll have to apply for foreign aid.

**APPA**

Huh?

**AMMA**

This job of rebuilding morale and good cheer seems to need a special project.

**APPA**

You are the party's greatest asset. You are the one who gives us stability! *(Amma holds his hand. They look at each other briefly. He withdraws his hand awkwardly, looks off. One waits for the other to continue.)*

**AMMA**

The party has a bright future – there is a son to the dynasty!

**APPA**

Actually, I'm a bit worried about Ramki.

**AMMA**

In what way?

**APPA**

What does he want in life? One day this, one day that – I wish he'd settle down to something solid.

**AMMA**

But he's just over twenty.

**APPA**

Twenty-three.

**AMMA**

Okay, twenty-three, if you must be particular.

**APPA**

On his way to being twenty-four.

**AMMA and APPA** *(Together)*

Now, when I was his age, you know that... *(Amma grins. Appa continues)*

**APPA**

I wish I knew what he is planning to do with that expensive engineering degree that will soon be decorating the wall.

**AMMA**

Do you want me to ask him?

**APPA**

No, that's not what I meant. I mean, do we have to really ask our own son what he is planning to do? 'Please, our son, kindly consider the matter above and convey your decision to us at the earliest and oblige. We remain, yours faithfully... '

**AMMA**

Things are not what they used to be in your time. For that matter, even in my time. College life nowadays is so busy, busy, busy all the time. There is so much to do.

**APPA**

Yes, of course. So much to do all over town, no? You have to be loafing, loafing, loafing all the time. He and his motorbike and his motorbike gang.

**AMMA**

He is a careful driver.

**APPA**

And his 2-in-1. You know he is at home only because the 2-in-1 is on, blaring away. 2-in-1 Ramakrishnan they should call him.

**AMMA**

That is a clever one!

**APPA**

What?

**AMMA**

Did you know you just cracked a very original one? 2-in-1 Ramakrishnan! Now you can call Natraj's son 3-in-1 Sivaramakrishnan?

**APPA** *(Laughs)*

Yes, that sounds good. You are right, it is quite funny.

**AMMA**

You haven't lost your sense of humour – your Sunday evening humour. You are just a bit tense, that's all.

**APPA**

You have done quite well yourself – even without foreign aid.

**AMMA**

You know, I think deep inside, you do believe that Ramki is a fine young man, that he is growing up just fine.

**APPA**

Do you think so? He is growing up fine?

**AMMA**

He takes after you in so many ways. It's not always clear – not in so many obvious ways – but it's there. You two should be seen together more often for the similarities to be noticed.

**APPA**

It's funny. I was thinking the other day that we are so alike in being so different.

**AMMA**

Oh?

**APPA**

You know, when I was his age, or even younger, I had to make such an effort to appear phirangi. Wearing a tie correctly, using cutlery, being proper in speech, 'no thank you' and 'how do you do' and a smattering of Beethoven and Victor Sylvester. Or Brahms for the heavier pretensions– more Brahmanical. Of course there was nothing more to it at all. At heart, I was all thairsatham and little else. We were all like that – Natraj, Panchu, Vicky, even Kurien, and that Sharma fellow from the rich business family. Even getting our first jobs – we had to look cultured. Which meant European, or American, or English or whatever – nobody knew the difference. And now I see Ramki – he has to try so hard to be Indian, to appear Indian.

**AMMA**

Isn't that good? Isn't it nice to know that something like that always comes back?

**APPA**

I'm not sure. I can't help thinking – if this is what he is trying so hard to put on, what is underneath? What is it he'll fall back upon?

**AMMA**

You mean if it will be hamburgers?

**APPA**

Hamburgers, hot dogs, pizzas, steaks...

**AMMA**

They all come in vegetarian versions. That's what Ramki and his friends order anyway.

*(Pause)*

**APPA**
Time to leave?

**AMMA**
If you say so. It's past 7:30.

**APPA**
Nah – let's walk round the plaza one more time.

## SNIP THREE

*Pavi, Abhi, and Sushi at a school meeting. Father Principal is studying some exercise books. The trio wait at a distance.*

**PAVI**
Do you think we'll have to go for tuition?

**SUSHI**
What on earth for? His grades are not bad.

**PAVI**
But they all say, 'Could do better.'

**SUSHI**
They said that in your marks card and mine – twenty-five years ago.

**PAVI**
Still, he must get more As. He can't get used to bringing home so many Bs.

**SUSHI**
Where is the time for tuition now? The homework itself takes up to dinner time almost.

**PAVI**
And where do I go round looking for a tutor? Will they be there in the yellow pages?

**SUSHI**
Forget it! I can easily spare an hour most evenings. Four days a week maybe. I'd love to be able to help Abloo with his studies.

**PAVI**
If they insist?

**SUSHI**
Then it means they have somebody in mind from the school. That's what the PTAs have become – an extracurricular employment exchange.

**FATHER**
Abhishek! *(They step up)* Abhishek?

**ABHI**
Good evening, Father.

**FATHER**
Good evening. And which of these is your... ?

**PAVI**
I'm Abhi's mother, Father. I mean his father is not here. He's on tour, Father. The slip said mother or father or both. So I've come, Father. I'm Abhi's mother, Father.

**FATHER**
And this is... ?

**PAVI**
This is Sushila, Father.

**SUSHI**
Good evening, Father.

**FATHER**
Good evening.

**PAVI**
Good evening, Father

**SUSHI**
I'm just accompanying them.

**PAVI**
She's like a member of the family, Father. She's Abloo's favourite Aunty – that's Abhi. He's called Abloo at home.

**FATHER**
Abhishek, you can go out and wait. I'll call you later. *(Abhi looks at his mother.)* You can watch the cricket practice if you like. Go on. *(He leaves)*

**PAVI**
Is something wrong, Father? *(Pause)* Abhi's father will be back in three days, Father. He can deal with any... *(Pause)* Yes, Father?

**FATHER**
Abhishek is showing signs of a learning disability. *(Pavi and Sushi look at one another.)* He can't retain things.

**PAVI**
Is that why his grades... ?

**SUSHI**
But his grades are not bad.

**FATHER**
Is that what you think? Well, our computerised cumulative tracking index doesn't think so.

**PAVI**

Oh, Sushi...

**FATHER** *(Continuing)*

There has been a steady decline in the index in almost all subjects.

**SUSHI**

Decline? We haven't noticed.

**FATHER**

Except poetry and drawing, although he insists on colouring parrots blue and gold, and making them bigger than necessary.

**PAVI**

Parrots? Bigger than... ?

**FATHER**

Parrots! Bigger than the cat, bigger than the hen, bigger than the boy and girl.

**SUSHI**

It might look interesting. Another way of...

**FATHER**

They are not important subjects anyway.

**PAVI**

No, father.

**FATHER**

Look at history. Down 2.5 points.

**PAVI**

But he loves the subject.

**FATHER**

You should see the test papers.

**SUSHI**

I remember his doing the revision with me. I thought he was good.

**FATHER**

Here's an example. The lesson says, 'Phoenicians were very good sailors.' Abhishek's answer, 'The Phoenicians were able seamen.' Lesson on the Harappan civilization. The correct answer is, 'Mohenjodaro was located in the north-western part of the Indian subcontinent.' Abhishek's answer, 'In present-day Pakistan, north of Karachi, lie the ruins of Mohenjo-daro, a fine example of Harappan civilization.' He even writes the name as two words, with a hyphen in between.

**SUSHI**

The answers are not wrong, Father.

**FATHER**

They are not right! It's the same thing in arithmetic, science, environment studies. Long division – one bracket on the left, one on the right. Abhishek's long division? He puts the numbers on top, above a line. Definitions of solid, liquid, gas – he puts gas first, solid last. It won't do. Solid–liquid–gas. In that order. Why can't he learn to do things the proper way?

**SUSHI**

And environment studies?

**FATHER**

We have hardly started. There is so much to cover by the end of the year. Air, water, energy, wild life sanctuaries, and what not. But he must go off at a tangent and write some silly essay on Man's Best Friend, The Bicycle.

**SUSHI**

I see. Then I suppose we all must...

**PAVI**

I'm sorry, Father. I'll talk to his father. You are right, Father. I was telling Sushi the same thing – that we all must work harder to help Abhi in his studies.

**FATHER**

Good. That is a positive attitude.

**PAVI**

Thank you, Father. You will tell us what to do, Father?

**FATHER**

We'll see. *(A pause and a glare)* You may need some specialised help.

## SNAP THREE

*Ramki's room. Amma is tidying up. Among other things, she recovers several audio cassettes from various points and stacks them neatly. She decides to play one on the 2-in-1. A blast. She doesn't like the sound, tries another one. That's better. She continues with the tidying up, picks up a book covered with a newspaper from under his pillow, flips through, and decides to sit down and read a page or two. Ramki enters quietly and watches Amma awhile before speaking.*

**RAMKI**

Naughty, naughty!

**AMMA**

Oh, Ramki! You gave me such a scare...

**RAMKI**

Room door open, music on, personal belongings disturbed out of their usual place *(Indicating the neatly arranged things)* – it is an open-and-shut case, m'lord. The intruder was somebody who knew the household very well, perhaps an insider, perhaps... a woman. And the one woman with the strongest motive for breaking into the victim's premises m'lord was... the mother! *(He turns off the 2-in-1.)*

**AMMA** *(As Judge)*

Does the accused plead guilty or not guilty? *(As herself)* Not guilty, m'lord. *(As judge)* Overruled. In the case under trial there is no provision for a not guilty admission. *(As herself)* Well, then, m'lord – guilty, with a small 'g', followed by a star in parentheses, which as explained in the birth certificate of the plaintiff dated September 3, nineteen hundred and seventy one, that is in the year of the lord, m'lord, permits the natural mother of the plaintiff at any time...

**RAMKI**

Case dismissed! However, as a deterrent to future misuses of the generosity of this court, the accused is directed to pay a token fine of rupees one hundred and fifty only per month, which may be annexed to the monthly allowance of the plaintiff.

**AMMA**

Permission to appeal to higher court, m'lord?

**RAMKI**

It may be considered. Until this court delivers judgement on the appeal, the accused may remit to the plaintiff an earnest deposit of rupees seven hundred and fifty only as security.

**AMMA**

So that he may continue to drop donations into the Postal Department hundi?

**RAMKI**

Postal... ?

**AMMA**

Or cybercafé print-outs. For catalogues from American universities? Each application must cost twenty to twenty-five rupees in postage in the first round, and another fifty to sixty in the next round. *(Pause)*

**RAMKI**

Amma, you're always like this. All fun and chatter for a while – you lead me on – and then thup! You toss a googly.

**AMMA**

Do you really mean that? Has that upset you? Or is it just the awkwardness of being found out?

**RAMKI**

Why awkward?

**AMMA**

Like playing I Spy as kids. You think you have found the cleverest, most secret, hiding place and somebody just gets there straight without the slightest effort.

**RAMKI**

I was not hiding anything. It's not meant to be a great big secret. I would tell you about it anyway...

**AMMA**

When the right time came along!

**RAMKI**

Come on, Amma. Half the world finds out about American universities some time or the other.

**AMMA**

Have you talked about it with Appa?

**RAMKI**

Not yet. I will, by and by. Anyway, I was planning to talk to you first.

**AMMA**

Oh? A domestic courier service?

**RAMKI**

He is unpredictable. He is moody and irritable.

**AMMA**

Is he? Appa?

**RAMKI**

No, not all the time. Just – I don't know, I can't say – he wasn't like this earlier. I thought I should approach him later. Carefully.

**AMMA**

Ramki, it's not like Appa to be this way. You know that.

**RAMKI**

No, it's not him. He is strict and strong minded, but not...

**AMMA**

You should also know that it's not like him to take out his problems on people around him. *(Pause)* He is passing through a very difficult time at the office.

**RAMKI**

Appa? What kind of difficulty?

**AMMA**

It is a long story. And too complicated for me to understand fully. But to put it very simply, he is being denied a promotion.

**RAMKI**

This happened recently?

**AMMA**

Over two years ago. Almost three now.

**RAMKI**

Somebody else... ?

**AMMA**

That's the sad part of it. They haven't got another person for the senior position after Narayan uncle retired. Although Appa has been handling the job as in-charge ever since.

**RAMKI**

Why? What is it that Appa doesn't have for the job?

**AMMA**

As far as I could make out, Appa has every possible quality for the post. Every requirement, except one thing.

**RAMKI**

What thing?

**AMMA**

He doesn't have the three magic letters after his name – MBA.

**RAMKI**

As a matter of fact, he doesn't have any letters after his name. He is not even a graduate.

**AMMA**

You could add SC, I suppose, for the Senior Cambridge certificate that was so highly valued once. But it has quite another meaning today.

**RAMKI**

But Appa – they can't do this to him. He has such a fantastic record in the business.

**AMMA**

Times change.

**RAMKI**

Do you remember the citation on the silk scroll he got when he completed twenty-five years in the company? Everybody thought...

**AMMA**

That's just it. His first and last job – that's what he always said. Started with a bag in his hand, door-to-door, walked all over the country. Worked his way up with grit and loyalty. His first and last job. To be treated like this in his last five years must be so... *(Pause)*

**RAMKI**

Do you remember the Canara Bank order? There was a special issue of the house magazine. I think I was in eighth then. There was so much written about Appa's approach and perseverance in that job.

**AMMA**

Two years later they had a young fellow as Product Manager, hardly out of his pimples.

**RAMKI**

The one who botched up the Sri Lanka order.

**AMMA**

Because he rubbed everybody the wrong way from Purchase to Packaging.

**RAMKI**

Amma...

**AMMA**

Good god, what am I doing? Getting sucked into Appa's office politics like this!

**RAMKI**

I didn't know at all.

**AMMA**

Now you know, how does it help? You can't do anything about it. That's what he always said – you can't do anything about it.

**RAMKI**

How much longer... ? When are they going to settle the appointments?

**AMMA**

Your guess is as good as mine – which is as good as anybody else's. Meanwhile, the number of management-type youngsters has steadily increased. The old-timers and the youngsters are in two opposite camps. And life in the office has become hell. Appa doesn't say that – he only thinks it has become uninteresting.

**RAMKI**

Don't you think he should fight for his rights? Make a representation or something?

**AMMA**

Unthinkable! Against the rules of the game. That's exactly what he thinks the youngsters would do in the slightest of difficulties in company life. No, Ramki, Appa's rule book is a 1955 edition. *(Pause)*

**RAMKI**

Is there something I can do?

**AMMA**

Of course, you can. In his own words, 'study hard, work hard, be a good engineer.'

**RAMKI**

Amma, I...

**AMMA**

No, no need to feel bad about anything. Times change, everything must change. You must grow up in your own future.

**RAMKI**

It is all so different now. When Appa started work...

**AMMA**

He had a bicycle till the day he got married. He cycled to school, he cycled to work, he cycled to meet friends. He might have cycled to the wedding, if it wasn't for Thatha's raised eyebrows. Even after we got our scooter, he went on the bicycle to meet his friends in the Sunday routine – walk round the plaza – a masala dosai – walk round the plaza again – coffee – cycle home. *(Pause)* Riding doubles sometimes.

**RAMKI**

Does it mean so much to him – for me to be an engineer?

**AMMA**

It means a lot to him. He doesn't want you to suffer the same... you know the way the world looks at you today if you have solid qualifications... he wants that for you. He thinks you'll be a great engineer.

**RAMKI**

He wants to fix me up as an Officer Trainee in the Company!

**AMMA**

He doesn't want you making a living selling shampoo – or kitchen scrubbers or wax polish or whatever – although you can make a fortune in the line they say.

**RAMKI**

Amma, it's not enough getting an engineering degree. Not anymore. Just like you can't do much with an MBBS anymore. Who'll look at a mere graduate engineer? I'll end up selling screws and washers in a hardware shop.

**AMMA**

It keeps getting longer, doesn't it?

**RAMKI**

What?

**AMMA**

The schooling – the preparation for whatever it is we call life and living.

**RAMKI**

It does. And I have miles to go!

**AMMA** *(Wistful)*

You know when I went to my first school? When I was five years old. In Hyderabad. You know when Appa went to school? When he was seven!

**RAMKI**

But Amma...

**AMMA**

But no – there is no point in these comparisons. You are different, living in a different world, in a different time. You started nice and bright when you were two and a half. And you are going to become a super-specialised engineer.

**RAMKI**

And do I get a chance to change my plan?

**AMMA**

Out of guilt or remorse – no.

**RAMKI**

Out of clear thinking, if found necessary?

**AMMA**

Change in specialisation? Why not?

**RAMKI**

Yes, change in specialisation. I suppose I can choose the right specialisation for a good future.

**AMMA**

But you will be an engineer all the same, won't you?

**RAMKI**

At the base, yes, I will be an engineer.

**APPA***(Offstage)*

Listen!

**AMMA**

Oh, it's Appa. *(Replying)* I'm up here.

**APPA**

I need some help with the garden tap. I must change the washer before we lose all the tank water.

**AMMA**

Ramki is here. I'll send him.

**APPA**

Ramki home? What is he doing up there?

**AMMA**

He is... working. He is studying some technical catalogues and making notes.

**APPA**

Oh, then don't disturb him. I can manage if you come and hold the pipe while I...

**RAMKI**

I'll come, Appa. No problem.

**APPA**

Good. It will be better with an engineer on the job. *(Ramki prepares to go. Amma stops him as he leaves.)*

**AMMA**

If it has to be an MBA... so let it be. But don't go and do something rash with your life.

**RAMKI**

Amma, you are simply... *(He rushes out)*

*(Amma looks after Ramki awhile. She then puts the newspaper-covered book in place with other books, papers. She switches on the 2-in-1, adjusts the volume to a comfortable level, and proceeds with the tiding up.)*

## SNIP FOUR

*Sister Principal walks in with Munni, holding her hand. She leads Munni in light and dreamy dance steps to her position and seats her on the floor. She sings in an assembly hall voice.*

**SISTER**

What are little girls made of?
What are little girls made of?

**MUNNI** *(Reciting)*

Sugar and spice
and everything nice.
That's what girls are made of.

**SISTER**

What are little boys made of?
What are little boys made of?

**MUNNI**

Snips and snails
and puppy dog tails.
That's what boys are made of.

*(Sister gives Munni an exquisite set of drawing colours and an art book. As Munni begins to draw, she watches indulgently for a while and then slips away in the same light-stepped way. Munni is alone for a while, absorbed. Abhi enters with a catapult around his neck, walks past Munni, stops, and looks intently at Munni's drawing. Munni does not respond. Presently Abhi takes the caty off his neck and begins to play with it. Over the next minute or so, the two very gradually increase their attention on each other's playthings, until they are at last looking at each other. Abhi places the caty on the floor. Munni slides over to the caty even as Abhi positions himself at the drawing. He continues Munni's drawing, getting completely absorbed in it, huddled on the floor. Munni is all concentration, stalking and shooting down a tiger with the caty. The tiger despatched, she takes a second look at Abhi, moves quietly up to him, drops to her knees, and watches him at work, fascinated. Abhi finishes, is pleased with what he has done, and rises slowly to his knees. They look at each other briefly and turn their attention to the drawing again... as the lights fade out.)*

*End of Act I*

# ACT II

## SNIP FIVE

*A spot picks up Munni and Abhi at their homework. They are in school uniform. There are two enormous school bags next to them on the floor. There is an occasional glance and enquiry into each other's workbooks. They finish triumphantly at about the same time.*

**MUNNI** *(Handing workbook to Abhi)*
I love maths!

**ABHI** *(Handing workbook to Munni)*
I love drawing!

**MUNNI**
I hate poetry!

**ABHI**
I hate science!

**MUNNI**
Thanks for this.

**ABHI**
Thank you too.
*(They pack up their bags, punctuating it with a series of hates and loves – anything from school subjects thru palak bhaji to uncles, aunts, teachers, to be improvised by the actors. They end with...)*

**MUNNI**
I hate boys!

**ABHI**
I hate girls!

**MUNNI**
Yeaahhukk!

**ABHI**
Oooahhukk!

**MUNNI**
Double yeaahhukk!

**ABHI**
Treble Oooahhukk! *(They are done. They take off their shoes; put them away neatly. Before they can take their socks off, they are sleepy.)*

**MUNNI**
What will you do when you leave school?

**ABHI**
I will work for the poor people in the country.

**MUNNI**
So nice.

**ABHI**
Then I can travel to so many other countries.

**MUNNI**
Can I come with you?

**ABHI**
I don't know. What about you?

**MUNNI**
I want to be a minister.

**ABHI**
A minister?

**MUNNI**
A chief minister. Then I can have my statue everywhere. I can name so many things after me. Parks, roads, buses, even cities.

**ABHI**
You can do that only after you are dead.

**MUNNI**
Who says?

**ABHI**
That's the rule. You have to be dead first.

**MUNNI**
I will change the rules. *(They curl up next to their school bags.)*

**MUNNI**
Will you help me with my drawing homework again?

**ABHI**
Yes.

**MUNNI**
Tomorrow?

**ABHI**
Okay. Will you help me in maths?

**MUNNI**
Okay. Poetry?

**ABHI**
Okay. Science? *(Munni does not reply.)* Science?

**MUNNI**

Huh?

**ABHI**

Science. *(Munni is asleep. Pause)* I hate science. *(He turns and goes to sleep. Pause)*

**PAVI** *(Offstage)*

Abhi-Munni! Have you finished with your homework? It's past ten already. You must come down for your dinner now!

## SNAP FOUR

*The park. Amma is seated. Appa has a packet of potato chips in his hand. He offers some to Amma.*

**AMMA**

Sit down and take it easy. He will come.

**APPA**

He might have gone off to the other side of the plaza.

**AMMA**

Nonsense! He knows which is which. He knows the exact stone seat we will be sitting on.

**APPA**

Everything has changed here. He might not...

**AMMA**

Nothing has changed. These seats have been here the last hundred years. And you've been sitting on this one the last forty years.

**APPA**

Why is he late then?

**AMMA**

He is not late. We are early. There is still a clear half-hour before the show, and we have the tickets in advance. So, sit down and eat your chips in peace.

**APPA**

If you start arguing with me on every little thing...

**AMMA**

I'm not arguing with you!

**APPA**

There you go again.

**AMMA**

I'm just trying to make you see...

**APPA**

Every little thing! Everything I say, everything I do – there has to be something wrong. Only me. There has to be something wrong only in me all the time! *(He stops. She motions him to sit. He does. Pause)*

**AMMA**

I'm sorry. I didn't mean to upset you.

**APPA**

It's all right.

**AMMA**

You know I didn't.

**APPA**

Why is he late?

**AMMA**

He is not late.

**APPA**

Is it a good movie?

**AMMA**

We will know in a little while. *(Pause)* You've heard reports?

**APPA**

Some. Not many. Some good, some not so good.

**AMMA**

We are talking about...

**APPA**

It is important to spend one Sunday in a month together. *(Pause)* A movie together, or dinner, or both sometimes.

**AMMA**

At least once a month. You have been very particular. He must be looking for a parking place.

**APPA**

That's no problem on this side of the plaza. Badshah and Pinto and the other fellows are all there. They've known him since he was a baby. He might not recognise them, but they know him.

**AMMA**

He is quite a capable boy himself, you know.

**APPA**

Do you think so? Yes, I think he is capable. Gets lost in the City Market and the RTO Office, but on the whole...

**AMMA**

He is very proud of you.

**APPA**

He said that to you?

**AMMA**

Not in so many words...

**APPA**

He says things to you he never even... I hope he doesn't become dependent on his Mummy's hand-feeding.

**AMMA**

Does he look as if he might be?

**APPA**

No! You are right. He is a capable sort of boy. On the whole.

**AMMA**

You've heard reports?

**APPA**

Some.

**AMMA**

The new MD...

**APPA**

He's going ahead with the plan. Take it or leave it. It will be introduced on the first of April.

**AMMA**

April Fool's Day... How much time will they give you?

**APPA**

Oh, a couple of months. Not more than three months, I suppose.

**AMMA**

And then it will just go through, you think? No protests, no appeal?

**APPA**

Who are we to protest? This way you leave the Company with something in your hand at least. That is why they call it a handshake. You try your protest-lotest, and you can end up spending the rest of your life writing letters to the Great Wall of China.

**AMMA**

You people have an Officers' Association, don't you?

**APPA**

They organise the annual table tennis tournament. That's all! Have you forgotten what our Venky has gone through?

**AMMA**

Poor Venky.

**APPA**

No job, nothing to do the last three years, and no money either. It's all held up somewhere, god knows where.

**AMMA**

How many have decided?

**APPA**

Poor Viji's marriage held up with all that... If he had waited and quietly taken the scheme this year...

**AMMA**

How many of you?

**APPA**

All of them, I suppose. It is not the golden handshake they make it out to be, fourteen carats maybe. But what is the alternative?

**AMMA**

And you?

**APPA**

I don't know. Should I tell you? I really don't know what to do. *(Pause)*

**AMMA**

You don't have any grievance against the Company... No major complaint...

**APPA**

I suppose you are right.

**AMMA**

They have been good with you.

**APPA**

On the whole.

**AMMA**

So, why leave with bitterness? It is not as if you are leaving one company to join another company.

**APPA**

That is the trouble, you know. It is clear that people like us are not wanted anymore, but where do we go? Who will take us seriously?

**AMMA**

You will stay?

**APPA**

It is not so easy. I have, what, another two years before retirement? Till recently I could have expected an extension of another year or two. I wouldn't have to say, 'Please, sir, will you give me an extension?' They would ask me to continue. They may still do that – who knows? But they may not too. They may not even give me a grade change – now or after two years. So, what do I do? Leave now, collect my money, and have nothing to do the whole day from next month? Or continue for the salary and Company medical benefits, but bear the humiliation of being ignored by all around me all the time?

**AMMA**

The company will not persecute you. You can at least be sure of that.

**APPA**

No, they might not do that.

**AMMA**

Not you. Not with your service record.

**APPA**

Thirty-five years.

**AMMA**

Next to Vishnu in the head office, you are the oldest employee.

**APPA**

The old MD used to say, 'Look at Achar, he has a head start!'

**AMMA**

Absolute gentleman he was.

**APPA**

First in the family to start working, first to get a car, first to build a house, first to send a son to engineering college. Also, the first sales trainee in the Company to get into the management grade.

**AMMA**

The Company has been your life...

**APPA**

I don't know any other life.

**AMMA**

You'll stay? *(Pause)*

**APPA**

The new MD – he looks just a little older than Ramki.

**AMMA**

Is he good? Do people... ?

**APPA**

He is so powerful... so much power, at such a young age...

**AMMA**

Leave!

**APPA**

Huh?

**AMMA**

You should leave. You don't have to walk out making a noise. Just take the scheme and leave.

*(Appa does not reply. She moves closer to him, offers him chips. He is quiet. She takes out some and tries feeding him. He smiles, takes the chips, and feeds her in return. They laugh softly.)*

**APPA**

Scorpions, serpents, centipedes... Here comes Mastan... a talisman most delightful...

**AMMA**

No need to rush. You have two to three months. *(They munch the chips. Ramki enters, sees them together, absorbed. He poses as a photographer.)*

**RAMKI**

Khatchak! One more for The Hindu Sunday edition. Khatchak! One more to send to Mani Ratnam for his next superstar project...

**AMMA**

Here at last! Another two minutes and Appa would have organised a search party.

**APPA**

Where have you parked?

**RAMKI**

Right next to the cinema. Badshah had put his boys on the job. When they saw me coming, they just put the manhole cover back, removed the ring of bricks, and jisss I parked!

**APPA**

Good old Badshah!

**RAMKI**

When did you both get here?

**AMMA**

Oh, a little while ago.

**RAMKI**

You left home so early. What have you been... ?

**APPA**

Time to move. You have the tickets?

**RAMKI**

There is time for a coffee.

**APPA**

Yennaiah, it is 6:15 already.

**AMMA**

There is plenty of time. The seats are reserved.

**RAMKI**

What were you discussing so seriously when I came?

**APPA**

Discuss? What is there to discuss?

**AMMA**

What is there to discuss? Except you!

**RAMKI**

Me? Wow! The most discussed personality of the year! In the Achar household at least.

**APPA**

We were wondering what your next steps in life might be. You haven't told us anything.

**RAMKI** *(Looking at Amma)*

Actually...

**AMMA**

We were also talking about all the exciting things we can do when Appa stops going to the office.

**RAMKI**

Stop going to the office?

**AMMA**

When he retires.

**RAMKI**

When is that? *(He looks at both of them)*

**APPA**

It could be soon... but then, it may not be all that soon either.

**RAMKI**

You didn't tell us...
*(To Amma)* Did you know about this?

**AMMA**

Well, we both know his age... the thing would have come up one day or the other.

**RAMKI**

Appa retired – wow! So, what are your next...

**APPA**

There is enough time after today's movie to talk about these things. Now let's...

**AMMA**

One little plan is pukka anyhow.

**RAMKI**

You are both taking a trip to Singapore for a holiday!

**AMMA**

No.

**RAMKI**

Appa is starting his coaching classes for sales trainees, and you are joining the computer course.

**AMMA**

Wrong again.

**RAMKI**

Appa and you are both – no, I give up.

**AMMA**

We are going to start looking for a girl for you.

**APPA**

Yes, that's something we can start on straightaway!

**AMMA**

It takes time. It takes great care. We must do a nice, thorough job of it, right?

**APPA**

Come on, come on, let's move fast. I like to see the trailers before the movie. *(He moves off)*

**RAMKI**

Were you really discussing me?

**AMMA**

For a while.

**RAMKI**

Does he know? Have you... ?

**AMMA**

No, I haven't said anything.

**RAMKI**

Do you know what's happened today?

**AMMA**

Was that the post today?

**RAMKI**

Yes! Have you heard of Northwestern?

**AMMA**

No. Is it one of the places you applied to?

**RAMKI**

One of the places, yes. They have offered me admission!

**AMMA**

Yes? You've got in?

**RAMKI**

I'm in!

**AMMA**

What about... ?

**RAMKI**

Not full aid. Part aid they say. I have to manage the first year by myself. After that, they say they can give me part aid, and for the rest I can easily... *(He sees she is not with him)*

**AMMA**

Let's go now. We can talk about this later. We'll talk about it tomorrow.

## SNIP SIX

*Pavi and Sushi on the floor. There is a big pile of new-looking school books and notebooks on one side, a smaller pile on the other side, freshly covered in brown paper. Also seen is an ample supply of brown paper sheets, scissors, name labels, and other paraphernalia that goes with the starting term routine. A tea service tray. They are both busy.*

**PAVI**

It was all right till last year. We managed somehow. They have now gone and introduced 15 per cent marks for neatness. It's called turnout. Like some military parade. Turnout. It includes neatness of books and notebooks. 15 per cent, can you imagine? Poor kids! What do they know about binding with brown paper and labels and cellotape and what not. Bad enough having to learn about how many trees are cut for making how many tons of paper or something like that. The other day Munni came home and announced that she had taken a vow never to use toilet paper when she grows up. I can imagine things like clean socks and shoes and haircut and fingernails trimmed twice a week. But books and notebooks! They even want the exact same shade of brown. So we all have to buy the brown paper only from the school stores. Last year, we had to buy their sweaters from the school stores. Uniforms, I can understand. Sweaters! Fifty rupees more than the shop price. I refused. I'll buy sweaters for my children from the market, I said. There was a letter from the Principal. Chalo, I said. I agreed. I went along and bought them from the school. Next thing, Reebok will open a branch in the school compound. Everything from the school stores. Pencils, rubbers – school stores. Crayons, paint box – school stores. They have kept some lunch boxes in the school stores. Horrible plastic ones with prints of Snow White and Spiderman on them. Wait and see, next year those lunch boxes will be made compulsory. Plastic lunch dabbas!

The school bag will be stinking by the time they get home. You know how forgetful Abloo is. He forgets to have his lunch sometimes. Imagine all that in a plastic lunch dabba kept the whole day in his bag. They all need a bigger bag anyway. Five hundred each, these new bags. Twice as expensive as the old one. Half as durable. I doubt very much if all this will last three full terms. God! Let's get going with the first term for now. *(She stops. They have both just finished one set.)*

Well! That's not too bad for the first round. Some more tea?

**SUSHI**

Sure. Shall I? *(She reaches for the tray)*

**ABHI** *(Off)*

Mummy, have you finished?

**MUNNI** *(Off)*

It's past ten already. You must come down for your dinner now!

## SNAP FIVE

*Ramki's room. Amma and Ramki are in the middle of a tangled discussion.*

**AMMA**

You can tell me straight. Is there some girl you have in mind already?

**RAMKI**

No.

**AMMA**

Are you sure? There is no harm in...

**RAMKI**

No. There is no one.

**AMMA**

Do you object to your parents looking out for a match?

**RAMKI**

No.

**AMMA**

You trust your parents, then?

**RAMKI:**

Of course, I do.

**AMMA**

We really don't have to make a great effort, you know. There are already so many enquiries. Word gets around. After all, you are quite a prize for any girl's family.

**RAMKI**

I don't want to get married.

**AMMA**

You won't marry? You said just now...

**RAMKI**

Not now. I don't want to get married now.

**AMMA**

Such a disappointment...

**RAMKI**

I am sorry.

**AMMA**

For all those sweet young girls...

**RAMKI**

Oh no!

**AMMA**

Who set their parents to hook you!

**RAMKI**

Amma, I know you are very good at this! You are flattering me...

**AMMA**

But you will not bend.

**RAMKI**

You don't have to make it sound like that.

**AMMA**

Put yourself in Appa's shoes. He gets one reference after another. All first class families, lovely girls. He feels very good about them too. He passes them on to you. You reject every one of them without so much as a comment.

**RAMKI**

I know how you both must feel.

**AMMA**

You know what he said yesterday? He said Ramki is simply passing papers. In tray, out tray.

**RAMKI**

It's true. I have been doing that. But how can I get Appa to see?

**AMMA**

To put himself in your shoes?

**RAMKI**

How can I even expect him to do that?

**AMMA**
What do you want him to see?

**RAMKI**
Everything! There is so much he must see. I don't know where we can begin.

**AMMA**
At the beginning most likely.

**RAMKI**
Wait a minute. Does he know?

**AMMA**
Maybe.

**RAMKI**
What does that mean? Have you told him?

**AMMA**
Was I expected to? It wasn't clear. Did you share a secret with me? Or did you confide in me so that I would let him know?

**RAMKI**
Come on, Amma, stop teasing me. Does he know?

**AMMA**
Maybe.

**RAMKI**
You've told him!

**AMMA**
No, I haven't. Since it was not clear, I decided not to.

**RAMKI**
Then how would he...

**AMMA**
He is your father!

**RAMKI**
How much do you think he knows?

**AMMA**
How much have you told him?

**RAMKI**
It is easy to say that. You know how it is when it comes to...

**AMMA**
He got you a motorbike.

**RAMKI**
That was long ago. The whole world has motorbikes.

**AMMA**

He didn't have to. In his heart he still does not accept that there should be so many motorbikes on the roads. He got you one anyway.

**RAMKI**

What do you think? How much does he know?

**AMMA**

My own personal estimate?

**RAMKI**

Your own assessment.

**AMMA**

Notwithstanding the subjective nature of the evidence, m'lord, it might be stated inter alia that inasmuch as...

**RAMKI**

Objection, m'lord, the witness is evading the question posed to her.

**AMMA**

Sustained. My personal estimate is that he knows something is cooking, but not much more beyond that.

**RAMKI**

What did you say when he asked you?

**AMMA**

You will be surprised. He hasn't asked me. To be honest, I'm surprised too.

**RAMKI**

God! I feel guilty about this – keeping him in the dark.

**AMMA**

What he knows and what he does not know have several shades of grey in between, I think. My personal estimate, that is. For instance, he knows very definitely that you are an engineer, and a pretty good engineer. He knows you want to study more, rather than work. He thinks he knows that. He has an inkling, I think, that you may be thinking of studying abroad. Lots of young people do that. Some of your friends are abroad, two of your cousins are, so why not... About admission offers and Northwestern and aid and so on – doubtful. I don't think he is in the know. What you are actually planning to study, I think, is quite unknown to him. My estimate purely. The MBA thing would be quite unexpected. There, I have given my testimony!

**RAMKI**

You think he knows about the American universities? *(Amma smiles)* He might know that something can come up?

**AMMA**

Possibly.

**RAMKI**
Then he should understand. This is no time to be rushing into marriage.

**AMMA** *(Smiles again)*
You should understand too.

**RAMKI**
Understand what?

**AMMA**
Why he is so keen on your getting married.

**RAMKI**
What?! But that's ridiculous!

**AMMA**
That is what his father did for him – when he decided to go to the big city for the big break in his life.

**RAMKI**
But my dad is different. He is well read, he is cultured, he has seen the world... He couldn't possibly...

**AMMA**
But he is your father! He is worried about you.

**RAMKI**
Gawwd!

**AMMA**
He loves you.

**RAMKI**
Shit!

**AMMA**
That is not the best description of his love for you.

**RAMKI**
I'm sorry... Look, we must decide on a couple of things before he gets back from the office.

**AMMA**
He is back.

**RAMKI**
What? He is home?

**AMMA**
He is in the garage. He will join us soon.

**RAMKI**
He is coming up here?

**AMMA**
I told him to finish what he was doing. I said I'd be here.

**RAMKI**

To prepare the ground, so to speak!

**AMMA**

He was fixing a leak in the radiator hose. *(She goes to the entrance and calls)* Listen! We are waiting for you.

**APPA** *(Off)*

Yes, yes, I am coming.

**AMMA**

Remember to lock the garage. *(She turns to Ramki)*

**RAMKI**

You are holding his brief, aren't you? You are taking his side.

**AMMA**

That is a silly thing to say.

**RAMKI**

I don't know what to say!

**AMMA**

Get a hold on yourself. You are quite capable of running your own life. We all know that. But do it with your God-given intelligence.

*(Pause. Ramki breaks away abruptly and busies himself, tidying up his shelves. Amma watches him sympathetically. Appa enters and surveys the scene. He has an audio cassette in his hand and an envelope sticking out of his shirt pocket.)*

**APPA**

Here, you left this on the dashboard. *(No response)*

Nice collection. When did you start listening to these? *(No response)*

It seems to be the in-thing. Lots of people listening to old film music nowadays. Do you have more of these? *(A mumbled response)*

There must be a cassette of Suraiya in our bedroom. Take it whenever you feel like it. *(To Amma)* Is he sulking? Or is there a death in the family that I haven't heard about yet?

**AMMA**

I was talking to Ramki.

**APPA**

That I think I know.

**AMMA**

He was saying...

**RAMKI**

Appa, I don't think I should be getting married now.

**APPA**

You don't want to get married.

**RAMKI**

No.

**APPA**

We'll accept that. We can just have the engagement for the time being.

**RAMKI** *(In a burst)*

There is no hurry. I'm twenty-three now. Only twenty-three. This is 1994. People don't rush into marriage at this age. There are lots of things to be done. There are lots of things I want to do. Study some more, get some experience, get more exposure...

**APPA**

What is a mere engineering degree nowadays!

**RAMKI**

Get a good job on the fast track, good prospects – that's right, a simple engineering degree does not get us far.

**APPA**

What is a motor car nowadays? What is a two-bedroom flat nowadays? You spend lakhs and lakhs of hard-earned money and all you get is defective wiring, defective assembly, defective plumbing – so many things incomplete. And then you end up paying for all of these things all over again.

**RAMKI**

It is a bit like that, I suppose.

**APPA**

I never should have sold off the old Morris Minor.

**RAMKI**

One day I will learn to clean the spark plugs, Appa. I promise.

**APPA**

That is not enough. You will have to learn to love cleaning the spark plugs.

**RAMKI**

I will.

**APPA**

The best thing any education can do to people is teach them...

**RAMKI and APPA** *(Together)*

How to look after things.

**APPA**

Hmm. So – we don't pursue this proposals business anymore.

**AMMA**

Suspended – till further notice.

**APPA**

No need to subject the bashful bachelor to the slings and arrows of his fan club.

**RAMKI**

Come on, Appa...

**APPA**

In tray, out tray.

**RAMKI**

You know I have always looked at the papers given to me.

**APPA**

There were three more enquiries. Two of them I dropped straightaway. Only this one seemed worth considering. *(He takes out the envelope)* I don't suppose you want to look at this now. *(Ramki shrugs)*

**AMMA**

Who is it anyway?

**APPA**

Referred by Janakiraman. The family lives in the US. A place called Houston, Texas. One son, one daughter, the boy is one year older than Ramki, working in some research project on growing tomatoes... *(He stops, realising they are both staring at him)*

**AMMA**

Go on.

**APPA**

The girl is twenty. She will be twenty-one in December.

**RAMKI**

Are they... ?

**APPA**

After high school, she continued with her training... Yes?

**RAMKI**

No, nothing.

**APPA**

She has continued with her training for a diploma in contemporary dance, whatever that means. She has had a traditional upbringing and has agreed to her parents looking for a boy for her.

**RAMKI**

How long has the family been in America?

**AMMA**

Are they returning to India now?

**APPA**

How does it matter? Now that we are not interested in these proposals...

**AMMA**

We are not slamming the door on people's faces! It won't do any harm to be polite and remain in contact. It seems a nice family.

**APPA**

They have been there for over fifteen years, but their ties to this country have remained very strong. They keep making contributions to all kinds of religious charities and programmes here.

**RAMKI**

I suppose they have settled down there permanently.

**APPA**

Not clear. They have American citizenship, but it says they have also retained their Indian passports.

**AMMA**

What do you say, Ramki?

**RAMKI**

Huh?

**AMMA**

Will you take a look at just one more proposal?

**RAMKI**

I don't know... We were just... I was thinking...

**AMMA**

No harm in taking a look, is there? You can do that much.

**RAMKI**

I didn't say I would not take a look!

**AMMA** *(To Appa)*

Give it to him. *(He does. An awkward moment)*

**RAMKI**

Why does she want – why do they want a boy from India?

**APPA**

Why do you long for Amma's rasam when you are in the NCC camp? There are some things to return to in everybody's life.

**RAMKI**

The girl?

**AMMA**

She was born here. Her first schooling was here. They must be coming back here every now and then.

**APPA**

Every two years, without fail, ever since they shifted.

**AMMA**

There you are! A very level-headed family, looks like.

**APPA**

You know what it says here? She has trained in classical Bharatanatyam for eleven years under the best known Indian teacher in the States, who has a centre for South Indian Classical Dance in Houston, Texas. She had her arangetram there.

**RAMKI** *(Whistles)*

Rangapravesam in Houston, Texas. Wow!

**AMMA**

I remember now. There was a performance here last December by a girl from Texas. Very highly praised, even by our severest critics. It must have been her!

**APPA**

She is devoted to her dance, driving seventy-eighty miles, three days a week, to the dance centre, year after year, for her classes. She drives her own car now.

**AMMA**

Ramki might like to know what car she drives!

**APPA**

So, shall I tell Janakiraman to hold on for a while?

**AMMA** *(Looking at Ramki)*

No harm, I suppose. It would be courteous to at least take a look... What Ramki?

**RAMKI**

Oh, yes, I suppose so. At least for courtesy.

**APPA**

You can take a couple of days.

**AMMA**

Very sweet of Janaki to have thought of us, really. You must thank him properly.

**APPA**

Actually, it seems the girl insisted on a boy from India as a first preference... She wants to go deeply into research in South Indian Classical traditions. She plans to return to India and make her future here. *(A stunned silence. Amma switches to crisis management.)*

**AMMA**

Marvellous! How nice that young people can have clear long-term plans for their lives.

**APPA**

She can easily set up her own dance school here in no time at all.

**AMMA**

All in good time. First she must complete her diploma course. She shouldn't give it up. Or rush through it either. She is only, what, twenty? She has her whole life ahead of her.

**APPA**

Meanwhile, the Achar family in one corner of South India must make do with leftovers for its evening meal.

**AMMA**

Certainly not! There is a Friday special waiting for some finishing touches. I'll go now and get things ready.

**APPA**

Is it a surprise?

**AMMA**

I'll know after you have taken your first bite.

**APPA**

We'll join you as soon as you call.

**AMMA**

It shouldn't take more than ten or fifteen minutes.

*(She starts to go, stops, looks at the two men)*

You can come down in ten minutes. Ramki, you were saying something about taking Appa's advice...

*(She leaves. Appa looks at Ramki, who avoids his gaze at first, but finally turns to him. Appa motions Ramki to come sit next to him. He does.)*

## SNIP SEVEN

*Sushi, Abhi, and Munni are sitting on the floor playing with cowries. The children have not quite mastered the art, but are completely absorbed.*

**ABHI**

Where did you learn this, aunty?

**SUSHI**

Oh, from my mother, I suppose – or the older girls. I don't know, I've forgotten.

**ABHI**

Did you have other games like this?

**SUSHI**

Like what?

**ABHI**

Like this. It is so much fun.

**SUSHI**

Is it fun? You like it?

**ABHI**
Yes!

**MUNNI**
Your turn. *(Abhi takes over)* Did you have Lego?

**SUSHI**
No.

**MUNNI**
You played with cowries all the time?

**SUSHI**
Of course not! There were lots of other games.

**MUNNI**
What games?

**SUSHI**
They came in seasons.
*(Through the following passage, the children's attention is divided between Sushi and the cowries, taking their turns in the game.)*
Like seven tiles. For about two months, everybody everywhere would be playing seven tiles. Then all of a sudden, it was kabaddi. We called it hututu. Wherever you went, you'd hear boys and girls going hutututututu. After some time, the boys would start off on tops, and we would go into house-house. We made all the houses ourselves from cardboard, coloured paper, crayons, and rice glue. We made the dolls too. We made all the dresses from paper. You could keep changing the dresses on the cardboard dolls. We had marriages for the dolls. We wrote out invitations, had hundreds of guests, wedding music, and, of course, a proper wedding feast – all made from sand and pebbles and flower petals from the garden. Outside the house, the boys counted the number of tops destroyed in the day's battles. By end December, we were all flying kites. Girls too. We had the kites with long tails that remained steady in the worst breeze. One month later, it was gulli-danda and hopscotch. Have you played gulli-danda?

**MUNNI**
Did you come first in class?

**SUSHI**
Not once!

**ABHI**
How did you become such a nice aunty?

**SUSHI**
Have you ever come second in class?

**ABHI**
Not once!

**SUSHI**
And you, Munni? Second in class?

**MUNNI**
Once. Mummy scolded me so much...

**ABHI**
She cried and cried and cried.

**SUSHI**
Would you like to be first in class forever?

**MUNNI**
No.

**SUSHI**
No? Why not?

**MUNNI**
Then Pinky will come second, and her mummy will shout at her.

**SUSHI**
You don't want Pinky to...

**MUNNI**
She is my best friend!

**SUSHI**
Would you like to be first in a class of one hundred children?

**ABHI**
Yes.

**SUSHI**
In a class of five hundred?

**ABHI**
In a class of one thousand!

**SUSHI**
Can you be tenth in a class of one thousand?

**MUNNI**
Okay.

**ABHI**
No!

**SUSHI**
If there were only two in your class?

**MUNNI**
We will take turns.

**SUSHI**
If there was only one? If you were the only one in your class? *(Munni giggles)*

**ABHI**

I will be first even if there are zero children in my class!

*(Munni laughs, claps her hands. Sushi rises)*

**SUSHI**

Why don't we all go out for a while, and I'll teach you how to play gulli-danda.

**MUNNI** *(Jumping up)*

Let's go!

**ABHI**

You go.

**SUSHI**

You won't join us?

**ABHI**

I want to play here – with this.

*(Sushi ruffles his hair affectionately, takes Munni's hand, and goes out with her. Abhi waits for them to leave, takes out a lesson book from his school bag, and starts to work on it. After a while, he closes the book abruptly, puts it away, collects the cowries, and runs out to join the other two.)*

## SNAP SIX

*Ramki's room. Appa is standing with an audio cassette and an envelope in his hands. Ramki is looking cheerful.*

**APPA**

Here, I thought you might enjoy this collection from the forties.

**RAMKI**

Thanks, Appa. *(Eyeing the envelope)* Is there something more?

**APPA**

Yes. It is in two cassettes. If you like this one, I'll pick up the second volume. *(He puts the envelope into his shirt pocket.)*

**RAMKI**

Shall I play it now?

**APPA**

No, not now. You can listen to it by yourself. Don't play it loud. This sort of music is enjoyable most at low volume, as if they are singing just for you.

**RAMKI**

Could you tell me about... ?

**APPA**

The music is entirely in the voice and the melody. The background instruments are heard but not imposed on you.

**RAMKI**

They all sound like they were performing on an open-air stage.

**APPA**

Well, many of them came from the stage anyway. They were all trained in classical or at least light classical music. The movies were influenced heavily by the drama companies.

**RAMKI**

Appa, when do you think... ?

**APPA**

In those days, the length of a song was decided by you know what? It was decided by the fact that one side of a 78 RPM record could run for a maximum of three minutes. So, all the songs were written to run between two-and-a-half minutes to three minutes maximum. Doesn't that sound funny today?

**RAMKI**

I didn't know... very interesting.

**APPA**

It was the same for all recordings. Have you heard the album of Mogubai? All three-minute pieces, one after the other. Before she even warmed up, the studio fellow must have been signalling to her that she had thirty seconds more!

**RAMKI**

Did they have air mail in those days?

**APPA**

Only the programmes broadcast live on radio were different. Your Frank Sinatra – he used to sing every Saturday with Dinah Shore, and for some time with Doris Day, on a programme called Your Hit Parade. They sang the seven most popular songs of the week. Live, with a full orchestra backing. The songs they sang were the songs people bought on records, but in the radio programme, they could extend it a bit, beyond three minutes, once in a while.

**RAMKI**

Appa, I thought you had a letter... Okay, I'll get back to work now.

**APPA**

Wait.

**RAMKI**

Yes?

**APPA**

Sit down. *(He does)*
I have some news.

**RAMKI**

Oh? From...

**APPA**

Yes. There is a letter from the family in Texas. *(He takes out the envelope)* It came yesterday.

**RAMKI**

I saw the cover on your table...

**APPA**

Yes, it came yesterday. I had to consult Thatha before talking about it.

*(A long pause through which Appa slowly and carefully takes out the contents of the envelope. He looks at Ramki.)*

**RAMKI**

They are well?

**APPA**

They are. They send their greetings and warm regards. Shyamala is looking forward to her visit to India with her parents. The whole family approves whole-heartedly of the match. *(Ramki is overwhelmed but restrained.)*

**RAMKI**

Oh, that's nice... that's nice... So, I suppose... You will tell us what the next steps must be...

**APPA**

You have a problem, Ramki.

**RAMKI**

Problem? With me?

**APPA**

It is not with you. It is not with us. It is with the match.

**RAMKI**

The match?

**APPA**

It seems this match cannot take place. Shyamala's horoscope was examined by Thatha. Poor girl, she is born with a Moola nakshatra. He ruled out the match straightaway.

**RAMKI**

What?! What does this – whatever it's called – what does it mean?

**APPA**

I know you will be disappointed, but look at it this way, it is good we found out in time before you went any further.

**RAMKI**
Found out what in time? What is wrong with her?

**APPA**
The Moola nakshatra says that she'll bring disaster into her in-laws home... It usually means the father-in-law dies soon after she enters the house.

**RAMKI**
Thatha told you this?

**APPA**
He is the most knowledgeable person in the family in these matters.

**RAMKI**
Why did you go to him? *(Appa does not reply)* Why did you go to him first? Why couldn't you talk to Amma? Why didn't you tell me about their letter before going to Thatha?

**APPA**
We would have to consult him sooner or later.

**RAMKI**
Consult him?! We could have informed him. I would have gone to his place and given him the good news.

**APPA**
It is not done that way. He would expect to hear about your marriage from Amma and me first.

**RAMKI**
Is there... Can we take a second opinion?

**APPA**
Ramki, a star is a star. It is there. It is like the colour of your skin or the shape of your nose. Given by birth. It is not somebody's personal opinion.

**RAMKI**
It is a verdict! It seals my fate. It seals her fate – once for all – no way out – sealed!

**APPA**
I feel sorry for her too. Such a lovely girl she appears to be.

**RAMKI**
Can't things be changed somehow?

**APPA**
You can't change your horoscope, if that's what you mean. It's not like paying a fee and getting your date of birth changed.

**RAMKI**
There must be a way around this. Our Shastras are full of little tricks to overcome the influence of the stars. Even the gods use these tricks all the time.

**APPA**

I hope you are not being disrespectful to your...

**RAMKI**

I am not being disrespectful, Appa. I am just trying to be what I thought you wanted me to be.

**APPA**

I did not want you to disrespect religion and tradition.

**RAMKI**

You did want me to have self-respect.

**APPA**

Yes, but not...

**RAMKI**

And lots of self-confidence. And courage to make my own life, live my own life. Like you did yourself.

**APPA**

All that stands. This is different. Here we are playing with...

**RAMKI**

With what? Is it something beyond us? Appa, I cannot accept this. I cannot accept this from you!

**APPA**

I am sorry, Ramki, but this matter is something... something beyond me. *(A long pause. Ramki picks up some courage.)*

**RAMKI**

Appa, suppose I insist?

**APPA**

What do you mean? You can't go ahead by yourself.

**RAMKI**

No, suppose I insist that you go ahead with this match. Either this girl or no match at all.

**APPA**

You know what you are saying...

**RAMKI**

Suppose I take the responsibility of your health and long life? Shyamala and I together – it is her star after all – we will take the responsibility of keeping death out of this house!

**APPA**

I am not scared of dying! When it is time to go, we go!

**RAMKI**

Then... ?

**APPA**

It's just that... it does not make sense to know about things and still...

**RAMKI:**

Appa...

**APPA**

Knowing there are thieves roaming the streets, if you keep your door open at night...

**RAMKI**

What can the thief possibly take away, Appa? Where will he strike? Thatha is not part of this house, so he's safe. Amma? She is capable of giving any thief the thrashing of his life. You? You will kill yourself with worry before any Moola nakshatra has even put you on its list – running around and worrying about us all the time. *(Pause)*

**APPA**

This girl... you are very keen on this girl?

*(Ramki quietens, but does not answer)*

Your heart is set on her? Come on, where is that self-made-man son of mine? Answer my question. You are set on Shyamala?

**RAMKI**

Yes, I have decided.

**APPA**

We will get a second opinion then.

**RAMKI**

Appa...

**APPA**

You will have to give me some time. I have to do this slowly. Carefully. Things have gone too fast so far.

**RAMKI**

Is there anything I should... anything I...

**APPA**

No, let me handle this.

**RAMKI**

Yes, Appa.

**APPA**

It is not such a simple matter. We will have to do this very carefully.

**RAMKI**

I have an idea!

**APPA**

Already?

**RAMKI**

This Moola nakshatra – it seems to be in geostationary orbit only over the Deccan plateau of our planet. So, it cannot find victims anywhere else, right? Suppose you and Amma shift to the US for a while? If the evil star can't spot you, it will stop looking for you.

**APPA**

There might be a good business opportunity there – finding hiding places in the world for people like us. *(Father and son look at each other, smile. Appa extends his hand. Ramki takes it.)*

I'll see what I can do. I can't make promises just now.

**RAMKI**

Yes, Appa. I understand.

**APPA**

Whatever happens, we will still have to get around Thatha. We cannot cut him off like that.

**RAMKI**

We'll put Amma on that job! *(They laugh)* I must go now. Thanks, Appa.

Ramki dashes out. Appa puts the papers and the envelope back into his pocket, looks around the room, picks up the audio cassette he had given Ramki, puts it into the 2-in-1. It plays... Toofan mail... Duniya, yeh duniya toofan mail...

## A SNIP SNAP

*The park. Appa and Amma are seated. He is munching chips. She is reading a letter.*

**AMMA**

'... Soon after enrolment, we were all given a library assignment. We had five days to complete it. It was a tough assignment. There was a lot of information and data to be put together. I was really nervous when I started, but the library facilities are so good here that I myself was surprised by how much I could do in the first three days. Back home, I hated going to the library. Anyhow, there was some good news after that. I was called to the Dean's office and told that I would be given part aid even in the first year. I can start saving something from next month and Appa can repay the Canara Bank loan faster.'

**APPA**

Tell him not to do anything so foolish. I can take care of the loan business. Let him buy himself some good things – some good books, instruments, good tools. Good hardware stores there – tools you will never get here.

**AMMA** *(Continuing)*

'... Shyamala is a very good cook. She is fully vegetarian. We get everything here for running our kitchen. She transferred to a Fine Arts School in a neighbouring university. They welcomed her because the three semesters in her previous Centre were regarded very highly, along with her earlier training. She has to drive a good distance to her school, but she reaches quite fast. She drops me off first, and then it takes her about three quarters of an hour to get there. I am not driving yet.'

**APPA**

I wonder how much time is spent each day sitting inside a car.

**AMMA**

Three quarters of an hour... It's funny. I have never heard him use an expression like that. He would say forty-five minutes.

**APPA**

There will be other changes, one by one.

**AMMA**

You think he will change a lot?

**APPA**

He will change.

**AMMA**

I'll be surprised if he does.

**APPA**

I'll be surprised if he does not.

**AMMA**

Why do you say that?

**APPA**

Because he is a sensible fellow. He has his head screwed on right. And he is young. He can change easily.

**AMMA**

He can adapt intelligently. He will. I hope he doesn't change.

**APPA**

It's the same thing.

**AMMA**

It is not.

**APPA**

It is. What happens to those other boys and girls, we call change. What happens to our boy, we call intelligent adaptation.

**AMMA**

I hope he does well at the University. I pray every day that he will do well.

**APPA**

And do us proud?

**AMMA**

I am sure he will do well. What do you think?

**APPA** *(Taking his time)*

An American MBA will be good for him. It will give him a solid base for whatever line he chooses later. *(Pause. Amma looks at him, smiles.)*

Whatever line he chooses.

**AMMA**

Shyamala is such a nice girl. I wish we had more time with her.

**APPA**

We will.

**AMMA**

She has brought such joy into our home... *(Pause)*

**APPA**

Even Thatha thinks highly of her, I gather.

**AMMA**

Thatha is getting old.

**APPA**

He can't be getting younger.

**AMMA**

He is still quite sharp though.

**APPA**

Thatha is a wise old man.

**AMMA** *(Continuing)*

'... Last Saturday, when we were out on a picnic lunch, I saw for the first time how many different shades of brown and gold there can be in the falling leaves of autumn. They call the season fall here. It is a beautiful sight. When you decide to come and visit us, I hope you will be able to see the beautiful season of autumn.' *(She keeps the letter down. They are both silent. Munni darts in, circles around the seat, and hides behind them.)*

**APPA**

Amma, if anyone comes looking for a little girl, what will you say?

**AMMA**

I'll say I haven't seen any girl here.

**MUNNI**

Shhh! Please!

**APPA**

Some little girls can be heard, but not seen.

**MUNNI**

Please, please, please!

**AMMA** *(Passing the chips behind without looking)*

Can some little girls eat but not be seen!

**MUNNI**

Thanks! Shhh!

*(Abhi rushes on, stops, and looks suspiciously at Amma and Appa. Amma offers him the chips. He hesitates, then takes some.)*

**APPA**

Hello, sir!

**ABHI**

Hello.

**APPA**

Are you looking for something? *(Abhi nods no)*

Looking for some people? *(No response)*

If you are looking for a little girl wearing a black and gold hair-band, she went that way.

**ABHI**

That way?

**APPA:**

Yes, she was going to Delhi.

**ABHI:**

She was going to Delhi?

**APPA**

She was going to become a pilot and fly planes, she said. So she was going off to Delhi. *(Abhi dashes off)*

**MUNNI** *(Emerging)*

Abbah! I fooled him!

**AMMA**

More chips?

**MUNNI**

How did you know I want to be a pilot?

**AMMA**

How did we know? Aha!

**MUNNI**

How did you know? How did you know?

**APPA**

Well, you were wearing a black and gold hair-band, you see. Only pilots wear black and gold on their heads.

**MUNNI**
Ohhh...

**AMMA**
Didn't you know?

**MUNNI**
Of course, I knew! That's why mummy got me this hair-band.

**ABHI** *(Entering with a bang)*
I spy! I knew you were here. Got you!
*(He runs towards Munni, who ducks behind Amma. Appa catches Abhi on the run.)*

**APPA**
Hello, sir!

**ABHI**
I got her!

**APPA**
And what are you going to become when you grow up?

**ABHI**
Me? I want to become a cook.

**APPA**
A cook!

**MUNNI**
Mummy says she wants a cook more than anything else in the world.

**AMMA**
Of course! Anybody can see he is going to be a great and famous cook.

**ABHI**
You can see?

**APPA**
From that coconut oil on your head. And the haircut. What a super-duper haircut. Just what a great Chinese cook would have.

**ABHI**
I love Chinese food!
*(By now Amma and Appa have Abhi and Munni on their laps, eating chips, looking rather like a family portrait.)*

**AMMA**
Have you come here by yourselves?

**MUNNI**
Mummy will pick us up. She has gone to park the car.

**APPA**
Does she know where to go?

**MUNNI**

Near the cinema. An old man there helps her park.

**AMMA**

You come here often?

**ABHI**

Lots of times. Every week.

**AMMA**

Well, you know how to look after yourselves. Can we go now?

**ABHI**

Okay. We'll play here till Mummy comes.

**AMMA**

Look after yourselves now. *(Amma and Appa stand the children on the seat and start to leave.)*

**MUNNI**

Uncle! The chips were very nice!

**APPA**

Ah! Here, you can keep this packet too.

**MUNNI**

Thank you, uncle!

**AMMA**

Do we see you again?

**MUNNI**

Next week. Here!

**AMMA**

Or when we travel in your plane.

**APPA**

Or when we eat in his Chinese restaurant.

*(Appa and Amma wave to the children and go out. A pause.)*

**MUNNI**

Ay! We didn't say 'bye to them.

**ABHI**

They are so nice.

**MUNNI**

The chips are very nice.

**ABHI**

Did we say thank you to them?

**MUNNI**

I said thank you.

**ABHI**

You didn't. You forgot.

**MUNNI**

I didn't forget.

**ABHI**

You did.

**MUNNI**

I didn't.

**ABHI**

You did.

**MUNNI**

I said thank you. You didn't.

**ABHI**

You didn't.

*(Through the following passage, the scene transforms to a snip, the lighting closing in on them.)*

**MUNNI**

YOU didn't. *(Steps down from the seat)*

**ABHI**

YOU didn't.

**MUNNI**

I'll tell Mummy you didn't say thank you.

**ABHI**

I'm sorry.

**MUNNI**

I'll tell Mummy.

**ABHI**

I said sorry.

**MUNNI**

Now say excuse me.

**ABHI**

Excuse me.

**MUNNI**

Say it was a mistake and you'll never do it again.

**ABHI**

It was a mistake.

**MUNNI**

You'll never do it again.

**ABHI**
I'll never do it again.

**MUNNI**
Now, dance!

**ABHI**
What?

**MUNNI**
Simon says dance!
*(Abhi catches on, dances on the seat)*
Simon says stop! *(He does)*
Simon says clap your hands! *(He does, now quite enjoying the game)*
Simon says pull your ears! *(She shows how, he follows. They both laugh.)*
Put your tongue out! *(She leads; he follows. She laughs louder.)*
Roll your head! *(She leads; he follows, quite lost in the comic act. She laughs at him.)*
Stop! Stop!! You are out. You can't go on. *(He does anyway.)*
Stop. It's over!

**ABHI**
I won't. You didn't say Simon says... *(He goes on)*

**MUNNI**
It's over! It's over!

**ABHI**
You can't fool me! You can't win. I'll win.

**PAVI** *(Off)*
Abhi–Munni! Finish with your play now. We must get back soon.

**MUNNI**
Ohho! You have to stop now.

**ABHI** *(Continuing)*
You didn't say Simon says stop, I'll win. I can go on till you give up.

**MUNNI**
I didn't say Simon says stop just now. But before that I didn't say Simon says for your tongue... *(Abhi has stopped. He steps down.)*

**ABHI**
Your turn.

**MUNNI**
My turn? I win?

**ABHI**
You said Simon says stop.

**MUNNI**
I didn't.

**ABHI**

You did just now.

**MUNNI**

I didn't.

**ABHI**

You did.

*(He advances on her. She runs. He chases. It is good fun. They are shouting 'you did' and 'I didn't' all the time. They run around the seat, around the stage.)*

**PAVI** *(Off)*

Abhi–Munni! Hurry up, now! There's a big pile of homework to be done before dinner!

*(Abhi and Munni stop dead in their tracks.)*

**ABHI**

Simon says stop. *(They stop)*

**MUNNI**

Stop.

**ABHI**

Simon says turn around. *(They turn around)*

**MUNNI**

Turn around.

**ABHI**

Simon says quick march.

**MUNNI**

Quick march... *(They march off)*

***Close of play***

# Evening Shadows

*An original adaptation in English of*
***Sandhya Chhaya** by **Jaywant Dalvi***

*Adaptation by **Vijay Padaki***

**FOR**
**JAYWANT DALVI**

## CHARACTERS IN THE PLAY

NANI AND NANA ........................ *An elderly couple, affectionately called Nani and Nana, although not grandparents. Nani is about sixty. She has a limp from a sciatica condition that makes her drag a foot slightly. She is in a simple sari, worn the traditional way. Nana is in his late sixties. His head is silver-grey. A fall in the bathroom, some time ago, has led to steel cups being implanted in his knees. He wears a dhoti, usually with just a vest above.*

MAHDU ........................................ *A part-timer servant in his twenties, slightly built. He is unlettered, but he runs the household with a mind of his own. His mouth is always full of paan, possibly the reason he never speaks.*

SHARMILA .................................. *A school-going little girl of eight or ten. She becomes Nana's telephone friend.*

DADA ......... *Sharmila's grandfather, protective, humourless, and business-like.*

VINAY BHOLE ............... *A young man, who gets to know Nana and Nani accidentally, and then becomes a regular visitor and friend.*

SHYAM DESHPANDE .................. *A visitor, a friend of Dinoo in the US.*

DINOO ............................... *The older son of Nana and Nani, living and working in the US since eight years, and uninterested in returning to India.*

Voices of postman, news reader, telegram bearer

### Time

The year is 1971. It is an India that might already be unrecognisable by many. Although the play can be given a contemporary setting, this script retains the socio-political context in the original version. The backdrop of the Bangladesh liberation war is also important to the mood of the play.

### Place

The action of the entire play takes place in the living room of the small first-floor apartment of Nana and Nani. It is a sparsely outfitted middle-class home. The bare essentials for the action of the play are described in the play script. The performing group may work around these features, retaining the basic character of the home.

## INTRODUCTION

I was introduced to the work of Jaywant Dalvi in the early 'sixties by the director of The American Cultural Centre (USIS) in Bangalore. After working with Marathi newspapers, Dalvi had an appointment in USIS in Mumbai, which undertook a programme to make good English literature available in other languages. Dalvi selected texts and able translators, and helped the cause. He was not so well known outside Maharashtra in those days except in literary circles. Years later, the film Chakra, based on his writing, was known more for the stars Smita Patil and Naseeruddin Shah than for the writer. My interest in Dalvi was rekindled when I saw Nadira Babbar's rendition of Sandhya Chhaya in Hindi. Alas, it was too late to meet him. He had passed away in 1994. I asked Nadira to seek permission from the family on my behalf for an attempt at an English language adaptation. She arranged that readily. She also gifted me the Hindi translation used in her production of the play. I completed the play script only much later.

It was not an easy job. Some challenges in translation-adaptation from an Indian language are well known, and a repetition here can be avoided. This adaptation has tried sincerely to strike a purposeful balance between the requirements of fidelity to the original and the requirements of performance in English on a contemporary stage. There is no assurance of complete success, of course. At best we can hope that a performing group will find a useful springboard from which it can attempt its own deep diving. The most important objective of the adaptation project is to make Jaywant Dalvi known to a wider Indian audience.

The adaptation has retained the length and detail of the original. It is a proper full-length play of over two hours with an intermission. It goes against the grain of current theatre productions being less than an hour and a half. In Evening Shadows, the ingenuity of the performing group will be tested further on a few special counts:

- How does an elderly lower-middle-class couple speak in English in the play?
- How do they convey inability to converse in English, as required by the play?
- Should the actors retain the Maharashtrian ethos, or seek a pan-Indian ethos?
- How should the couple handle the Gyaneshwari, a key ingredient in the play? and so on.

I have done my best to capture the rhythm of the spoken language, especially between Nana and Nani. I would like to believe that a liberal retention of Hindi words and phrases in their lines has helped. The actors need to be careful in not making it a gimmick. The atmosphere in the home of the lonely elderly couple appeared so very important. In the first reading of the play, the talented artistes recognised the dividing line between contemporary drama and a traditional form of melodrama, as well their own tendency to slip into stereotyped understanding of melodrama. The original play actually has layers of comic pathos that presents an unusual opportunity for the actors. Over to the artists now.

The story of Evening Shadows is set at the end of the 'sixties, crossing into 1971-72 when the Indian military was drawn into the Bangladesh liberation struggle. It is very important to retain the period in any performance of the play. It was also the time when many young Indians sought career paths in foreign lands, which meant the USA in most cases. They developed a loyalty for all things American and a contempt for all things Indian. My friend at the American Cultural Centre would have loved this play!

## Language Notes

*Booddha/booddhi:* Old man/old woman
*Booddhi ho gayi:* Turned into an old woman
*Kashayam:* An ayurvedic medicinal tonic,
*Ulta-seedha:* Turned this way and that
*Buss:* Enough
*Sharm nahi aati:* Aren't you ashamed
*Khamba:* Pillar, column
*Mayura:* Peacock
*Nakhra:* Being fussy, putting on dramatic airs
*Jhadoo:* Broom
*Lashkari:* Troop, gang
*Saala:* Literally brother-in-law, wife's brother. Expression used both as an abuse and as an affectionate gesture.
*Ulloo ka pattha:* Literally son of an owl, an out and out fool
*Bhoosa khopdi:* Skull full of hay
*Us zamane ke:* From those times
*Aaye bina:* Without coming, visiting
*Chup:* Quiet
*Satyanash:* Literally annihilation, a bloody mess
*Thappad:* Tight slap
*Dal-chawal:* Lentils-rice, simple/basic meal
*Bilkul ulta:* Completely upside down, the other way
*Na jaan na pehchan:* Not known, not recognised/stranger
*Dhatt tere ki:* Exclamation of surprise – Oh heck! Damn it!
*Gujiya:* A popular dumpling snack
*Poojya Nana:* Revered Nana
*Saprem Namaskar:* Namaskar with deep love
*Jeethe raho beta:* Live long, son
*Udaa diya:* Knocked it off, polished it off
*Andar aaiye na:* Won't you come in

*Baitho na:* Won't you sit
*Rishtedar:* Relative
*Kya pata:* Who knows
*Wahan hai kya:* What do you have there
*Aapko ek baat kahoon:* Shall I tell you something
*Zaroor:* Certainly
*Tu kahoon toh chalega:* Can I call you 'tu'? 'Tu' meaning 'you' is used affectionately, for loved ones.
*Haan haan:* Yes, yes
*Vagairah:* Etcetera
*Tujhe maloom hoga:* You might know
*Yeh nahin hai, woh nahin hai:* This not there, that is not there
*Tu ingineer ban jayega:* You will become an engineer
*Badhiya:* Fine, excellent
*Masti:* Fun, rollicking
*Kaam-chor:* Shirker, lazy person
*Mirch-masala:* Spiced up
*Dahi:* Curd
*Achcha mila aaj:* Good find today
*Bada khana:* Big meal, special meal
*Badam:* Almond
*Mufat:* Free
*Zara ruk na:* Stay awhile
*Chup nahi rahegi:* She won't stay quiet
*Aisa khana khilayegi:* She will give you such a meal
*Chalta hun:* I am going, will leave
*Aata hun:* I will come (again). Considered inauspicious to say 'I will go' when leaving; more correct to say 'I will come'.
*Jamaai:* Son-in-law
*Shandaar:* Grand
*Kya kaam hai:* What do you want?
*Aap kaun:* And you are? (Aap is used in respect for you)
*Hazir:* Present, on duty
*Lagta hai:* It looks like
*Baraat:* Wedding procession
*Nath:* Nose ring, worn on ceremonial occasions
*Ziddi:* Persistent, stubborn
*Kaisa hai woh:* How is he?
*Naukri ka mamla:* Matter of employment, livelihood
*Pet bharne ke liye:* To fill one's belly
*Ghus:* Barge in
*Shrimati:* Respectful reference to the wife
*Bhaiya:* Brother

*Theek hai:* It's all right
*Gujri bazaar:* Flea market
*Tagda:* Solid, muscular, sturdy
*Bakwas:* Nonsense
*Chaddi:* Undie, in this case diapers
*Mangalsutra:* Necklace received at wedding, considered sacred
*Bhasha:* Language
*Hum Jeetenge ya marenge:* We will win or we will die
*Chalta hai:* It goes on
*Farmayish:* Request, asking
*Besura:* Out of tune
*Roti, kapda, makan:* Bread, clothing, shelter
*Some gadbad happening:* Something happening, brewing
*Char:* Four
*Kutte-billiyon ke havale:* In the custody of dogs and cats
*Aapki tabiyat kaisi hai:* How is your health, how are you keeping
*Hadbadi:* Ruckus
*Khel khatam:* End of game, close of play
*Gadha ka bachcha:* Son of an ass
*Tere peechche peechche:* Following you all the time, your shadow
*Zabardasti:* Insistence, also compelling
*Ganapati Bapa:* Lord/father Ganesha; reference to idol installed at home during annual Ganesha festival
*Gana-bajana:* Band and music
*Bhajan mandali:* Group singing bhajans, devotional music
*Pandharpur:* Town in Maharashtra with renowned annual pilgrimage
*Lota:* Tumbler
*Odhni:* Head cloth
*Bahu:* Daughter-in-law in the house
*Maane:* Meaning
*Samadhi:* Final resting place
*Nahin:* No

# ACT I

## SCENE 1

*The living room of Nana and Nani. On one side of the room is an exit that leads off to the inside of the home, the kitchen, and the bathroom. On the other side of the room is an exit that leads off outside. Upstage is an exit to a balcony from which a street lamp is visible. There is a potted plant in the balcony, a flowering creeper. An optional feature would be an unseen entrance to the balcony from the kitchen area. On one side of the balcony wall is a large window that lets in light. Under the window is a stool which is used frequently by Nani. There is a desk-table with a chair (or any other simple seat). There is a lamp on the table. There is a stand or stool with a telephone. There are two single beds, also very simple.*

*Periodically there is a phone call conversation with a person in another location. The performing group can decide where to locate the other telephone and how to depict the two separated spaces.*

*Nani enters from inside the house. She has washed her hair. She walks over to the seat under the window and sits, drying her hair in the sunlight streaming in.*

*Nana enters from inside the house. His dhoti is wet. He has a hand on his back, which is slightly bent, and he appears to be in some pain.*

**NANI**
Pulled your back, na?

**NANA** *(Snapping, trying to straighten)*
Why would I pull my back? Am I a booddha or what?

**NANI** *(Laughing to herself)*
Still, a woman's job should be done only by...

**NANA**
Oho, soaping hair is only a woman's job or what? Then what is it I put on my hair, haan?

**NANI**
Soaping your hair is one thing, my hair is another thing.

**NANA**
What is another thing about your hair? Apply sabun, same. Rub it in, same.

**NANI**
Very nicely you have soaped and rubbed my hair. It's all knotted up now, and both my arms will give way before it is straightened out. Look

at it! The oil hasn't even gone yet. For a whole month you keep pestering me – I'll wash your hair, I'll wash your hair, and now this!

**NANA** *(Mock scolding)*

Buss! You are like that only. You get things done for yourself all the time, and then find some fault or the other.

**NANI**

For myself? What things do I get done by you?

**NANA**

I soap your hair... I rub oil on your forehead when you don't get sleep at night. I rub the oil, and you make all the fuss about the oil getting into your ears. Fussing and complaining all the time! It's an old habit of yours. Booddhi ban gayi, but the habit does not leave you.

**NANI**

Haan haan, Booddhi, main. Let me be the booddhi! And you...

*(Nana has suddenly straightened up)*

Why don't you go in and change into a dry dhoti?

**NANA**

Change and do what?

**NANI** *(Annoyed)*

What do you mean do what? The dhoti is wet. You'll start sneezing... then coughing... then you'll ask me to rub the Vicks all over you... then I'll have to make the kashaya for you. I can't do all this anymore.

*(Pause. Nana goes in. Nani rises.)*

Goes in to change leaving the dhoti here! Thank god he doesn't leave the mug outside before going into the toilet.

*(Nani takes down a dhoti from a peg on the wall. Nana enters looking for his dhoti, sees Nani with it, snatches it from her, and goes in again. Nani sees the calendar on the wall. She places the stool against the wall, climbs on it, not without some effort, and tears off the page of the month that has passed. She climbs down, places the stool next to the window, and sits on it once more. Just then Nana enters, adjusting the ends of the dhoti just worn. )*

**NANA**

Don't you start thinking I have become an old man.

**NANI**

Me? I am not thinking any such...

**NANA**

No? You were saying just now that...

**NANI**

When did I say that you had become a booddha? The other way, you were the one to call me boodiya!

**NANA**

There you go, always turning things ulta-seedha. When did I say you were booddhi?

**NANI**

Go ahead and call me a boodiya! It won't hurt if you do. I am a boodiya after all.

**NANA**

You are no boodiya-vudiya. How can you be a boodiya?

**NANI**

How can I what? I am a boodiya after all.

**NANA**

Buss! This is a bad habit of yours! Picks up a point and goes on and on with it. Sits down and keeps grinding away. Not just today, it's an old habit of yours. Booddhi ho gayi but she...

*(Nana walks about the room, annoyed. He sees the calendar on the wall and goes to it to change the page.)*

Month over? *(Realising that the page has been torn off)*

Who tore off the page?

**NANI**

What did you say?

**NANA**

Who tore off the page on the calendar?

**NANI**

I did. Why?

**NANA**

Why?

**NANI**

That's what I said.

**NANA**

Why?

**NANI**

Meaning? I tore it off, that's all. What more is there to... ?

**NANA**

How did you reach the page?

**NANI**

Why, I put the stool there and stood on it.

**NANA**

Stood on the stool! Sharm nahi aati, telling me? What fancy did you take to climbing on a stool? You'll fall once and break your knee, then you'll know. As it is you have such big fat khamba legs!

**NANI**

Okay, okay, I have big fat legs. What about you? You have the legs of a peacock, no?

**NANA** *(Teasing, clapping a beat, and mocking a dance step)*

Dance, mayura, dance! Dance for your lover, ambuva ke van mein *(In your lover's garden)*! Dance, mayura, dance!

**NANI**

Now he starts dancing like a little kid! But mind your knee! Your own knee!

**NANA**

But tell me, was it wrong what I said?

**NANI**

What did you say?

**NANA**

If you fell off the stool?

**NANI**

When you fell down in the bathroom and broke your knee, were you standing on a stool?

**NANA**

There you go again! You keep twisting things ulta-seedha – a wretched old habit of yours!

**NANI** *(Mischief)*

Booddhi ban gayi, the habit still hasn't gone.

**NANA**

Now, I did not call you booddhi!

**NANI**

Call me, then. It won't matter.

**NANA**

But I didn't! Oho... look, it's you who keeps making fun of my knee all the time. Do you think I went and cracked open my knee on purpose?

**NANI**

Did I ever make fun of your... ?

**NANA**

All the time! From the first day! When they put the stainless steel cup in there, all you could say was you could do with the katori to measure the dal.

**NANI** *(Smiles)*

I said that?

**NANA**

Grinning away! Didn't you say that?

**NANI**

Maybe I did, once, long ago, in fun. You are the one who keeps repeating it every now and then.

**NANA**

No, baba, no, I don't say anything. You are the one poking fun all the time... joking about my knee that doesn't bend... that hurts...

**NANI**

Oh no, it hurts? But you were singing and dancing just a minute ago... 'Dance, mayura, dance!' Dance for me some more, no!

**NANA**

No!

**NANI**

Come on, now, dance for me!

**NANA**

No!

**NANI**

Why the nakhra? Just once now, one little dance. Here, I will sing for you... Dance, mayura, dance...

**NANA**

No... my leg hurts.

**NANI** *(Worried)*

Really? It's hurting now?

**NANA**

Then what?

**NANI**

Then... why did you start to dance?

**NANA**

Where did I dance?

**NANI**

Why did you come to soap my hair?

**NANA**

Me? You were the one who kept saying, 'Oh, won't you soap and massage my hair for me? The oil doesn't go when I do it by myself.'

**NANI**

But has the oil really gone? It's still...

*(Nana slaps his forehead. Just then the doorbell rings. Nana goes to the door. Mahdu enters with a broom in hand. He is dressed in khaki half pants and a faded vest or T-shirt. In one long, continuous, swift move, he completes sweeping the room and goes into the kitchen area, leaving Nana and Nani staring.)*

**NANI**
Done! His jhadoo has graced the floor!

**NANA**
Just the way I did it when I was in the college hostel!

**NANI**
Once in how many days?

**NANA** *(Glaring, as she controls her laughter)*
Twisting things always! Old nasty habit! *(He looks at the wall clock.)* It's Thursday, right?

**NANI**
Yes, why?

**NANA** *(Brightening)*
Must wind the clock. Let me get the key.

**NANI** *(Going up to him)*
Don't you climb on the stool, now. I will get the key for you.

**NANA**
You'll climb on the stool?

**NANI**
Why, have I never got on a stool?

**NANA**
And I have never climbed a stool in my whole life!

**NANI**
When we run out of matches, and I say, why don't you go and get some, you say your leg hurts... can't go up and down the stairs. But getting on a stool to...

**NANA**
It's different. I have to exercise the leg correctly. If I keep telling myself the knee can't take it, the knee can't take it, then I'll never be able to climb a stool.

**NANI**
No need for you to climb this stool. I will get the key and wind the clock.

**NANA**
No! I will wind the clock today!

**NANI**
Now, stop behaving like a little brat. Not at this age.

**NANA**
I don't know all that, I am going to wind the clock today!
*(Both try to get on to the stool. Just then Mahdu enters, goes directly to the stool, climbs it, winds the clock swiftly, closes the clock cover, gets down, and goes straight back to the kitchen. Nana and Nani are frozen, looking at each other.)*

**NANI**

Chalo, that job is done.

**NANA**

Oversmart lashkari! Who asked him to saala wind the clock?

**NANI**

Let him wind the clock, no.

**NANA**

How can I let him? You will tear the calendar page, he will wind the clock... saala what must I do then?

**NANI**

What need is there?

**NANA**

Need?

**NANI**

For you to do anything?

**NANA**

Must do something, na? Can't sit and stare at the wall the whole day.

**NANI**

Do that. Just sit and relax. No need to busy yourself unnecessarily.

**NANA**

Just sit and relax! I can't do that, I won't do that. What do you take me for?

**NANI**

Then I'll tell you what.

**NANA**

What?

**NANI**

Fill up a lota and water the creeper in the balcony.

**NANA** *(Cheerful)*

Yes! Nobody has watered the creeper today.

*(He goes to the kitchen. Just then Mahdu enters the balcony with a lota and waters the creeper in the pot. Nana returns with a lota and stops, staring at Mahdu, who soon finishes watering the creeper and returns to the kitchen through the living room. He takes away the lota from Nana's hand as he passes him. Nani watches with some amusement. Nana grunts in annoyance.)*

**NANI**

What happened?

**NANA**

What happened what? That ulloo ka pattha, I won't let him go on like this!

**NANI**

Who?

**NANA**
That Mahdu! I'll break open his skull, saala.

**NANI**
Oh, him! He is only trying to ease things for you, no.

**NANA**
Stop giggling! Bhoosa khopdi!

**NANI**
Let him be... I'll tell you what you can do.

**NANA**
What?

**NANI**
Look, there's good sunlight today. What we can do is put all my silk sarees out to sun them.

**NANA**
Me? Put sarees out in the sun?!

**NANI**
Yes. Why not?

**NANA**
Class I Auditor, me, that's what I was in the Railways. Not for putting your sarees out in the sun! You have a sunstroke or what?!

**NANI**
All right, baba. I will put them out in the sun. You will at least pull out that trunk, I hope. *(Nana shuffles to the bed. He lowers himself slowly to pull out an old steel trunk from under the bed. Just then Mahdu enters from the kitchen, goes directly to the bed, pulls out the trunk, sets it on the bed before Nani and goes back to the kitchen, leaving Nana gaping. Nani hides her amusement under her saree pallu.)*

**NANA**
What's so funny?

**NANI**
Funny? What are you talking about? *(Nani cannot conceal her laughter. Nana paces about the room in anger. Nani takes out a silk and zari saree from the trunk and lays it on the stool and window sill.)*

**NANI**
This saree... you got it for me, didn't you?

**NANA**
I know nothing!

**NANI** *(Matter of fact)*
No, no, this came from the bride's side.

**NANA**

Yes, yes! From the bride's side! Nothing came from that side except you! Came from the bride's side! *(Nani conceals her laughter)*

It was... I got it for you... from Banaras.

**NANI**

That's what I was saying! But you – you won't listen, you won't let me finish... It was for a hundred and twenty-five, wasn't it?

**NANA**

What one hundred! Say eleven hundred! Us zamane ke eleven hundred!

**NANI**

You remember? It was when Dinoo was born, right?

**NANA**

What is there to not remember?

*(He goes to the trunk and takes out another saree)*

This one... I got you this one too.

**NANI**

This is not a saree, it's an odhni.

**NANA**

Maybe it is. *(He puts it back)*

**NANI**

I never wore this saree... I thought... when Dinoo gets married, our bahu will wear this...

**NANA**

She'll wear it, she'll wear it! Of course she'll wear it! Dinoo and our bahu, keep thinking about it!

**NANI**

Stop your steaming! She will wear it! Let Dinoo get here. This time I will not let him return without getting married. We will definitely have a bahu in this house now... she'll wash my hair, comb my hair... I can't go on like this at this age, everything by myself...

**NANA**

No, no, you can't manage by yourself. How can you when Nana's there?

**NANI**

For what?

**NANA**

For washing your hair, for combing it, of course.

**NANI**

There you go! Just once – it was my mistake – I let you soap my hair, and you'll go on about it like a stuck record. Listening to you my hair will start falling!

**NANA**

Let them fall! I'm there to rub oil on your head. But listen, before you lose your hair, get your son fixed up.

**NANI**

Of course, I'll get him fixed up, as if I'll let him off. We'll also have to get a bigger flat then.

**NANA**

Yes, yes, we'll get everything, but let Dinoo get here from America first.

**NANI**

He'll come. Aaye bina how can he... he must come.

**NANA**

But when? It's eight years already. I don't know...

**NANI**

Of course he'll come! Don't go on getting muddled about it. What else can he do? What does he have there? Who will look after him there? What is there in America?

**NANA**

What is the point in your blabbering about this to me? You should ask him, ask Dinoo these questions.

**NANI** *(A change of tone)*

All this is because of you after all.

**NANA**

Stop pasting the blame on my head again and again.

**NANI**

Why not? You are the one who sent him off to America.

**NANA**

What do you mean sent him off? I didn't ask him to stay there forever, did I?

**NANI**

I ask you, what was the need to send him in the first place? He became an engineer here, buss. Who was dying to be educated there?

**NANA**

Arrey, but what crime did I... ?

**NANI**

Now, please – chup. He had a good job here, no? You got him to give it up and... you sent him off so far.

**NANA**

And why? So that when he gets back from there and he lands a nice job, he will be well off... and buy a car, and get a bungalow, and...

**NANI**

It's your more-and-more that did it. Satyanash! Once this more-and-more demon raises its head, there is no end to its craving. There must be some dignity in things, no? Having happiness from less, and not more? Your more-and-more... eight years have passed already! He is still there, making more and more money, no sign of him here.

**NANA**

God knows if he has got himself a wife there...

**NANI**

Now don't start mouthing such... inauspicious thoughts. He is not one to do something like that. Even if he does marry there, it doesn't matter – as long as our bahu is one of us.

*(Mahdu enters wiping his hands on his pants. He goes out by the front door. Nana and Nani watch him go.)*

**NANA**

This man has true bliss. Does his work, fills his belly. Not a worry in his life... not like us.

**NANI**

There's going to be a baby in the house – his house.

**NANA**

That was bound to be. How could it not be? Wherever you look people are in such a hurry – hurry, hurry, baby, baby, hurry, hurry.

**NANI**

In what way were you not in a hurry?

**NANA**

Oho! It was a good thing then that nothing happened for seven years after you got married. You were the one in a hurry – all the pooja-paat, fasts, pilgrimage! Dinoo came after seven years! And she says I was in a hurry!

**NANI**

Let it be! I gave you two sons, right?

**NANA**

You gave me! One is in America, the other, a militarywala, in Kashmir... If we had our Malu today, she would at least keep us company. She arrived so soon after Nandu... and left so soon. *(A long pause.)*

**NANI**

First thing today, you should write a letter to Dinoo.

**NANA**

What?

**NANI**

Write. Come back at once. We don't want your American job. We don't want the money. Whatever little we have here, buss, that is plenty. What is the point in chasing money like a mad dog, running and panting till you collapse? Tell him, 'we must have you before our eyes.'

**NANA**

If you say so... well, I will write once again. But you know how many times we have said the same things – in our letters, on the phone. You know his reply, every time. What will I eat if I come back to India? Twigs and pebbles?

**NANI**

Yes, yes, tell him to hurry home for the pebbles. We are thriving on our daily pebbles, are we not? What did generations before him live on?

**NANA**

He means... what big difference will it make? He says if you fall ill, you can keep a nurse. He will take care of the expense. Take all the tonics and medicines you need, whatever the cost. He will send the money. You call every day, talk as much as you like, he will pay the phone bills. That is why he has given us this phone, na?

**NANI**

That phone can turn to ash! If he talks like that again, you can thappad his jaw for him. We have had enough of this from him, I am not taking any more. Write to him now. Tell him to come immediately. Say we will arrange marriages for him and Nandu together. This house needs filling – the grace of two bahus, the chatter of grandchildren playing. There are stories to be told, stories of crows and birds of many colours... I will tell them the stories, of course. God knows where all the stories have disappeared today. *(Nana is at the window, looking away)*

What do you do in an empty house? How do you pass the time? You keep staring at my face, I keep staring at yours... the same dal-chawal to be cooked, the same meal to be eaten because it has to be eaten... Who is there in the house to say what they would like to have? I want this today, I don't want that... That Nandu, at least he could have got a job somewhere here... he's gone too, flying a plane somewhere, in the name of serving the nation somewhere. Who'll be there to give us comfort in our old age? Bilkul ulta, we will only have sorrow to keep us company. Not one child to keep us happy. *(Nani chokes. She dries her tears, but continues to weep into her saree. Nana stands beside her and strokes her hair. He looks for a way to break the depressing mood. Just then a crow perches itself on the balcony and starts to caw. Nana and Nani turn their attention to the balcony.)*

**NANI** *(To the crow)*

Who will ever come to this house, baba?

**NANA** *(Putting on cheer)*

Of course somebody will come! Noisy crow on the wall, fly away now! *(Nana sees the crow fly away and claps his hands in glee)*

Did you see that? The crow flew away. We are going to have a visitor. Somebody will surely visit us now.

**NANI**

Who? Who will visit us?

**NANA**

Dinoo, from America. Maybe our Nandu, from Kashmir.

*(The phone rings. Nana goes to pick it up.)*

**NANI**

Who could that be?

*(Nana picks up the phone. A corner of the stage is lit, revealing Sharmila at the other end.)*

**SHARMILA**

Is that Dandekar saheb?

**NANA**

Dandekar? Oh yes, yes, Dandekar.

**NANI**

Who is Dandekar?

**NANA** *(To Nani, covering the receiver)*

It's a wrong number. I'm having some fun.

*(Into the phone)* Dandekar. And you are... ?

**SHARMILA**

I'm Sharmila.

**NANA**

Sharmila Tagore? *(Laughs at his own joke)*

**SHARMILA**

Oh, no! Sharmila Deekshit.

**NANA**

Sharmila Deekshit... good, good.

**NANI**

Who is it?

**NANA**

Sharmila Deekshit.

**NANI**

Who is that?

**NANA**

A girl.

**NANI**

Why are you talking to her? Na jaan, na pehchan.

**SHARMILA**
Who are you talking to?

**NANA**
Your dadi. Matlab, she is not booddhi, not yet. Her teeth haven't fallen off yet.

**SHARMILA** *(Joining the joke)*
Really? But is her hair silver or no?

**NANA** *(Looking at Nani)*
Yes, yes, the top is quite silver.

**NANI**
Whose top?

**NANA** *(To Nani)*
Mine!

**NANI**
What's going on here?

**NANA**
Just some fun, time pass. You have become a dadi.

**NANI**
Whose dadi?

**SHARMILA**
But who are you?

**NANA**
Me? The same. Arrey, your dada!

**SHARMILA**
Dada! What fun!

**NANA**
What kind of fun?

**SHARMILA**
I have two dadas from today!

**NANA**
Two? *(A change of tone)* Listen, will you take down my phone number?

**SHARMILA**
What is it?

**NANA**
Write it down!

**SHARMILA**
Wait, I'll put it down... Okay, tell me.

**NANA**
Put it down... 528... 2946... you got that?

**SHARMILA**

Yes, 528-2946.

**NANA**

What's your number?

**SHARMILA**

528-5352.

**NANA**

Wait, slowly... 52... ? *(He writes the number down)*

**SHARMILA**

528... 5352.

**NANA**

Right! Now, I'll tell you what you can do? Every day, in the afternoon, you can phone me once. You are home in the afternoon, na? When do you go to school?

**SHARMILA**

I have morning school.

**NANA**

Good! Then you will give me a call everyday in the afternoon, will you not?

**SHARMILA**

Why?

**NANA**

Just like that, to have some fun.

**SHARMILA**

How is that fun?

**NANA** *(A short pause)*

How? Arrey, I am your dada, na? Listen, I am, you know, old.
*(Another pause)*
There is no kid here to chat with... it feels good to chat with a little kid, na? You'll call?

**SHARMILA**

Okay. *(Sharmila's real dada has appeared beside her. Nana can hear the conversation between them. )*

**DADA**

Who are you talking to?

**SHARMILA**

It's a wrong number.

**DADA**

Put it down. *(Sharmila puts the phone down. The light goes out in her corner.)*

**NANA**
Hello? Hello... hello... *(He disconnects)*

**NANI**
Who was it anyway?

**NANA**
What a sweet kid she is.

**NANI**
You talk as if she was right in front of you.

**NANA**
Can't you tell from the talk? Sharmila... Deekshit.

**NANI**
How old is she?

**NANA**
Must be eight or ten.

**NANI**
Dhatt tere ki! I thought she was older... marriageable age. I thought you were getting to know her better... for Dinoo.

**NANA**
Arrey, she is a little kid. Talking to her I was thinking... It felt like I was talking to my own grand-daughter. If Dinoo had married when he was twenty, would he not have a daughter that age?

**NANI**
Why a daughter? Would he not have a boy that age?

**NANA**
Both your sons are causing you enough pain, and you still haven't lost your obsession with boys. Really, we must get the girl here.

**NANI**
How can we get somebody else's child here?

**NANA**
Getting her doesn't mean keeping her here. She'll stay an hour or two, play here, eat here, and then go back.

**NANI**
But who will bring her here? You can't climb up and down the staircase, your knees won't take it.

**NANA**
I will still do it, I will bring her here. I should find out her address.

**NANI**
You should have asked her right then. Always in a rush, forgetting important things!

**NANA**
Wait, I will call her and get the address.
*(Nana dials the number just noted. A corner of the stage is lit, revealing Sharmila's Dada at the other end.)*

**DADA**
Hello... *(Pause)* Who is this?

**NANA**
Is Madhuri there?

**DADA**
Madhuri who?

**NANA**
Madhuri Deekshit.

**DADA**
Madhuri Deekshit? Here?

**NANA**
Sorry, Sharmila. Sharmila Deekshit.

**DADA**
And you are... ?

**NANA**
I am... I am her dada.

**DADA**
Dada? How can that be? I am her dada. Wah! *(A pause)*

**NANA** *(To himself)*
Arrey baap re!

**DADA**
What? What was that? Hello... Hello...
*(Nana disconnects. The light goes off in the corner.)*

**NANI**
What was that?

**NANA**
Her Dada picked up the phone!

**NANI**
What did he say?

**NANA**
What did he say? He said, 'How can you be her dada? I am her dada!'
*(Nani smiles, shrugs, and leaves the room. Nana remains, a bit dazed. A rapid fade out. There is a knocking on the front door. The lights return to reveal Nana going to the door to collect the post. He opens one letter.)*

**NANI** *(Entering)*
Was that the post? Whose letter is that? Dinoo's?

**NANA**
Could be Nandu's.

**NANI**
How long it's been since we heard from Dinoo in America!

**NANA**
Fourteen days.

**NANI**
Call him tonight! He cannot take so long to write. *(Turning to the letter)* All right, read the letter. Did Nandu eat the gujiya I sent him?

**NANA** *(Putting on his glasses and reading)*
Poojya Nana, saprem namaskar.
*(Aside)* Jeete raho, beta.
*(Continuing)* Received your letter. It is two days since I got the gujiya parcel. They have come out really good. They were a great hit here, so I did not get much of a share for myself. The gang here ate up all the gujiya in a single sitting. Udaa diya!

**NANI**
Such foolishness! What was the need to display the parcel before all of them? Could he not keep the gujiya in his room?

**NANA**
Like mama, like baba, na!
*(Continuing)* But please ask Nani not to send any more gujiya, because next month I am going to take off on leave. I will be there myself to eat lots of it.

**NANI** *(To herself, reminiscing)*
Nandu and gujiya – it is his life force. And Dinoo – for Dinoo it's mithi roti. Who is going to make mithi roti in America? And feed him lovingly? Huh!

**NANA** *(Watches Nani, continues)*
There was a letter from Dinoo in New York. He is fine, theek-thaak.
*(Looking closely into letter)* Some lines scratched off here... something written and then scratched out.

**NANI**
See if you can make out what it was. *(Nana tries.)*
Here, give it to me, I will read it for you. You never did learn to read.

**NANA**
Here. *(Nana gives Nani the letter. She looks for her glasses. Nana takes off his glasses and gives them to her.)*
Here. *(Nani puts them on and tackles the letter.)*

**NANI**

Cursed if I can make out a single letter. He has written something about Dinoo and then cut it out. Maybe about his health.

**NANA**

His health? Nothing about marriage?

**NANI**

Why are you going off on that line now?

**NANA**

Just like that.

**NANI**

Could you make out the word marriage anywhere here?

**NANA**

No.

**NANI**

Dinoo is not the one to do something like that without telling us. But you must phone him tonight. Why not call just now?

**NANA**

We will call at night. He will be up then. We get the line more quickly at night. The line is also clearer then.

**NANI**

Okay, but put it down on that pad, or you will forget. And remember to write to Nandu too. Tell him there's no need to take a plane, he can just come by train.

*(A young man has appeared at the door. He is watching the old couple. Nani sees him and is startled.)*

**NANI**

Arrey Dinoo!

**NANA**

Who? Who?

**NANI** *(Breaking into a smile)*

I am so sorry, my mistake. He looked so much like... I thought Dinoo... *(To visitor)* I am sorry.

**NANA**

And you are ... ?

**VISITOR**

Is this the home of Mr Karandikar?

**NANA**

No, I am Abhayankar. Please... please come in.

**VISITOR**

I am sorry please forgive the intrusion. *(He starts to go)*

**NANA**

Oh, but please... Andar aaiye na.

*(Nana is insistent. The visitor, Vinay Bhole, comes in. Nana and Nani try to make him comfortable in their sparse surroundings, finding him a seat, fetching a glass of water, and so on. All the time they keep glancing at him, still wondering if it might not be the long-lost Dinoo. Nevertheless, they are happy to have a visitor. There are awkward attempts to start a conversation.)*

**VINAY**

My apologies. I thought this was where Mr Karandikar stayed. That is why...

**NANI** *(Thinking)*

Karandikar?

**NANA**

It could be them... the family there on...

**NANI**

No, that is the Rawalkar family.

**NANA**

Then it must be...

**VINAY** *(A newspaper cutting in his hand)*

CV Karandikar, Jai Mangal Colony.

**NANI**

This is Jai Mangal Colony all right.

**VINAY**

Block No 3.

**NANA**

Ah, this is Block No 1. The building on the other side of the road is Block 3.

**VINAY**

Right, thank you. *(Starts to leave)*

**NANA**

Arrey baitho na! No problem. *(Seating him again)*
Haan, Karandikar... Rishtedar?

**VINAY**

No, no. He had an ad in the papers – for a paying guest.

**NANA**

What does he do?

**VINAY**

Kya pata, no idea. *(Nani goes in.)*

**NANA**

We have no idea either. There are so many new residents here nowadays. And who is the paying guest?

**VINAY**

Me. I am looking for a place to stay. A paying guest place would be fine.

**NANA**

Tea? *(Calling)* Oh, Naniji, some tea would be welcome.

**NANI** *(Off)*

On its way!

**NANA**

And your name... ?

**VINAY**

Bhole. Vinay Bhole.

**NANA**

There was a Bhole in Railway Audit... in the sixties.

**VINAY**

I don't know of anyone in the Railways.

**NANA**

All right. Your parents – where are they?

**VINAY**

In Belgaum. We have a cloth shop there.

**NANA**

And what do you do?

**VINAY**

I am studying Engineering here – final year now.

**NANA**

Achcha, achcha. And after that? Off to America-shamerica, I suppose.

**VINAY**

No!

**NANA**

No? Why not?

**VINAY**

Wahan hai kya? Why should anybody go there?

**NANA**

Very good! I am so happy to hear that!

*(Nana is overcome. He thumps Vinay on the back, catching him by surprise.)*

**VINAY**

What? What happened?

**NANA**

Oh, nothing, nothing

**VINAY**

Something the matter?

**NANA** *(Controlling himself)*

No, it's nothing. Nothing to... Yes, something... Nowadays, you see, anybody who gets his backside off a chair flies off to America or Canada or Germany or some other place out there. They go off. And they stay there, buss. And we keep shouting brain-drain, brain-drain, here – shouting ourselves silly.

**VINAY**

The people who go there have brains, we can't deny that. But shouting about it here becomes a habit, and it does not help. That also can't be denied.

**NANA**

Absolutely! You are so right, my boy!

**VINAY**

And let me ask you, is there really a brain drain? What are the numbers? There are millions who don't go away. They stay here, and they also have brains. All we have to do is tap those brains.

**NANA**

Wah! Absolutely right! Aapko ek baat kahoon?

**VINAY**

Zaroor.

**NANA**

Tu kahoon toh chalega na? You won't mind?

**VINAY**

Haan-haan, why not? I am like a child to you.

**NANA**

Good boy! To tell you the truth, I don't think there is any need for you to even think of going to England, America, vagairah. You will get a good job right here. Things are picking up in this country too, you know. Tujhe maloom hoga. People keep shouting, shouting all the time, yeh nahin hai, woh nahin hai. It has become some sort of national social service, shouting about the country all the time.

**VINAY**

Haanji.

**NANA**

Griping, bitching, shouting. Take a name, gripe, gripe. Take another name, bitch, bitch. They won't do anything themselves, just shout.

**VINAY**

I know that well. *(Vinay watches as Nana gets carried away.)*

**NANA**

We also have good programmes here, na? So many schemes in our Five-Year Plans. Tu ingineer ban jayega toh you can get a good job right here. Even if you don't get one straight away, you are not the one to give up, are you? You can open a business of your own, you will make jobs for ten-twenty others. Better than running away to some godforsaken foreign land. What a state! Kids having all the means for all the comforts there, and old folks left here by themselves. Nobody to turn to. Counting hours left in the day, tick-tock, tick-tock, counting hours left in their lives.

**VINAY** *(Hesitantly)*

You have children?

**NANA**

The younger fellow is in the Air Force. He is posted somewhere in Kashmir now, we don't know exactly where. The older one... America mein hai... He is an engineer.

**VINAY**

Where in America?

**NANA**

Somewhere in New York. Eight years... Who knows, maybe...

**VINAY**

Maybe he won't come back now?

**NANA**

He will come, he will come. What is he going to do there all his life? He has to get back, he is the elder son after all. And you, how many brothers and sisters?

**VINAY**

My sister and myself, just two of us. *(Nani has entered with tea)*
Why did you take the trouble?

**NANI**

What's the trouble in this? You take tea, no? Or do you prefer coffee?

**VINAY**

No, no, this is fine. Still... *(He takes the cup of tea, offers it to Nana)*

**NANA**

For you, for you.

**VINAY**

Wah! Badhiya chai!

**NANI**

Wait! I'll get some gujiya for you! You'd like some?

**VINAY**
Gujiya? Of course! My mother likes to make Gujiya too.

**NANI**
Our little fellow, no? Nandu?

**VINAY**
The one in Kashmir?

**NANI**
You know him?

**VINAY**
He just told me.

**NANI**
Gujiya is his life! Let me get some for you. *(She goes in.)*

**NANA**
Just the two of us here. Nandu, in Kashmir, the older fellow, Dinoo, in America... just us and this whole house. You slave the whole of your life for what? For some joy in later life, na? For your kids, na? To see them grown, to see them married... to see their kids running around the house... their laughter, the masti. The blossoming, you want to watch every moment of that... first the outer-most petals opening, then the inner, then the deepest part of the flowers revealing themselves. *(Nani enters carrying a plate of gujiya.)*

**NANI**
Here we are! This is no kaam-chor gujiya, haan – chop, chop, chop, dump in artificial ghee, buss, ready. This gujiya needs special care, special technique. It is a pleasure making it for people with good taste. *(She gives Vinay some)*
What do you think?

**VINAY**
Wah! Very special! So nice and crisp.

**NANI**
Good. I can get you some more. What was I saying? Yes, just recently I sent a dabba full of it to our Nandu. His friends... well, they polished it off in no time. Chalo, at least people enjoyed themselves there. We can't do that here. He can't take fried stuff, I am off mirch-masala.

**NANA**
Just dal, chawal, dahi – that is our routine.

**VINAY**
Shall I... ?

**NANI**
Wait! I will get some more for you.

**VINAY**

No, no, please!

**NANI**

Didn't like it?

**VINAY**

It is excellent, really. But I have to be careful.

**NANI**

Some more tea, then. It is ready. *(She goes in)*

**NANA** *(Grinning)*

Achcha mila aaj! Nobody here to talk to, na. You must be wondering... I step in here to find out about Karandikar, and here she is jabbering away non-stop! It is an old habit, talking too much...

**NANI** *(Entering with tea)*

Whose habit are you talking about?

**NANA**

Our old habits, you know.

**NANI**

Yes, it is an old habit of his, jabbering away all the time! But only with outsiders, mind you, not with his own people at home. With his own people he goes chup! Now that you are here, you can expect him to go on non-stop! He will ask you all kinds of things. *(Gives him the tea)*

You have brothers, sisters?

**VINAY**

Just two of us. I have one sister.

**NANI**

Married?

**VINAY**

Who, me?

**NANI**

The sister.

**VINAY**

Not yet. We're looking out now. It has to be someone she likes after all.

**NANI**

How old is she?

**VINAY**

Twenty six. I have an uncle here, my mama. He is looking out for us, but you know...

**NANA**

Our Dinoo, he is of marriageable age. Thirty-one years, bilkul eligible.

**VINAY**
He is in America, right?

**NANA**
He is coming back. He has to come back.

**NANI**
Does she look like you?

**VINAY**
Oh, she is much nicer than me – in every way.

**NANI**
Then she'll be fine for our Dinoo. *(To Nana)* You have to call him tonight, remember? Tell him about...

**NANA**
Just wait!

**NANI**
Why?

**NANA**
I was going to say... *(To Vinay)*
You were going to stay here as a paying guest, na?

**VINAY**
Where?

**NANA**
That Karandikar place.

**NANI**
Who's Karandikar?

**NANA**
Will you please... ! What was I saying? *(To Vinay)*
Yes, you were going to stay as a paying guest with Karandikar, right?

**VINAY**
Yes, but... I will have to see. I have to go there first and...

**NANA**
What will they give you there?

**VINAY**
Morning tea, breakfast, hot water for bath.

**NANA**
Buss? And how much will they take?

**VINAY**
At least five hundred, I suppose. More – a thousand, maybe twelve hundred.

**NANI**

Oh, look how the costs have gone up. When Dinoo was in the hostel, he got two whole meals for four hundred. Plus bada khana on Sundays. That's at least four times a month.

**NANA**

Oho, hold on a bit! *(To Vinay)*

What was I saying? Yes, you... why don't you stay here? Breakfast, lunch, dinner – yes, morning tea – a glass of milk at bed time...

**NANI**

With badam. Nowadays you get a ready mix of badam-pista. I have it with me. Just add in hot milk, stir, go. Badam milk ready! You know how it was in the old days – crush the badam, put it into the milk, boil till it softens, add the saffron, stir every half a minute...

**NANA**

Stop, will you?! *(To Vinay)*

And for all this, you will have to give us... let's see... not a single rupee.

**VINAY**

Mufat?

**NANA**

Bilkul Mufat.

**VINAY**

But how does this...

**NANI**

You are our third son! You will bring some brightness into this house.

**NANA**

Zara ruk na! *(To Vinay)* A bright young fellow like you, level-headed, no thought of running away to a foreign land, so well-behaved... We will have your company. Tomorrow you will be a big engineer, then we will be able to say with pride, 'he studied here!'

**NANI**

Then what! And we are, you know, well on our way. If one of us takes off, you know, one fine day, one of us goes dhupp – there must be somebody around to gather half a dozen people, no?

**NANA**

Chup nahi rahegi! That's not what we want him for. Nobody is 'taking off' here just now!

**NANI**

Who knows whose number is coming up next?

**NANA**

Stop butting in all the time!

**NANI**

I think I can do better inside. *(She goes in. A pause. Nana looks at Vinay.)*

**VINAY**

I will tell you later. Let me... how much space do you have here?

**NANA**

Just this. What space do the two of us need? When Dinoo returns, which will be anytime now, and Nandu also gets back, we'll take another place, a big place. But you won't have any problem here. *(Nana moves about the room, explaining)*

**NANA**

I will just get another cot and set it up for you. Her cot can be shifted to the kitchen – it's a big kitchen. And Nani, she will feed you well – aisa khana khilayegi, you will never...

**NANI** *(Entering)*

Just tell me what you want and what you don't want, buss. Leave it all to me. *(A short, awkward pause. Vinay is watching Nani's limp.)*

It has been that way for some time. No effect on the service!

**VINAY**

Achcha, chalta hun.

**NANI**

You must always say 'aata hun'.

**VINAY**

Yes, of course. Achha, aata hun.

**NANA**

What is the big hurry? Sit for a while.

**VINAY**

No, I have to go now.

**NANA**

All right, all right. You are coming tomorrow, right? You can move in tomorrow if you like.

**VINAY**

I will tell you...

**NANA**

Take down our phone number *(Takes out a note pad)*

**NANI**

You will also have the phone here, you can call anybody you like.

**NANA**

Here, take it down. *(Vinay does)* 5-2-8-2-9-4-6. Call tomorrow. Better still, come over yourself. We can sit down and gupshup over chai.

**VINAY**

I'll come I'll come. *(To Nani)* Aata hun, maji.

*(Vinay, Nana, Nani exchange good byes. Vinay leaves.)*

**NANA**

Looks bilkul like our Dinoo, na? Just a little on the thin side.

**NANI**

Why thin? Dinoo is the same.

**NANA**

How can you say? It's eight years since you saw him.

**NANI**

Since we saw him.

**NANA**

It will be good if this boy comes to stay with us. This house...

**NANI**

He will come. Of course he will.

**NANA**

He will?

**NANI**

He will.

**NANA**

You think he'll come.

**NANI**

Who else will give him a place to stay for free? All meals thrown in?

**NANA**

An interesting boy too. If our Mala was here today, we might have had him as a nice jamaai.

**NANI** *(Cutting in firmly)*

Enough! *(A short pause)* Now, if his sister is good looking, that will do. We will make her a bahu. No need for any dowry-showry. But we'll make sure it's a grand wedding. *(Taking out a zari sari)* Bilkul shandaar! I will wear this saree just once, and then hand it over to Dinoo's wife. And this other one, this will go to Nandu's wife. And these, I have kept these...

**NANA**

Haan, haan, give them all away! You will have something left to cover yourself, I hope. Or will it be time for your...

**NANI**

The schoolboy in you always! Don't go cracking your dressing-undressing jokes when that boy Vinay is here.

**NANA**

Nice boy, really. He tells me he will not go abroad after getting his engineering degree. What is there abroad, he asks.

**NANI**

Our Dinoo, he was like that too. When was he ever keen to quit his job and go abroad?

**NANA**

Achcha achcha, now put all these sarees away carefully.

**NANI**

You can fold them carefully, and I will put them away carefully.

**NANA**

I will do that soon enough. Wait! I think I will call that little girl.

*(Nana goes to the phone and dials. The other telephone corner is lit. The grandfather picks up the phone.)*

**NANA**

Hello...

**DADA**

Hello, kaun?

**NANA**

Sharmila hai?

**DADA**

Kya kaam hai? Aap kaun?

**NANA**

I am the... *(He disconnects hurriedly)*

**NANI**

What happened?

**NANA**

What happened maane? The same old man again! He will ask, *(Mimicking him, enjoying this)* Aap uske dada kaise? Main uska dada!

*(Nana and Nani are putting the sarees away. The street lamp is on. The sound of a wedding band and procession is heard, getting closer.)*

**NANI**

What a racket!

**NANA**

It's a wedding procession. *(To the balcony)* It's a baraat, heading this way!

**NANI**

A wedding! Whose?

**NANA**

Yours!

**NANI** *(Joining in)*

There you are! You have arrived in such style!

*(They playact their own wedding day for a few moments. Nana is impatient. He interrupts.)*

**NANA**

We must hurry. Let's go down and take a look. We can even join in!

**NANI**

In the baraat?

**NANA**

In the baraat!

**NANI**

Go on! God knows whose wedding it is.

**NANA**

Who cares! We just join in.

**NANI**

Just like this?

**NANA**

Here, wear this zari sari. Now, some jewellery. Put on this nath. And let me look at you! Let me see how you'll look in Dinoo's wedding.

**NANI** *(Snatching the nath from Nana)*

Give it to me first. Take out the set in that box.

**NANA**

Hurry! And I will put on something nice too. The marriage party mustn't think I am one of the servants sneaking in.

*(He hurriedly takes out an old coat and puts it on. He then finds a cap which he fits carefully on his head. He looks out from the balcony.)*

Come on, hurry up! The baraat is almost here!

*(The sound of the procession is nearer. Nani is absorbed in her jewellery. She is fixing a nath with great care. Nana watches her intently and then whistles in glee.)*

**NANI**

Oh, you! *(Trying to look into a mirror)* Move aside! Or you can help me with this chain... Why are you looking at me like that?

**NANA**

I imagined you seated in the mandap.

**NANI**

Go on! Enough of your natak flattery!

*They move excitedly to the balcony to watch the approaching procession. They turn and look at each other with a new fondness.*

*Fade out.*

## SCENE 2

*When the lights come on, Nana and Nani are at the entrance.*

**NANI**

I tell you! I thought it was my Dinoo seated on the horse.

**NANA**

Your Dinoo! Seated on a horse!

**NANI**

Of course he will be on a horse! I am not going to let him off. We will take out a baraat just like this one. Even more grand!

**NANA**

You will take out a baraat! A grand baraat, you will take out! Now go and get out of that fancy dress.

**NANI**

You are the one who told me to get dressed up. Just for these two hours. Now you say take them off, put on the old rags.

**NANA**

So, don't. What is the need to wear anything when you are...

**NANI**

Enough of your stale jokes. You are going senile or what?

**NANA**

All the women in the procession were craning their necks so hard to get a good look at you.

**NANI**

But why were you looking so hard at all those women?

**NANA**

You and your ziddi habit of talking back! You will be just the same over a hundred years! *(A young man has appeared at the front door. He knocks at the door and coughs.)*

**NANA**

Who?

**VISITOR**

I am Shyam Deshpande.

**NANA**

Shyam? Deshpande?

**SHYAM**

Yes. Sorry, were you going out?

**NANA**

No, no. Please come in.

**SHYAM**

Then you must have just come in. Oh, I know. From that wedding.

**NANA**

Yes, that's right. Sit, please sit.

**SHYAM**

Whose wedding was it?

**NANA**

Oh, that was... it was a distant relative.

**SHYAM**

Achcha achcha. *(Pause)* I have come... I have just come today from New York.

**NANI and NANA** *(Together)*

New York? *(They look at each other)*

**NANI**

We have a son there, Dinoo. Do you know him?

**SHYAM**

Yes, as a matter of fact. That's what brings me here.

**NANI**

You know Dinoo? Kaisa hai woh?

**SHYAM**

Achcha hai. He is fine, keeping very well. He is doing well at work too.

**NANI**

Yes, yes, but why is he not coming here? We have been asking him for such a long time.

**SHYAM**

He will come. It's not pukka when, but he will definitely come.

**NANA**

He has been saying that the last eight years! Tell me, how long have you been there?

**SHYAM**

Two years. Just two years.

**NANI**

See? You could come away in two years. What is the problem in Dinoo doing the same?

**SHYAM**

Naukri ka mamla hai. It is not easy getting a good job here.

**NANA**

And you? You had no problem?

**SHYAM**

It's different with me. My father has a factory here.

**NANA**

After all the higher studies there, you can't get a good job? I don't understand it. Just our fate, this is a poor country, na, backward. There is no way a boy like that will get a job for fifteen-twenty thousand here.

**SHYAM**

Sir, forget about fifteen-twenty. Even if they get five or six thousand here, they will be happy to leave and return. But they won't do that if the job is just pet bharne ke liye, and they are left doing nothing.

**NANA**

So... what's to be done?

**NANI**

What to do with old folks like us?

**SHYAM**

Point. You have a point. But what to do? People like you have a point, and people like Dinoo have a point. What can be done?

**NANA**

I'll tell you what can be done! Make me the President of India. I will pass an order that no young man will go abroad for so-called higher studies. And after completing all studies here, they will work only here.

**NANI**

Why do you let your blood boil unnecessarily?
*(To Shyam)* Now, tell us about our Dinoo. He is all right, no?

**SHYAM**

Very fine.

**NANI**

Any message? News?

**SHYAM**

No message, but he has sent some money.

**NANA**

Huh! *(He turns away in anger)*

**SHYAM**

Dinoo gave me two hundred dollars and asked me to exchange it and give you the rupees here. *(He holds out a bulging envelope. Neither Nani nor Nana takes it from him. Shyam places the bundle on the table.)*

**SHYAM**

You can check the amount.

**NANI**

It's all right. Let it be there. Did he say anything about coming here?

**SHYAM**

No, he didn't say anything about that.

**NANI**

But he must come.

*(To Nana)* You must phone him quickly.

*(To Shyam)* We have found a nice girl for him.

**SHYAM**

For whom?

**NANI**

For Dinoo.

**SHYAM**

But Dinoo is married. *(Awkward pause)* Didn't you know?

**NANA**

Married?

**NANI**

When?

**SHYAM**

A week ago, last Sunday. I left soon after the reception.

**NANI**

The girl... where is she from?

**SHYAM**

From there. She is American.

*(A difficult silence. Nana moves away to the window. Nani sits down.)*

**NANA**

I had a feeling...

**SHYAM**

She is a very nice girl, you needn't worry about that. Nowadays, marriages like that... many marriages... *(A long pause. Shyam looks about nervously. Nani is controlling her sobbing, wiping her tears. Nana remains motionless at the window, looking out.)*

**SHYAM**

Achcha, I am sorry if... I am very sorry. I have to go now... If you don't mind...

*(Shyam leaves. Nana takes off his coat and cap. Nani takes off her jewellery. Nana sits at the table, lost, plays with the table lamp switch.*

*Fade out.)*

## SCENE 3

*Morning, a few days later. Nana is watering the potted plant in the balcony. Nani is seated on the stool at the window. Nana takes the water jug inside, re-enters, and sits at the table, stares at the ceiling, picks up the newspaper, and looks at it without reading it. Nani watches him for a while and then addresses him.*

**NANI**

No other work or what? *(There is no response)*

I am asking you...

**NANA**

Huh? You said something to me?

**NANI**

Who else will I talk to here?

**NANA**

What was it?

**NANI**

My head!

**NANA**

But what was it?

**NANI**

Lagataar you are lost inside that paper. At night when I ask you to read the Gyaneshwari, your eyes are tired, you say. And now your eyes are glued to the newspaper.

**NANA**

Who's reading what paper? It was lying here, I picked it up. What else to do?

**NANI**

A man must be saying something all the time. He must be heard all the time – making demands at meal time.

**NANA**

To tell you the truth, I feel too tired to talk now. Talk about what? I say something, you listen. You say something, I listen... day after day, month after month, years. Who else is there to speak to, listen to?

*(He looks up)* Except that sparrow...

*(They both look up at a sparrow flitting about. After a while Nana picks up the newspaper again.)*

**NANI**

Paper neeche rakhiye.

**NANA**

Kyon?

**NANI**

I am telling you, that's why. Put down that paper first.

*(Nana puts the paper down and looks at Nani. He then grimaces.)*

**NANA**

I have a really bad tummy today.

**NANI**

What did you eat to get a bad tummy?

**NANA**

What did I eat, she asks! What did I eat! After stuffing me with that rock heavy paratha.

**NANI**

It was ajwain paratha, good for you. It doesn't cause any tummy troubles.

**NANA**

Maybe good for you. Not for me. Makes my tummy bhari.

**NANI**

No bhari-wari, nothing. Just walk about a bit, instead of sitting there staring at the newspaper all the time. For that, the first thing you have to do is get up. Get up now!

**NANA**

For what? Get up for what?

**NANI**

Walk about a bit. Get up and walk about.

*(Nana rises and paces back and forth in the room.)*

**NANA**

But I'm telling you right now, I am not eating anything you make tonight. Even if I am on the floor dying, don't try to feed me anything.

**NANI**

How can that be? I have already prepared the sooji. You will have to eat at least a bit of the laddu. It will be good for you. As if I don't know your tummy problem. It's all since the news of Dinoo's marriage. Khana-peena... completely upset.

**NANA**

How did you get that in your head? Dinoo got married to an American girl. So? Why should that bother me?

**NANI**

No need to keep up this natak for me. Actually I should also be upset, just like you. But I have courage.

**NANA**

Haan haan, courage-wali! Cries every time she sits and stands. You think I don't know. *(Nani sobs into her sari end)*

Listen, you remember what we decided, na?

**NANI**

What?

**NANA**

We will not talk about Dinoo's marriage. We will not bring it up again and again and make ourselves upset.

**NANI**

Where am I talking about it? Where am I upset? He got married, he got what he wanted, buss. What's it to us? We are here today, gone tomorrow.

**NANA**

Here today, gone tomorrow. We have said that the last eight years. We can say the same thing the next eight-ten years.

**NANI**

No need for so many years. What is there to live for anyway?

*(A long pause. Nani controls her weeping. Nana watches her intently, seated.)*

**NANA**

No news of that Vinay. Maybe we won't see him again.

**NANI**

Why do you say that?

**NANA**

You are the one, na? Telling him that he should be here when one of us drops dead? To gather a handful of people for the last rites?

**NANI**

Was that wrong?

**NANA**

No, of course not. Just what has to be said to drive somebody out of the house.

**NANI**

Nothing wrong with that. Suppose something happens in this house – tonight, in the middle of the night. Suppose something happens to me. Where will you be? What will you do? And if something happens to you, god forbid, what will I do?

*(She weeps, unable to continue. Nana watches without reacting. The phone rings. In another corner we see Vinay on the phone.)*

**NANA** *(Picking up the phone)*

Hello? Hello?

**VINAY**

Hello, is Nana-saheb there? This is Vinay Bhole here.

**NANA**

Arrey, you keep saying I'll come, I'll come, that's all. When will you show your face here?

**NANI**

Is that Nandu?

**VINAY**

Nana-saheb, how are things there?

**NANA**

Stop calling me saheb. Just Nana is all right. No sahib, no bibi, no ghulam here, only Nana-Nani. *(Vinay and Nana laugh)*

Yes, so what happened?

**VINAY**

My mama who lives here, he is alone.

**NANA**

Alone meaning?

**VINAY**

He has no children, he is a widower.

**NANA**

Arreyre.

**NANI**

What? What happened?

**NANA**

Nothing! *(Motioning her to be quiet)* Yes...

**VINAY**

So, my mama was asking why do I have to go and stay somewhere else? I have to stay right there, he said. Maaf keejiyega. I hope you understand.

**NANA**

Unhuh. It's all right.

**VINAY**

I would really have liked staying with you.

**NANA**

It's all right. All these things are part of... It's fate.

**VINAY**

But I'll keep coming there now and then. We will talk on the phone too. I hope that's okay?

**NANA**

Oh, yes, yes. There's a phone at your mama's place, na?

**VINAY**

No, no phone there.

**NANA**

Unhuh. So... what other news?

**VINAY**

The other news is that I wrote to my father in Belgaum.

**NANA**

Right...

**VINAY**

You know, about my sister who is ready for marriage, and your older son who...

**NANA**

Younger son, not older.

**VINAY**

What? Is the older one fixed up?

**NANA**

Not fixed up, he is married.

**VINAY**

Married? So soon? And you didn't even let me know?

**NANA**

Where did we have your whereabouts? How could we let you know?

**VINAY**

Where is the bride from?

**NANA**

Bride? *(Nana disconnects quickly and stands staring ahead.)*

**NANI**

What happened?

**NANA**

Vinay was asking... who is Dinoo married to. He has a sister na, to be married...

**NANI**

Why are you acting like that? As if we are thieves or something. Dinoo got married on his own right. What is our crime? Why can't we tell everybody the truth? Why hide it? *(The phone rings again. Nana hesitates, and then picks it up.)*

**NANA**

Hello?

**VINAY**

Sorry, the line got cut.

**NANA**

Yes...

**VINAY**

So, let's do this.

**NANA**

What?

**VINAY**

We can think of your younger son.

**NANA**

Nandu? But he is about twenty eight or so.

**VINAY**

It's all right. We will see. After all we are the ones who must look into this, right?

**NANA**

It is all fate, baba... fate.

**VINAY**

Do you people want the girl's horoscope and so on?

**NANA**

Not now. Give it another eight or ten days. Nandu is expected here himself.

**VINAY**

Arrey wah! Then there will be a gujiya treat again.

**NANA** *(Laughing)*

Yes, yes, but you know, the gujiya can be made for you also.

**NANI**

Here, ask him when he is coming. I will make all the gujiya he wants, just for him. We need someone here who will sit down and eat heartily

**NANA**

You heard that? Nani is asking when you will come and have the gujiya made specially for you. Khane wala chahiye koi!

**VINAY**

I will come. Zaroor aoonga.

**NANA**

So we will wait for Nandu and then fix up a programme to see the girl. Can your sister come here? It is a little difficult for us to travel now.

**VINAY**

She will come. We will bring her here.

**NANA**

That is fine then.

**VINAY**
My namaskar to Nani.

**NANA**
No, I will not give your namaskar to Nani. You have to come here yourself and do that.

**VINAY** *(Laughing)*
I will come, sure, I'll come.

**NANA**
Aur kya khabar?

**VINAY**
Aur to... nothing special. Achcha, I will close now.
*(He disconnects quickly. Nana is disappointed.)*

**NANA**
I get the feeling the girl will click with our Nandu, this Vinay's sister.

**NANI**
Don't say things out of turn. Who can tell who is tied up with whom by which string of fate? All that is important is her nature. Otherwise she will take away Nandu and set up another house.

**NANA** *(Irritated)*
This is a bad habit of yours! Jumping the gun, kuch na kuch bolti rahegi. Let them get married first. Once that is done, our responsibility is done. The two of us can then go away in peace, some place far away, and take our samadhi.

**NANI**
Samadhi? Yes, yes. Right now will you take some tea?

**NANA**
Is it ready?
*(Nani smiles and moves into the kitchen. Nana waits a moment, picks up the phone, and dials. The light in the corner reveals Sharmila's dada. He picks up the phone and speaks, 'Hello, hello. Who is it?' Nana does not respond. He sticks out his tongue, disconnects, and puts the phone down. Nani re-enters.)*

**NANI**
There's one thing I must tell you now.

**NANA**
What's that?

**NANI**
Once Nandu gets here you must not let him go. Tell him there is no need for his military pulav and biryani. Simple home food is good enough for all of us. Even if he has no job, fine. We have your pension to feed us. He has to stay with us, buss. We must be able to see him before us.

**NANA**

I will hand over the bank pass book and tell him, do whatever dhanda you want with this. Open a radio shop if you like, start anything you want to.

**NANI**

Yes, but say all this to him, not to me. When he comes, you will sit chup! I have decided – this time if he talks about going back, I will bang my head at his feet and give up my ghost. You and he can do what you like after that.

**NANA**

Yes, yes, but you were talking about tea just now.

**NANI**

You want it garam, no?

*(Nani goes back to the kitchen. Nana picks up the phone again and dials. The light in the corner reveals Sharmila's dada once again. He picks up the phone and speaks, 'Hello, hello. Who is it?' Nana does not respond. He covers the mouthpiece and says 'Yell, go ahead, yell some more.' Dada yells in annoyance, 'Hello! Hello!' Nana, laughs to himself. Dada disconnects. Nana puts the phone down. Nani enters with tea.)*

**NANI**

Whose phone?

**NANA**

I tried calling Sharmila, but the phone had hardly rung once and there was that dada, hazir! *(He picks up the phone and mimics Dada)*

Hello. Hello! Who is this? Who is calling?!

*(Admonishing)* Your dada! Put the phone down now!

*(Putting the phone down)* Lagta hai, he is a military type. Tries to bark his commands on the phone also.

**NANI**

He must be guarding his grandchild very well.

**NANA**

Guarding against what? As if I am going to abduct her or something!

**NANI** *(Laughing)*

Who can tell?

**NANA**

Why don't you try dialling the number?

**NANI**

Where is the number?

*(She looks at the number and dials. Sharmila appears at the telephone in the corner)*

Hello... Kaun, Sharmila?

**SHARMILA**

Haanji. Aap kaun?

**NANI**
Bete, I am your dadi.

**SHARMILA**
Which dadi?

**NANI**
That dada who phones you, no?

**SHARMILA**
Oh, yes, the wrong-number-dada.

**NANI**
Yes, yes, I am his shrimati. That means I am your what?

**SHARMILA**
My wrong-number-dadi.

**NANI**
Cheeky chokri! What are you doing? Not going to school?

**SHARMILA**
I was just getting ready. What is dada doing?

**NANI**
Well... *(Looking at Nana)* At the moment your dada is not in a good mood. *(Nana gestures in anger)*

**SHARMILA**
Why?

**NANI**
Old habit of his. Why don't you talk to him? *(Nana grabs the phone from Nani)*

**NANA**
Arrey Sharmila!

**SHARMILA**
Why are you in a bad mood?

**NANA**
I'll tell you later. First, let me hear you call me dada.

**SHARMILA**
Da-da!

**NANA** *(Pleased)*
Aisa! How nice that sounds!

**SHARMILA**
Has your bad mood gone?

**NANA**
Haan, bilkul!

**SHARMILA**

Has Nandu bhaiya come?

**NANA**

Not yet, but he will come soon.

**SHARMILA**

When?

**NANA**

He should be here within a week.

**SHARMILA**

You must call me when he comes. I have to see him.

**NANA**

Oh? You have some work with him?

**SHARMILA**

Yes, I want two things from him.

**NANA**

And they are... ?

**SHARMILA**

First, I want to see him in his pilot's uniform.

**NANA**

Achcha, achcha. And the second?

**SHARMILA**

The essay topic for the exam this term is going to be, 'The life of a pilot'. I am dying to talk to him about his life.

**NANA**

Arrey, what is the need to wait for him? I will ask him to write to you directly. *(Sharmila's dada enters.)*

**DADA**

Who are you talking to?

**SHARMILA**

Nobody. *(Sharmila disconnects quickly.)*

**NANA**

Okay, na? Hello... Hello... ?
*(He puts the phone down)*

**NANI**

What happened?

**NANA**

What else?! That booddha dada of hers got in there again. When the two of us want to have a talk on the phone, I don't know why this grumpy old man must ghus and... Why do you think he does that with me?

**NANI**

That is up to you and him. You asked me to connect, and I connected.

**NANA**

A big favour you did me, thank you! You should have found out who all were at the phone, especially senile old men lurking in the corner. All you could think of was sweet talk. *(Mimicking)* 'Yes, yes, I am his shrimati. That means I am your what?' Don't tell me!

**NANI** *(Laughing)*

Theek hai.

*(She pretends to be serious. He looks at her. She smiles. They exchange glances. Nani then moves to a corner and picks up the broom.)*

**NANA**

What do you think you are doing?

**NANI**

Zara jhadoo ...

**NANA**

Why? Is Mahdu not coming?

**NANI**

You can see how he sweeps, no? All the dust as is where is.

**NANA**

What dust? How can there be dust here?

**NANI** *(Rubbing her foot on the floor)*

What do you think this is?

**NANA** *(Moving to take the broom away from Nani)*

The slaving to death in the kitchen is enough for you. What if your back gets stiff tomorrow? I will have to do everything then. Here, I will sweep the floor. See how the room gets clean!

**NANI** *(Mock annoyance)*

It's my job! Give me the broom, will you! *(Changing)* I know how you swept the place every time I went to my mother's. The house would turn into a gujri bazaar, don't I know that!

**NANA**

In those days, I had a lot of other things to do. What work is there now? Can't find something even for time pass anymore. *(Nana starts to sweep. Just then there is knocking on the door.)*

**NANI**

Will you see who it is?

*(Nana goes to the door. It is Mahdu. He snatches the broom from Nana's hand and immediately sets himself to the task in his own way. In one long, continuous, swift move, he completes sweeping the room and goes into the*

*kitchen area. Nana watches in embarrassment. Nani conceals her amusement in her sari end.)*

**NANA**

Saala, bandit! How he snatched it away from me! I could have given him one – ek thappad saale ko… But he would have also run away. He is the only one to be stuck with us all these years.

**NANI**

It's a habit right from childhood.

**NANA**

My childhood?

**NANI**

No, no, Mahdu's. We took him in when he was a little boy, like that. He has had this since then, always in a big hurry, always restless.

**NANA**

But snatching the jhadoo from me… If I had known he was going to do that, I would have gripped it so hard, saala even his tagda father would not be able to take it away from me. *(Nani starts to laugh, and controls herself. She moves to the window and sits down, continuing to conceal her laughter.)*

Now, what's so funny about that? It must be something about me, then. No? What is it? What's so funny?

**NANI**

Kashi railway station, the platform. I just remembered.

**NANA**

You remembered what?

**NANI**

When the thief snatched the bag from your hand and ran away, you said exactly the same thing… 'If I knew he was going to do that, I would grip it so hard, saala even his… Nobody would be able to take it away from me.'

**NANA**

All right, laugh! Very funny! All you can do is laugh. You didn't even know what was in the bag.

**NANI**

Sixty rupees, ten rupee notes, six of them.

**NANA**

Whatever the amount… it was not from your ammaji's place.

**NANI**

Why do you have to bring ammaji into this?

**NANA**

Why not? She always comes into the picture anyway. As if I didn't bring any money into this house.

**NANI**

Yes, yes, that's why for every single delivery in this household I had to go away to...

**NANA**

What every single delivery? They were your deliveries, na?

**NANI**

Of course, mine. It's the done thing for the first delivery. You toh got every one of them done at ammaji's place. Did you pay one paisa to baba for the expenses? You were sharp in counting the notes in the dowry bundle!

*(Nana has sat down in annoyance)*

Now you sit there and make that face!

**NANA**

With you rattling away there, what else can I do, but sit and watch? And that too when the topic is ammaji's home. *(Nani remembers something and laughs, which makes Nana even more annoyed.)*

And now she starts giggling again!

**NANI**

Do you remember? How you cried when I was going away for my first delivery?

**NANA**

Nonsense! Why would I cry?

**NANI**

Tell the truth, now. You didn't cry? Thinking whether I would come back or not?

**NANA**

Bakwas! As if that was anything to think about. You made sure you went back for the second delivery in no time at all.

**NANI**

Buss, buss. But tell me first, did you cry or no? Even baba was wondering...

**NANA**

All right, all right, I cried. Satisfied? A little bit. But why that should make you laugh so much now...

**NANI**

And another thing.

**NANA**

Now what?

**NANI**

I just remembered. This Mahdu's wife is also expecting. It will be any time soon, I think. Just call him, no.

**NANA**

You keep track of everybody's affairs.

*(Nana calls out. Mahdu appears, mop cloth in hand, mouth full of paan as usual. He asks in gesture what they want.)*

**NANI**

Any letter from the village? Any news about your... ?

*(Mahdu shakes his head)*

When is it going to happen?

*(Mahdu gestures with two fingers that there is time)*

In two days?

*(Mahdu shakes his head and gestures again)*

Two months?

*(Mahdu shakes his head and tries again)*

**NANA**

Maybe something will happen in two years! Enough! You can go in. *(Mahdu goes in.)*

**NANI**

We must give him some clothes for the baby.

**NANA**

You have any to give?

**NANI**

Lots! I had them made for Dinoo's kids. But now his kids... they are not going to wear things made here. They'll just lie there. I can keep them for Nandu's kids, of course, but I can easily give three or four of them to Mahdu.

**NANA**

Give them all away...

**NANI**

Why all? My second bahu is still to come. And if her kids are going to be anything like Nandu, they will be wetting their chaddies away every hour. We need lots of clothes for them.

**NANA**

And what will happen when you dump them on Dinoo?

**NANI**

Who said I was giving them to Dinoo?

**NANA**

The other night, on the phone, when Dinoo called – what were you jabbering about, huh?

**NANI**

You are the limit! My child calls from America, and I shouldn't talk to him?

**NANA**

Talk to him! What were you talking to him about?

**NANI**

About his coming here. About so many things.

**NANA**

About sending things. Sending what things?

**NANI**

What was wrong in that? If I want to send a mangalsutra for a bahu – what was wrong in asking?

**NANA**

And what did the bahu have to say about that?

**NANI**

She spoke in that American bhasha. How could I... ?

**NANA**

I could have taken the phone.

**NANI**

Ohh... Let's stop this now.

**NANA**

No, wait. Tell me this – when you talked about the mangalsutra, what did Dinoo have to say? No go, that's what, na?

**NANI**

Stop, I tell you. Why must you get so worked up about this?

**NANA**

Worked up? Who's getting worked up? *(Walks about agitated)*

Worked up about what? We had our children, we brought them up, they sprouted wings, they have to fly away. They must fly. Who are we stop that? *(Nana goes to the telephone, picks it up, and starts dialling. Mahdu enters wiping his hands on his pants, takes away the receiver from Nana, puts it down, dusts the phone, and puts it in its place. He then makes his way to the door.)*

**NANI**

The sleeping pills are over, right? Ask him to get them. Mahdu! *(Mahdu stops)*

**NANA**

That's right, the tablets.

*(He takes out a prescription and some money from the cupboard and gives them to Mahdu)*

Here, show them this. You know which shop, don't go anywhere else.

*(Mahdu asks for a clarification in gestures. Nana replies in gestures, mimicking him. Mahdu understands and leaves.*

*Nana returns to Nani. Continuing his mime, he asks her for a cup of tea. She acknowledges and moves to the kitchen. Just then there is knocking on the door.)*

**NANI**

See who it is.

**NANA**

Kaun?

*(There is a postman at the door. Nana takes a letter from him.)*

**NANI**

Whose letter?

**NANA**

It looks like Nandu's writing. *(He opens the envelope. Nani gives her glasses to him. He starts to read.)*

**NANI**

He must be on his way.

**NANA**

He... *(Sits down speechless)*

**NANI**

What does he say?

**NANA**

He is not coming now.

**NANI**

Not coming? What does... ?

**NANA**

All leave cancelled. All units mobilised. The country is going to war.

**NANI**

Why do they keep fighting like this? War, war, all the time... Why can't they grow up? When will they stop? How long will it be? Why can't parents see their boys home during festivals... ? *(She moves to the window)*

**NANA**

Who knows? *(The street lamp comes on. Nani offers a namaskar and moves towards the kitchen.)*

Where are you going?

**NANI**

To light a lamp in the puja corner. It's all so...

**NANA**

Don't upset yourself too much. What is the point in worrying anyway?

**NANI**

Where am I getting upset? No harm can come to this home. We have done no harm to others. *(Nani goes in. Nana moves to the table, plays with the table lamp as before. He turns the radio on and puts his head to the set, listening at low volume. A patriotic voice is heard: 'Hum jeetenge ya marenge...' Nana turns off the radio quickly, and paces about the room. Fade out.)*

# ACT II

## SCENE 1

*A few days later. Nana is seen alone in the room. He is at the window. The phone rings. Nana goes to it and picks it up. The light comes on in the corner to reveal Sharmila.*

**NANA**
Hello, kaun?

**SHARMILA**
It's me, Sharmila.

**NANA** *(Matter of fact)*
How are you? All right, na?

**SHARMILA**
Dadaji, Nandu-bhaiya must be having a good time, no?

**NANA**
What do you... ?

**SHARMILA**
Now that we have a war, he will fly his plane fast and dhadadhad drop bombs all over the enemy.

**NANA**
Yes.

**SHARMILA**
They will be turned to dust.

**NANA**
Haan.

**SHARMILA**
Then he will get a gold medal, no? It will be a grand ceremony. When they put it on his chest, they will take hundreds of photos, how handsome he will look!

**NANA**
Yes, yes. *(Nana disconnects quickly)*

**SHARMILA**
Hello... Hello dadaji... *(An engaged tone)*

**NANI** *(Entering)*
Who were you talking to?

**NANA**
That girl...

**NANI**
What was she saying?

**NANA**
Nothing.

**NANI**
What do you mean nothing? Say something.

**NANA**
What can I say?

**NANI**
Anything. So it feels like somebody lives here. Say something.

**NANA**
What should I say?

**NANI**
Anything at all. Let there be some human voices here. The silence is frightening here.

**NANA**
She was saying...

**NANI**
She means who?

**NANA**
Arrey, that Sharmila.

**NANI**
Achcha, achcha, what was she saying?

**NANA**
That right now Nandu must be zooming through the sky in his plane, and...

**NANI**
Something else! Talk about something else!

**NANA**
What else?

**NANI**
Something else – something to brighten up things.

**NANA**
Something... to... brighten things...

**NANI** *(Brightening)*
You remember? Kashi railway station?

**NANA**
Haan, haan. What happened there?

**NANI**
What happened there? You are asking what happened there? As if you don't remember a thing.

**NANA**
Really, no.

**NANI**
That thief – the bag in your hand – what happened then? *(Nani tries to laugh. She cannot. Nana is unresponsive. Nani falls silent.)*

**NANA**
Yes... yes.

**NANI**
What did you say at that time?

**NANA**
What did I say?

**NANI**
You don't remember?

**NANA**
I don't. Why don't you tell the story?

**NANI**
What did you say... you said... *(She can't remember)* Oh, forget it.

**NANA**
I'll tell you what.

**NANI**
What?

**NANA**
Let us go out for a stroll.

**NANI**
A stroll? Dragging this foot along?

**NANA**
Achcha, I have another idea.

**NANI**
What now?

**NANA**
A phone call.

**NANI**
To Sharmila?

**NANA**

No, not her.

**NANI**

Then who?

**NANA** *(Picking up the telephone directory and handing it to Nani)*

Here, pick a number, any number.

**NANI**

Just like that? Jan-na-pehchan?

**NANA**

As if there was jan-pehchan with Sharmila. A wrong number, and I became her dada. They are all bonds from our previous births, all set long ago. Nani, you know what...

**NANI**

What?

**NANA**

I think our Malu... she went away, na, our Malu. Couldn't she be this Sharmila? She simply found us now, that's what.

*(A pause. Nani stares at Nana, who turns silent, then looks away. Nani regains her composure.)*

**NANI**

So, should I give you a number?

**NANA**

Number?

**NANI**

You asked for any telephone number from this...

**NANA**

Yes, a number. Go ahead and... Oh my god, the receiver is off the hook. *(Replaces it)*

Yes, you were giving me a number. And you will take two hours to do it. Here, give the book to me, I'll do it. *(The telephone rings. Nana picks it up.)*

Hello! *(The light comes on in the corner to reveal Vinay.)*

**VINAY**

Hello, is that Nanaji?

**NANA**

Yes...

**VINAY**

This is Vinay here.

**NANA**

Arrey, but where?

**NANI**
Is that Nandu?

**NANA**
No, it is Vinay.

**VINAY**
Who is that?

**NANA**
Nani was asking whose call.

**VINAY**
How is she keeping?

**NANA**
Chalta hai. What's there to be said about us now? But how are things with you?

**VINAY**
I'll be there in a day or two.

**NANA**
Yes, I'll be there, I'll be there – we hear that all the time.

**NANI**
Ask him if he can remember when he was here last.

**NANA**
You heard that? Nani is asking you.

**VINAY**
Sorry! Tomorrow or day after, definite.

**NANA**
Achcha, what other news?

**VINAY**
I called to tell you...

**NANA**
You have some news.

**VINAY**
Actually to ask you – apka Nandu, when is he coming?

**NANA**
Nandu... this war business – how can he come till it is all over?

**VINAY**
I had the same doubt, about his not being able to get here. The thing is we have arrived just today from Belgaum.

**NANA**
But Malu can't meet you today, beta.

**VINAY**

Malu? Meeting me?

**NANA**

Which meeting are you talking about?

**VINAY**

My sister – with your Nandu.

**NANA**

Your sister? Haan, haan, she has arrived? So, bring her over tomorrow. We'll get to see her. Nandu can meet her later. Of course he will like her.

**NANI**

Tell him to make it tomorrow.

**NANA**

You heard that? Tomorrow itself, no delay. She can't wait to set her eyes on the bahu.

**VINAY**

Our good fortune, really. But the question is how long should she stay here?

**NANA**

Why? She has to be taken to some other places or what?

**VINAY**

Two other places.

**NANA**

Theek hai. Your sister after all. What authority do we have over... ?

**NANI**

She is going to be the bahu in this house. We have all the authority in the world over her.

**NANA**

You heard that? She is going to be our bahu.

*(To Nani)* When we have had no authority over our own children...

**VINAY**

What are you saying?

**NANA**

Arrey, what I am saying is this. You must do what you think is right, but as for me, I know where all this is heading. When something pops up from nowhere and then takes hold of my mind, showing up again and again in my thoughts, it is a sure sign that it is going to happen. I know this for a fact. It has been that way all my life. Now, you – that first day you came into this house... I knew from that moment that your sister was going to be the bahu in this house. Don't worry about Nandu. He will come soon enough.

**NANI**

And he will not be going back to his military job. Tell him.

**NANA**

Yes, he will not be going back to the military life, he will stay here. We have decided. He will get married and stay here. With us, rey.

**NANI**

He will get married, she will have kids...

**NANA**

Nani is in a hurry too. She wants kids, grandkids. She has kept clothes ready for them. To tell you the truth, we are quite bored boxed in here. How nice it will be with kids running around the house, the noise, the mischief...

**NANI**

I am longing to have food cooked by another pair of hands.

**NANA**

Nani's farmayish. Does your sister cook or no?

**VINAY**

Very well. First class khana.

**NANA**

Mutton-wattan? Not for us, but Nandu is a great non-veg.

**VINAY**

She is good at everything.

**NANA**

Matlab, everything is pukka.

**VINAY** *(Tying to close)*

Yes, let's see where her... there are a couple of other places to go...

**NANA**

Yes, yes, but you will bring her here tomorrow, na?

**VINAY**

Let's see. I will ask mama about it.

**NANA** *(Trying to continue)*

So, what else on your side? *(Vinay disconnects. The corner is dark.)* Hello... Hello? *(He keeps the receiver down.)*

**NANI**

It's very true, what you said.

**NANA**

What?

**NANI**

I feel the same way too.

**NANA**

What about?

**NANI**

That Vinay's sister will come only into this home.

**NANA**

She will come, no doubt about that. But I have another feeling, you know.

**NANI**

About what?

**NANA**

That Sharmila... she is definitely our Malu.

*(Nani is silent. Nana opens the cupboard and rummages inside.)*

**NANI**

What are you looking for?

**NANA**

Our old photos.

**NANI**

For what? You will turn the whole cupboard inside out.

**NANA**

Here! *(Bringing a photograph to her)*

Look at this. You... me... Dinoo, Nandu... and in your lap, little Malu. Look at her face! She was two and a half then, right?

*(Nani does not react)*

Look at their faces... gems, every one of them.

*(He kisses the photograph)*

Madcap kids!

*(Nani moves towards the kitchen)*

Where are you going?

**NANI**

What is on that side of the house? What do I go there for? I have to heat up the milk. *(She goes in)*

*(Nana watches her go in, then moves to the radio, switches it on, and listens to it at low volume. The voice of a news reader is heard.)*

**READER**

The news. Our air force went into action on the Eastern front, striking deep in enemy territory. There was heavy bombardment, leaving behind huge fires and complete destruction of the chosen targets. A thick blanket of smoke remains over vast areas even now. Eight enemy aircraft were shot down in decisive engagements. Our air force has so far lost only two aircraft.

*(Nana switches off the radio quickly. Nani enters.)*

**NANI**

Anything on the radio?

**NANA**

Nah! Somebody singing something – besura saala.

**NANI**

Lies! *(Switches on the radio)*

**NANA**

Me? What makes you... *(The newsreader's voice is heard)*

**READER**

On the Western front, the attack on an enemy air base wiped out almost the entire fleet before they could even take off. There was no resistance in the sky from any enemy aircraft. All our aircraft returned to base safely, mission accomplished. End of news bulletin. The next bulletin will be one hour from now.

*(A sigh of relief from Nana, as he looks at Nani, forcing a smile. Nani does not respond. She goes back to the kitchen. Nana sits at the table, plays with the table lamp. He then picks up the Gyaneshwari and reads a verse.)*

**NANA**

Hote hain jahan sab nidrit *(Where one and all are asleep)*
Hota hai vah wahan jagrit (*There is one awake)*
Jahan hote hain sab jagrit *(Where one and all are awake)*
vah sota hai *(There is one asleep)*
*(Nani enters with a cup of milk and keeps it before Nana.)*

**NANA**

I don't feel like having it. I am tired of milk-milk all the time.

**NANI**

What do you mean don't feel like it? Don't take your milk, and you'll be complaining tired-tired all the time.

**NANA**

All right, baba, I will not complain anymore!

**NANI**

Fine, but take your milk now.

**NANA**

No, really, I don't feel like having it.

**NANI**

Shall I make some paratha?

**NANA**

No.

**NANI**

Put a slice into the milk?

**NANA**

Nahin, baba, kuch nahin! I don't want anything now.

**NANI**

That's why I am giving you the milk, no? Didn't I have mine?

**NANA**

Don't try to fool me. You have your milk at night, with the sleeping pill.

**NANI**

I'll have the pill with water tonight.

**NANA**

If you are giving me the milk, you might as well give me the pill. Here, you can take half of this milk.

**NANI**

No need, I will get mine.

*(Nani goes in. Nana takes out a bottle from the table drawer and puts two pills into his palm. Nani enters with her cup of milk. Nana takes a pill with his milk. Nani stretches out her hand.)*

**NANI**

Give me mine.

**NANA** *(Giving her the pill)*

I can't be giving you this every day. It will become a bad habit.

**NANI**

You can give me the whole bottle one day. I will sleep happily ever after. No waking up bother.

**NANA**

Madness! Sleep happily, no waking up! What happens when Nandu comes back and calls from the stairs 'Nani! Nani, Nani!'

*(Nani hears the sound of Nandu's voice echoing in the room 'Nani! Nani, Nani!' She is startled.)*

**NANA**

What happened?

**NANI**

I don't know... Did you hear?

**NANA**

Hear what?

**NANI**

His voice... 'Nani, Nani... '

**NANA**

Nonsense! That thing must be going to your head. I told you, na. Here, give me the cup.

*(Nana takes the cups and goes into the kitchen. Nani sits on the cot, lifts her legs up slowly, and lies down. She covers herself. Nana enters.)*

**NANI**

No call from Dinoo in a long time.

**NANA**

Go to sleep now! Time to put down your worldly cares.

**NANI**

What about you?

**NANA**

In a few minutes.

**NANI**

Read the Gyaneshwari for a while. I will get good sleep listening to it.

*(Nana sits at the table, opens a page of the Gyaneshwari, and reads aloud.)*

**NANA**

Jiska chitt hai sadoditt *(A mind that is ever emerging)*
Pata prasannata akhand *(Finds delight unending)*
Wahan pravesh nahin samast *(Never can emerge there)*
Bhav-dukhon ka *(Ideas of despair)*
Jaise amrut ka nirjhar *(As the stream of nectar)*
Bahata jiska udar... *(Creates a flow for... )*
*(The phone rings. Nani sits up.)*

**NANI**

Dinoo's phone! It rings just like that.

**NANA**

*(Picking up)* Hello?

*(The light comes on in the corner to reveal Dinoo)*

**DINOO**

It's me, Dinoo.

**NANA**

Dinoo... Dinoo...

*(Nani lifts herself up and comes to the phone)*

We were just thinking of you beta, we were talking about how long it was since we heard from you.

**DINOO**

The news on the radio – have you been following what is happening in the war?

**NANA**

We are so worried about that. He was to be here this week on leave. We got a short letter that all leave is cancelled. Then this news about war... Nani is so scared, Dinoo.

**DINOO**

Naturally, Nana. But what is the point in getting scared?

**NANA**

It's just that there is nobody here, na. If you were here, we would feel a bit comforted, not so lost.

**DINOO**

I understand, but...

**NANA**

And Nani is getting so nervous. She keeps hearing things. She hears you calling her.

**DINOO**

From America?

**NANA**

The mind plays tricks, rey, it's the mind getting old. You can't know till you get old yourself. *(Dinoo laughs)* Don't laugh. You will understand when it happens to you. Listen, let me tell you something. You have to come here now. Nani can't manage anymore, not at all.

**DINOO**

Nana, you say that all the time. Suppose, I did manage to come there, just supposing, what difference will it really make? What seva can I do there? Instead of that you should keep a nurse. Keep a paying guest, even staying free if you like. Find a cook. Don't bother about the money, whatever these things cost. How much can it be? I'll send the money.

**NANA** *(Unable to control himself)*

Money, money, money! Arrey, you don't know anything, and you care about nothing. What feasting can the two of us do? Roti, kapda, makan – I hardly use up my pension. Who is here anyway, huh? Who needs your... donation?

**NANI**

Don't talk to him in such anger.

**NANA**

You... talk to Nani.

*(Nana gives her the phone, sits at the table, burying himself in the Gyaneshwari, playing with the table lamp.)*

**NANI**

Dinoo... Dinoo bachchu, when are you going to come now?

*(Dinoo laughs)*

Why are you laughing?

**DINOO**

Nani, you are still calling me bachchu.

**NANI**

Dinoo, you are still my child, no?

**DINOO**

But Nani, very soon I will be old enough to be a father.

**NANI**

Ohhh... ? Some gadbad happening?

**DINOO**

No, no, nothing like that. I just said...

**NANI**

Fine, then. Now, listen Dinoo, you must return at once. Enough of your America. Start a life here now. Arrey, how long can the two of us go on like this, staring at each other's faces all the time? That Nandu, he kept saying no, no, and still went off to be a militarywala. And now this war. Can you imagine what we are going through? *(She weeps)*

**DINOO**

Nani... Nani, why are you crying?

**NANI**

God wills it, that's why I am crying.

**DINOO**

Don't cry, Nani.

**NANI**

I can't stop it. It will go on till you return. Dinoo, please tell me you will come back.

**DINOO**

I will come. It's not as if I want to stay here.

**NANI**

But you have been saying that god knows how many years.

**DINOO**

I will come, Nani. Don't I also feel like seeing you? Seeing Nana?

**NANI**

Really? You feel like that sometimes?

**DINOO**

Yes, Nani, it's the truth.

**NANI**

I've heard you say it, that is enough. I will be able to sleep in some peace tonight.

**DINOO**

Good. I am going to put it down now.
*(He disconnects. The light goes off in his corner.)*

**NANI**

Come soon. Try. *(She puts the receiver down)*

**NANA**
What did he say?

**NANI** *(Pleased)*
He said... he feels like seeing you.

**NANA**
He said that, really?

**NANI**
Yes. He said that. That is enough. Now I am going to sleep well. Will you read a bit of Gyaneshwari?

**NANA**
Yes. Yes, I will.
*(Nani lies down, covers herself, and turns around. Nana reads aloud).*

**NANA**
Jahan pravritti pangu hoti
Tark drishti andhi hoti
Indriyan sab bhool jati
Vishay sang
Mit-ta mamatva man ka
Aur shabdatva shabd ka
Jisme milta gyan ka
Gyey matr
*(Fade out. When the lights return, the room is dimly lit and eerily coloured with streaks of light circling the room. Nana is lying next to Nani. The voice from earlier, calling 'Nani! Nani, Nani!' echoes repeatedly. In a dream, Nani sits up, a nath on her nose, and a bright odhni on her head. At the door is the figure of a young man in Air Force uniform. We do not see his face. Nani moves towards the figure, adjusting her nath and odhni.)*

**NANI**
Shall we go? But listen, Nandu, Vinay's sister is a nice girl. We know that already. Don't find faults with her just to have something to say. Just say 'Yes' as soon as you see her, buss. She will also be happy. Once you have settled down, wah, chutti for us. Let's go now, quick.
*(She steps out. The lights continue in the room. The sound of a funeral procession is heard passing the house, the bhajan being sung to the beat of a dhol. Sounds of 'Shriram Jayaram' are intertwined with the lyrics of the bhajan. The performing group can choose the lyrics. Here is a specimen:*
*Surat kalari bhai matwari*
*Madwa pi gayi bin toley*
*Hunsa paye Man Sarovar*
*Taal talaiya kyon doley?*
*Nani returns frightened to the door, awake. She slams the door shut, screams, and collapses on her bed. Nana wakes up. He sits up and looks at Nani.)*

**NANA**

The nath on your nose?

**NANI** *(In a daze)*

Where is it? *(It is not on her)*

**NANA**

I saw it in front of me... You were there, the nath on your nose... It must have been a dream.

**NANI**

A dream?

**NANA**

It was Nandu's baraat. You were dressed up, a grand odhni on your head...

**NANI**

I had a dream too. Nandu had come home. We were going to that Vinay's place, to see his sister. I went...

**NANA**

Yes?

**NANI**

I went to the doorstep and there... there was a funeral procession. I rushed back I was in great fright. Then I woke up... *(A pause)*

Can you hear that?

*(The sound of the funeral procession is heard at a distance)*

I was frightened... because... what if I tripped and fell at the stairs?

**NANA**

Go to sleep now!

*(She lies down and turns over. Nana adjusts his side of the bed.)*

As for that girl...

**NANI**

Which girl?

**NANA**

Vinay's sister. This is the house she will come to. Now, go to sleep.

*(They go to sleep. Fade out. When the lights return, the room is dimly lit. There is knocking at the door. Nani sits up. There is more knocking. She wakes up Nana.)*

**NANA**

What is it?

**NANI**

Someone at the door.

**NANA**

Go to sleep. Always imagining things.

*(The knocking is heard again)*

Who could it be at this time?
*(He gets out of bed)*

**NANI**
Ask who it is first.

**NANA**
Who is it?
*(A voice calls out 'Telegram'. Nana opens the door and steps out.)*
From where? Whose telegram?
*(A pause. Nana steps into the room in a daze. There is a long wail.)*
NANDU!!! Dinoo, arrey Dinoo! Come home! Come back quickly. Our Nandu is no more!

**NANI**
Nandu...

**NANA**
From his Commanding Officer. They will send another officer in person soon...

**NANI**
Nandu...
*(Nana and Nani struggle to the cot and seat themselves, dazed. Images of Dinoo... Sharmila... Vinay appear in different sizes and colours in different parts of the room, looking down on them, grave in countenance.)*
*Fade out.*

## SCENE 2

*Nani is seated on the stool at the window. Nana is changing the month on the wall calendar. A crow is seen/heard cawing from the balcony. Nana and Nani turn to look at the crow. It flies away.*

**NANA**
You want us to say that somebody is coming? Fly away! Who is going to visit us now?

**NANI**
When did Dinoo say he was coming? Was it from Delhi?

**NANA**
He will come sometime... from somewhere.

**NANI**
Don't talk like that. He might have changed with all this...

**NANA**
Huh! You are mad to think that...

**NANI**

Yes, yes, I am. So?

**NANA**

Do you know how long he has been here in India? *(Nani looks blank)* How many times has he been here since then? Finding his way from that Intercontinental Hotel, where he has deposited his wife?

**NANI**

Why do you talk like that? They came here every day, didn't they, he and the wife?

**NANA**

And now he is on a chakkar with his wife... Delhi, Agra... showing her the Taj Mahal and whatever else he wants her to see!

**NANI**

I was the one who told him to go and get some fresh air. What's the point in sitting here and brooding? She is here for the first time, he might as well show her something of the country. We should be happy we have seen our child after so long... that he came here in the first place.

**NANA**

You think he came here to see your face! Foolish woman! The return ticket is a bargain – that is why he is here. To show his bibi the Taj Mahal – that is why he is here! Show her the country! Show her around! *(He starts to cough)*

**NANI**

Why must you work yourself up like this? Just sit down and relax. Better still, lie down. You hardly sleep at night.

**NANA**

And you? As if I don't know how much sleep you get!

**NANI**

And those sleeping pills are also useless. Char char goliyan, and still no proper sleep. Hardly a nod, god knows where the sleep disappears. I keep hearing voices, calling out Nani, Nani! Like it was Dinoo.

**NANA**

Dinoo, Huh! More likely Vinay. He has been the only one around when we were in need.

**NANI**

Such a nice boy. Such a help. More than even our own...

**NANA**

Help? Such a lot more! He was here for days on end, by our side all the time, sleeping on the balcony. And this Dinoo – he can hardly take time off from his Delhi-Agra chakkar.

**NANI**

Right, you better lie down now, instead of getting so... All this gets your blood pressure up.

**NANA**

Let it go up! I mean, look at that little girl Sharmila. How old must she be? She has been here twice already. Made her booddha dada bring her here, cried her dear little heart out. And this Dinoo?! Tells us to ree-lax, gives us some bakwas about time as the great healer. In that American accent! Healing is faster in American English, na?!

**NANI**

All this is no good for anybody you know that. All you will do is kill yourself, making sure you go up ahead of me. That's what you really want, right?

*(Going into the kitchen)*

What do you care what happens to me then? Kutte-billiyon ke havale.

**NANA**

And as if I don't know why you are leaving the room? You want to wipe your tears in there and come back.

**NANI** *(Enters wiping her eyes)*

When is Dinoo coming in from Delhi?

**NANA**

In today. Out tomorrow, back to America.

**NANI**

When is he coming here?

**NANA**

What for? To make mithi roti, na? Because he loves mithi roti, na?!

**NANI**

He has come at such a... I haven't been able to make anything for him. Why isn't he here yet?

**NANA**

There! Pick up the phone. Call that In-ter-con-ti-nental Hotel, find out.

**NANI**

Why can't you call?

**NANA**

Never! *(The phone rings)*

**NANI**

Pick it up! It must be Dinoo.

**NANA**

You want to talk? You pick it up!

**NANI** *(Picking up the receiver)*
Hello... ?
*(The light comes on in the corner to reveal Sharmila.)*

**SHARMILA**
Hello, Nani? Aapki tabiyat kaisi hai?

**NANI**
Theek. I am all right.

**SHARMILA**
And dadaji? What is he doing?

**NANI**
He is sitting and...

**SHARMILA**
Please tell him...

**NANI**
Wait, talk to him yourself.

**NANA**
I'm not coming!

**NANI**
It's not Dinoo. Sharmila on the line.

**NANA** *(Getting to the phone quickly)*
Ay, guddi! What is it?

**SHARMILA**
What were you doing?

**NANA**
Sitting, waiting for you.

**SHARMILA**
Lies!

**NANA**
Sacchi! *(Nani looks away, wiping her tears)*

**SHARMILA**
You know what? I was in the radio station the whole day.

**NANA**
What for?

**SHARMILA**
Recording a play. It will be on tonight. You will listen to it on your radio, won't you?

**NANA**
Won't we? What does that mean, silly girl? What time will it be?

**SHARMILA**
Ten o'clock tonight.

**NANA**
Right!

**SHARMILA**
Pukka?

**NANA**
Pukka.
*(Nana waits for Sharmila to say something more, but she has disconnected.)*

**NANI**
What was she saying?

**NANA**
A play, on the radio, tonight. She is in it.

**NANI**
What play?

**NANA**
I forgot to ask. Should I call her?

**NANI**
Let it be. We will know when we put on the radio.
*(A pause. They are looking at each other.)*
Say something, no.

**NANA**
What to say?

**NANI**
Put on the radio then.
*(Nana switches on the radio. It is the news channel.)*

**READER**
The news. This afternoon there was a formal ceremony in which the Pakistani military force in the East laid down arms and surrendered to the Indian military. The Indian Prime Minister, Mrs Indira Gandhi, has ordered an immediate end to the war effort. Wrap-up operations are already underway.

*(Nana switches off the radio and walks about the room, wiping a tear on his sleeve. Nani walks out of the room and re-enters, wiping her nose and eyes. A long and heavy silence fills the room.*

*Two blades of dry grass fall from above on Nana. He looks up.)*

**NANA**
What is this muck in the room?

**NANI**
What?

**NANA**
Muck... *(He picks up the grass and moves to the window)*

**NANI**
Don't throw it out. Put it down.

**NANA**
In here?

**NANI** *(Pointing up)*
She will come down for it. Madam sparrow, she is building a nest up there.

**NANA**
She has to build here...

**NANI**
Let her! And if you keep standing there, she won't come down for it.
*(They both move away and watch the sparrow's movements quietly.)*

**NANA**
Look, she is sitting up there... but she is not looking down.

**NANI**
She will. She knows everything.

**NANA**
Shall I bring the nest down?

**NANI**
Why on earth... ?

**NANA**
The nest, up there – the eggs breaking there...

**NANI**
Nothing of the sort. You know nothing about such things! Everything will be fine up there – eggs laid, eggs hatched, sparrow chicks out, wings sprouted, and off they will go.
*(They look at each other. The telephone rings. The light in the corner reveals Vinay. Nana picks up the receiver.)*

**VINAY**
Hello... Nana, this is Vinay.

**NANA**
Achcha.

**VINAY**
Has Dinoo left?

**NANA**
No. Expected today. In from Delhi today. Off to America tomorrow.

**VINAY**
Didn't consider staying here... ?

**NANA**

Unh... What news from you?

**VINAY**

Theek.

**NANA**

Your sister's marriage?

**VINAY**

Nothing known yet. It is not going well. Three good boys seen in the last week or so – all dropped out.

**NANA**

How come? They didn't like your sister?

**VINAY**

They liked the girl all right, they all did, but the horoscopes didn't match for any of them.

**NANA**

It is all written up there...

**VINAY**

With all this hadbadi, I could not come over. But I will come, definitely. Not today, tomorrow – first thing in the morning.

**NANA**

Yes, come.

*(Vinay and Nana disconnect)*

This girl's fate – I don't understand it.

**NANI**

Vinay's sister? What happened?

**NANA**

What else? It is not getting fixed. Some hitch or the other.

**NANI**

Oh, no, poor thing!

**NANA**

I can't help wondering...

**NANI**

It will work out sooner or later don't worry.

**NANA**

No, I was thinking about you know what? I think her fate was tied to Nandu's. Then when you have khel khatam there... and poor girl, she is left stranded.

**NANI**

Put that thought out! She will find a match any day now.

**NANA**
Shall we ask for her horoscope?

**NANI**
What?

**NANA**
We should see how it matches with Nandu's.

**NANI**
No need for any such thing!

**NANA**
Just to ease the mind. I keep thinking again and again, if the match between her and Nandu was pukka, we would have thirty-six out of thirty-six virtues in place.

**NANI**
It's all over now. Why go on and on about that?

**NANA**
I will tell Vinay. I will tell him when he calls. If there is no headway in her marriage, he must bring her here. She should come and stay here. We will look after her as our bahu.

**NANI**
How can she stay here?

**NANA**
Of course she can. If Nandu had returned a month earlier, according to his plan, he would have gone back married. And then with his... she would be here with us...

**NANI** *(Shouting)*
Stop it! Stop raving like a madman – blabbering anything that gets into your head!

**NANA** *(Lost)*
Am I sounding like a madman?

**NANI**
That will do! No more talk, just sit there. Sit quietly there.
*(Nana sits.)*
*Slow fade out.*

## SCENE 3

*When the lights return, it is evening. The street lamp is on. Dinoo is seated on a stool, his coat draped over the chair. Nani is seated next to him, stroking him now and then. Nana is seated at a distance, annoyed and restless. He paces about the room as he is inclined to do and sits on the bed.*

**NANA**

That is all you can talk about. Money! How much money we need, how much money you can send!

**NANI**

Who wants the money? What do we do with the money? Keep somebody here for what?

**NANA**

Luring us with the bricks of gold in Lanka!

**DINOO**

You tell me, Nana, what do you want me to do?

**NANA**

One step in the grave already, what could we possibly want? As if it matters what we want!

**DINOO**

You can at least tell me what you want.

**NANA**

As if it makes a difference my telling you!

**NANI**

Listen to me, beta. This chase after money, comforts, more money, more comforts... where does it get you? How long will the chase go on? You can only burst on the way. What we have here is enough, isn't it? It is from our soil after all.

**DINOO**

Achcha, so it is your turn now?

**NANA**

Look at you! Studies to be an engineer here, goes there to build bridges. We don't need bridges here?

**DINOO**

So, for that I should join the PWD and work for four hundred and fifty a month? Is that what you want? Work under some gadha ka bachcha boss because of his seniority? Push files whole day with those stained brown and yellow sheets of government paper?

**NANA**

All right, don't. You can start a business of your own, can't you? Put that money of yours in a business here. Build some bridges here and show us. Short of money? I will get it for you!

**NANI**

It's for your own good, Dinoo. Don't you worry about the money. I will keep one bead of the mangalsutra and sell off all my jewellery to make sure you have enough.

**DINOO**

How do I make you understand, Nani? You can't.
*(To Nana)* At least you must understand.

**NANA**

Understand what?

**DINOO**

Start a business, start a business, so easy to say that! Start a business in this country?

**NANA**

Why not?

**DINOO**

O bhagwan! Those government papers! They don't move an inch for years. You have to coax them to move, making a fresh offering for every step to be taken. If you talk about quality, the papers get thrown back – or thrown out. Go to Delhi once and see for yourself. Every official at every level is working so dutifully – making money for the official above him. And look at the names of the widest roads – Satya Marg, Niti Marg! No place there for people like us. Only thieves can survive there.

**NANA**

If people like you pack up and go away, only the thieves will be left behind to thrive, na?

**DINOO**

Let them thrive.

**NANA**

What happens to the country, then?

**DINOO**

To tell you the truth... I don't care. I don't feel this is my country.

**NANA**

Whose then? The thieves?

**DINOO**

Yes! The thieves! And all others who are left helpless, hopeless – people beating their chests and crying out, 'My country, my country'. It is their country, not mine!

**NANA**

Dinoo! What is wrong with you?!

**DINOO**

Wrong?

**NANA**

This country...

**DINOO**

This country! It is what you are supposed to say when you stand in front of the flag. It means nothing. What matters is what I see. This country... of losers... by the losers... for the losers. They just love to have their brains, their talents, and their hopes ground to dust here.

**NANA**

It was not always a country of losers. It has become one now. And people like you have helped in a big way to make it that. If you have the guts, if you think you know what has to be done, why don't you show them the way? Just sitting there griping and bitching! You people have turned this country into a huge complaint box. You keep dropping complaints into the box with every fart. Whose job is it to open that box and do something about it? Who will dirty their hands? All you want to do is run off to America and wash your hands in the holy waters of rivers there. And graze on the holy grass of green pastures there. All those brains and talents and hopes that you talk about, put them to work here! And show us!!

**DINOO**

Very easy to talk like that, Nana. If we want to do something...

**NANA**

Do it here!

**DINOO**

Yes, here! You go to a post office for a five-paise stamp, and you waste five hours. The pen that they keep there to write with – if they don't chain it to the table, it gets stolen. It's the same everywhere – banks, railway stations. People stealing things. Stop a taxi, and he won't come if it is some place nearby. The shopkeepers – they don't know how to talk to customers. These people, this country – I don't feel I am one of them. These people, who steal pens from the post office on Satya Marg and clips from the bank on Niti Marg – I want nothing to do with them.

**NANA** *(Shaken)*

All right, baba, all right. This country is only for the useless.

**DINOO**

About that I have absolutely no doubt.

**NANA**

Our Nandu, why did he give his life for a country like this?

**DINOO**

His misfortune. How many times did I tell him, 'Come away to America, you can also do well here.'

**NANA**

But he did not go, tere peechche peechche.

**DINOO**

He was stubborn. He was the chest thumping type, crying 'My country, my country' all the time, the needle stuck in that groove.

**NANA**

He was one of many hundreds who gave their lives for this country. I wonder why. There is nothing in this country, you say, and people fight to defend it, and are prepared to die for it.

**NANI** *(Restoring order)*

This is not getting anywhere. No need to make it a shouting match. Those who give their lives, give their lives. How does this arguing change that?

*(To Dinoo)* And you, Dinoo, please don't overdo this. Talk to Nana properly.

**DINOO** *(Calming down, to Nana)*

Yes, let's drop it. Pointless getting into this argument, there is no end to it. Nandu died in the war... that is why I am here... to see you, to be with you. Why should there be bitterness on top of the sorrow.

**NANA** *(Muttering to himself)*

Sorrow! Bitterness! *(To Dinoo)*

Right. You have come here at this time... that is good enough.

**NANI**

You should lie down now. What is this with you today?

**NANA**

What is what with me? *(He lies down)*

**NANI**

Just lie down and rest. Let me talk to Dinoo for a while.

*(She sits next to Dinoo, strokes him)*

Don't take it to heart... All this talk... it is all part of...

**DINOO**

It's all right, Nani.

**NANI**

So... What have you thought about it?

**DINOO**

About?

**NANI**

About staying back here.

**DINOO**

Oh, Nani! How can I... ?

**NANI**

No need to stay in this house. You can take another place, live your own... you know, as long as we can see you now and then.

**DINOO**

And what do I do staying back here?

**NANI**

He was telling you, no? Start something of your own.

**DINOO**

Ohho, now you too! When will you understand?!

**NANI**

All right, I am a hopeless case, I will not understand your state. But my children's love, I will understand that, no? Or is that another fault?

---

**[OPTIONAL: THIS PASSAGE IN THE ORIGINAL]**

**DINOO**

Those days are gone, Nani, that kind of show of love, maa-baap seva and all that – children carrying their parents to Kashi, buying the train tickets or maybe air tickets. We must have money for the tickets!

*(Nana glares at him)*

**NANI**

Nobody is saying anything about going to Kashi! We have been there already. We went when you were that little. Your lips and cheeks were cracked from the cold, we remember that well. It's like yesterday. No Kashi now, please! No SEVA, nothing, if you ask me!

**DINOO**

So – why should I be here?

**NANI**

How can I explain, beta? These are not things to be explained, they are things to be understood. You won't understand... until you reach our age. Maybe you will remember this conversation then. We won't be there, of course, but maybe you will remember us.

*(She drifts into memories)*

You came into our lives... It was a blessing. We were married long. There were no children. We went on pilgrimages, made offerings, took oaths. What for? We did not want any support in our old age from the state. What support can any state give? All we wanted was a living presence in the home, a son, a bahu, some living persons. Look at the two of us here. I can't even wash my hair. He has to help me, in his own clumsy way. He can't even change the month on the calendar...

**DINOO**

That is why I have been saying all the time – keep a maid here, keep a nurse if you like. I will pay for them. How does my staying here help?

**NANI**

It's not money that is needed, rey. It's what your own loved ones can do, and nobody else. A son who comes in and demands his favourite dish from me, a bahu who insists on cooking and feeding me, grand-kids who scream for more, but only from the grandma... where does all this come from? Who can replace it? When you went away, we thought, well, Nandu is always there. And then... he left us... and this is what we are left with. Can I help it if I sometimes think – and this is no zabardasti or anything like that – who are we to make any demands – here today, gone tomorrow – I can't help thinking, there you are in America, you have done well, you are making a lot of money, and we are here, two old folks who watched you grow up and saw you off, we don't need the money, all we need is... a peaceful end to our lives.

---

**DINOO**

Nani, you are talking as if...

**NANI**

I am not saying anything. Not asking for anything. We want to go away, with you beside us.

**DINOO**

This is nonsense! Just look at old folks there. They are so active, and in full control of their lives to the last breath.

**NANI**

Don't tell me about them. Them is them, us is us. Look, we have not brought a Ganapati Bapa into the house for over two years. Who will bring him here? Who will take him out? Diwali comes and goes. Who eats sweets? Who runs around in excitement with fireworks? Whose little hand can we hold with the sparkler and wave it around?

*(Nana can stand this no longer. He rises and moves to the kitchen, guardedly wiping his tears. Nani looks at him. Dinoo turns away and looks down.)*

It is all dried up. There is nothing to wake up to anymore.

*(Nana has entered with a pot and is going to water the plant in the balcony. A long pause.)*

Why did she not come?

**DINOO**

She is tired.

**NANI**

Am I going to give her work here?

**DINOO**

She said she wanted some rest. She had fallen asleep when I left.

**NANI**
Call her. You can both eat here.

**DINOO** *(Laughing lightly)*
How can she eat here?

**NANI**
Something wrong with my cooking?

**DINOO**
Her food and our food – they are different.

**NANI**
You can eat her food, but she can't eat your food?

**DINOO** *(Laughs it off)*
Let it be now.

**NANI**
If you could only stay another four-six days... coming here after such a long time... I haven't been able to make anything nice for you, all of us tied up in this... Stay a little longer, no.

**DINOO** *(Just a bit firm)*
No, Nani, I have to go tomorrow. And I have to leave now. We will drop in tomorrow. We will have chai here. It will be on the way to the airport.

**NANI**
It means you are set...

**DINOO**
Yes. I have to go. But I will come back soon, once a year.

**NANI**
We have heard that before – and waited eight years. Sit for a while!

**DINOO**
No, I must leave – she is all alone there.

**NANI**
Five minutes? Can't sit for five minutes? We wait for years.

**DINOO**
Chalta hun main.

**NANI**
Offer your namaskar there... And your father.

*(Dinoo bows before the puja corner and then goes to Nana to touch his feet. Nana raises him before he does and wipes his tears.)*

Dinoo... Come and sit here – here next to me.

*(Dinoo sits at her feet. Nani holds his head in her hands and gazes long into his face.)*

**DINOO**
Aisa kya...

**NANI**

I want to take in your face fully. It may be the last time we meet.

**DINOO**

Come on, now! I will be back!

**NANI**

But I may not be here then. Don't you worry about us. Live happily, both of you. What will be, will be, it's all written. Who can change that? Yes, come tomorrow in the morning.

*(Dinoo moves to the door. Nani and Nana follow him.)*

**DINOO**

Achcha, chalta hun.

**NANI**

Tomorrow morning – you must drop in on the way. Don't run off directly from the hotel.

**DINOO**

How can I do that? I will come, definitely.

**NANI**

One more thing – for me specially.

**DINOO**

Not staying back! Not again!

**NANI**

Not ever again. No, it would be so nice if both of us – you know – if the two of us passed away when you are here.

**DINOO**

What sort of talk... ?

**NANI**

No, really, the last rites for us done by your hands.

**DINOO**

Ohho!

**NANI**

But that's not what I wanted to say.

**DINOO**

Tell me tomorrow.

**NANI**

It's come up just now, so I must tell you now. Who knows, it may disappear overnight.

**DINOO**

All right, let's hear it.

**NANI**

It is about you, that is why it is special. Are you listening? This running after money – yes, money, more money, more luxury, more stuff – all this for what? Is that all there is in life? Is that happiness? More money, more happiness? I thought happiness came from up here, in the head. So... that's it. No, I really want you to be happy. Oh yes, if you have a son, give him a name from this place. And say 'aata hun' not 'chalta hun'...

*(Dinoo is going down the stairs through the last part of Nani's appeal. Nana and Nani control their tears and go to the balcony and wave good bye to Dinoo)*

Dinoo! Remember to drop in tomorrow!

*(Nana returns to the room, sits at the table, plays with the table lamp switch. He flips through pages of the Gyaneshwari.)*

**NANA**

Hare Ram... Hare Ram... Hare Ram...

**NANI** *(Entering)*

It's like the trees in the courtyard, uprooted and taken away. A barren courtyard...

*(Nani sits on the bed and looks up at the sparrow's nest. Nana sees her and also gazes upwards. From a distance, we hear the sound of a drum and a bhajan group. Nana goes to the balcony.)*

**NANA**

A bhajan group.

**NANI**

God knows why we must have all this gana-bajana when we are carrying somebody off to the cremation. Can't let him go in peace.

**NANA**

It's not a funeral... Nani, come and see...

*(Nani joins him)*

**NANA**

Look, it is a bhajan mandali. They are going to Pandharpur.

**NANI**

I wish we could join them. We don't have to come back.

**NANA**

I wish we could too... If we only had the strength...

*(They watch the procession from the balcony. The lights from the gas lamps and the tops of furling pennants pass by. They offer pranam and return to the room as the sound of the procession and bhajan recedes. Nani sits at the window and Nana at the table. A long pause as they gaze upwards at the nest. A blade or two of straw drops into the room.)*

**NANI**

Tell me, what have you been thinking of the whole day?

**NANA**
Thinking of?

**NANI**
Let me guess. It is about staying alive, right? Whether it is worth it anymore? Yes, I feel the same way myself.

**NANA**
You do?

**NANI**
If we could lie down now, go to sleep, and never wake up again... It would be just right.

**NANA**
Just right...

**NANI**
Dinoo is here. He will carry us... light the fire... Do whatever is needed for the last rites. Who else can do all this later?

**NANA**
Enough talk! Go to bed now.

**NANI**
I will. Just add a few extra pills into the milk, ten-fifteen of them. I will sleep like never before.

**NANA**
And what about me? What sort of natak... Oh my god...
*(He remembers suddenly, switches on the radio)*
Sharmila's play, she is on the natak programme on radio tonight.

---

**OPTIONAL: THIS PASSAGE IN THE ORIGINAL**

*(Nani is not listening. She is lost in thought, looking at the nest above. The story of Shravan Kumar is playing on the radio. Shravan's parents are calling out to him, 'Beta Shravan... Beta Shravan, kahan gaya tu... ? We are dying of thirst... Are you here, beta... ?')*

**NANA**
They had Raja Dashrath to curse. Who do we turn our anger on? *(Pause)* When the son arrives, what will they call him?

**NANI**
Whose son?

**NANA**
Who else? You think they will take your parting advice?

---

*(Nani is jolted out of her thoughts. She switches the radio off. Nana plays with the table lamp switch. Nani moves away to the kitchen.)*

**NANA**

They will call him George, Jack, Tom... cut off from this family forever. What do they care how anybody here feels!

*(Nani reappears with two cups of milk. She places them on the table.)*

**NANI**

Drop them in there.

*(Nani goes back to the kitchen. Nana stares after her. He takes out the bottle of pills from the drawer, puts two each into the cups, and puts the bottle back into the drawer. He goes towards the kitchen. Just then Nani enters and goes directly to the table. She takes out the bottle from the drawer and puts a large number of pills into the two cups. She picks up her cup and starts to sip the milk. Nana reappears from the kitchen, wiping his feet. He joins her. They drink up. Nani takes the empty cups to the kitchen, comes back, and joins Nana.)*

**NANA** *(With new found energy)*

Shall we take a walk in the garden?

**NANI**

You found a good day for that. Read the Gyaneshwari instead. I am going to lie down. Join me as soon as you can.

**NANA**

Achcha, I will do that.

*(He sits at the table and reads)*

Aise anadi par brahm
Jagdadi vishram dham
Uska hai ek hi naam
Kaha teen prakar se

**NANI**

A little louder, please.

**NANA**

*(Starts louder, but cannot help dropping his voice)*

Sansar dukh se jo hain peedit
Jeev aate uske paas nit
Unko Woh deta hai sanket
Jo yah naam.

**NANI** *(Sitting up)*

What is this fragrance?

**NANA**

Why are you up?

**NANI**

Aren't you getting this lovely fragrance?

**NANA**

Fragrance? From the pills?

**NANI**

What comes from a person cleansed with sandal paste and haldi, surrounded with dhoop.

**NANA**

Go to sleep now, you and your...

**NANI**

I should have asked Mahdu about his wife this morning.

**NANA**

Go to sleep, baba.

*(He walks over to the balcony)*

**NANI**

Where are you going? Don't go out into the night air.

*(Nana goes into the balcony and plucks out the plant from its pot. He flings it to one side with a contemptuous laugh.)*

**NANA**

Go to sleep... Go to sleep. *(He goes to the cupboard)*

**NANI**

What are you up to now?

**NANA**

Looking for a picture. *(He brings one to Nani)* Look, look at our Malu. If she was with us today...

**NANI**

Don't burden your heart uselessly. Put it away... Wait... let me look.

*(She takes the photograph, kisses it and gives it back to Nana)*

I am going to sleep. Lie down next to me. Turn the radio on.

*(Nana switches the radio on. There is a bhajan. A specimen is given here.)*

'Prachi ki ore se jo pravah bahta
Usme ulta hi koi tairta
Uska hath avashya hi rahta
Paani kheenchta odh main hi'

**NANI**

I am falling asleep. Come to bed now.

**NANA**

I am coming.

*(Nana wanders about the room. He bolts the window and door. He turns the radio up. He picks up the Gyaneshwari and starts on a stanza. Just then there is loud knocking on the door. Nana opens the door. It is Mahdu. He shows Nana a telegram. Nana reads it.)*

**NANA**

You have a son, Mahdu.

*(Mahdu touches Nana's feet. He looks at Nani on the bed and enquires by gesture.)*

Yes, she is asleep.

*(Mahdu gestures that he has to go the next morning, by bus.)*

Yes, yes, you must go soon. Wait...

*(Nana takes out a bundle from the cupboard.)*

Here, these are for the baby. And take this chain too. It used to be Nandu's. It will be useful...

*(Mahdu falls at Nana's feet again. He gestures that Nani should be informed later. He leaves. Nana sees him off and goes back to Nani.)*

*The telephone rings. Nana picks up the receiver. It is Sharmila. She speaks excitedly, 'Dadaji, dadaji'. Nana does not reply. He disconnects. The phone rings again. It is Sharmila again. Nanaji replies, 'Wrong number'. He disconnects. He starts to read the Gyaneshwari. The radio is on too. The phone rings again. Nana rises and goes over to Nani, covering her with a sheet. He looks up at the nest as a blade or two of straw drops. He sits at the table and starts on the Gyaneshwari again. He is drowsy. The phone keeps ringing.*

*Fade out.*

*The lights return briefly to reveal Nana asleep at the table with his head on the Gyaneshwari. A hiss from the radio.*

*Fade out.*

*Morning light, held low. There is faint bhajan music from the radio.*
*Prabhuji! Tum Chandan, Hum Paani*
*Jaki Ang Ang Vaas Samani...*
*Prabhuji! Tum Deepak, Hum Baati...*
*There is loud knocking at the door. We hear Dinoo's voice, 'Nana! Nani! Nanaji!'*
*Low fade out.*

***Close of play***

# BANGALORE LITTLE THEATRE

## Six Decades of Wholesome Community Theatre

In 1960, a small group of committed persons in Bangalore sought a theatre experience that could be a genuine alternative to the order of the day that was called BBC Theatre – British Bedroom Comedy. The group included the talented couple, Scott and Margaret Tod, and at least four other expats, along with a handful of Bangaloreans. They had a vision of a Community Theatre best described by the slogan invented 25 years later: *Think Globally, Act Locally.* Bangalore Little Theatre came into existence with a play reading in the last week of September that year. The first production on boards in December 1960 was Moliere's *The Prodigious Snob*, more commonly known as *The Would-be Gentleman.*

In 1962, within a year of inception, BLT arrived at a character and identity for itself: to maintain pride in its strictly amateur status, but to conduct its affairs in a thoroughly professional manner. The group gave itself a constitution and, through that, a participatory style of functioning. The group was seen as belonging to a membership, and therefore to be managed transparently by an elected management committee. The founding members were the first to give way to younger members to take the group forward.

Way back in 1963, BLT produced its first Indian play in English, an original adaptation of *Mrichhakatika* (The Toy Cart of Clay) by a founder-member, Prof B Chandrasekhara. Since then, the group has maintained the conscious policy of producing Indian plays periodically – translations, adaptations, original scripts, by its own members and others. Not surprisingly, two of the six awards for contemporary playscripts instituted for the first time by *The Hindu* in 1993 landed in BLT. The first prize was for the play by Vijay Padaki, *Credit Titles,* a political satire on intellectual property rights for patenting life forms. A Special Prize was awarded to another member, Ambika (Poile) Sengupta.

Old-timers of BLT have often been asked the secret of the group's long life when, in contrast, we see hundreds of cases of groups starting with a bang and dropping by the wayside in a couple of years. The difference, it seems, is in the simple fact that BLT is a community-based organisation and, therefore, a membership-driven group. From this fact has followed a number of guiding principles that appear to have served BLT well over the years. For instance:

- The participatory and transparency principles in management (with all financial transactions completely open and made available to the entire membership)
- The highly open leadership structure around an elected Managing Committee (rather than being founder-centric or personality-driven)
- The constant development of new talent, including new directors (rather than being dependent on the same old hands or breeding star complexes)
- The pursuit of the higher purpose, the constitutionally-enshrined objective of promoting the theatre and related arts in Bangalore (rather than the attitude of 'let's do another play')

All of this actually makes it far more difficult to 'manage' the organisation. It is so much easier to let a charismatic leader take charge and 'run' the group as he (or she) wishes.

The significance of these principles is understood better when we see that a sizeable majority of the theatre talent in Bangalore, including the more recognised names, has been in BLT productions, workshops and training programmes earlier. They continue their affiliation with BLT even if they perform under other banners.

Related to this point is one other indisputably important feature of BLT. It is the only English-language theatre group in Bangalore (perhaps anywhere in India) with strong links to the local-regional theatre, building bridges across language divides. Many of the stalwarts on the Kannada stage and screen have been either life members of BLT or have been prominently involved in some capacity or the other. After all, among the founders were personalities like Prof B Chandrasekhara, Nani, Shivaram, Seetharam, V Ramamurthy and S Ramaswamy. Then there were CR Simha, Vimala Rangachar, SG Ramachandra, KC Sekhar, Suresh Heblikar, Paddu, Shankar and Arundhati Nag, Ashok Rao…. And many many more – including some who went on to become Presidents of Karnataka Nataka Academy! Indeed, BLT has been a substantial support to Kannada theatre groups in their start-up stages.

BLT has invested heavily in training and outreach activity. In the late 1970s, BLT introduced for the first time in Bangalore a comprehensive introductory programme for newcomers to the theatre, based on the Stella Adler system. Since the mid '80, the group has made its Summer Project on Theatre (SPOT) a regular training event. It has come to be recognised as the most prestigious training event in the city, because of the quality of inputs provided. And it continues to be a part of BLT's social commitment. Other groups and productions snap up the talent from these training projects.

In 1993, the group initiated an annual Festival of Short Plays (SHORTS), aimed at promoting theatre activity among the college and youth population. With the audience response as enthusiastic as seen, the scale of the Festival may well be enhanced considerably in the coming years.

As a socially-responsible theatre society, BLT has readily taken on many a fundraising production for worthy causes. In 1970-71, BLT's production of the new play by Badal Sircar, *Evam Indrajit,* was the first fundraising event to contribute to the Prime Minister's Fund for the Bangladeshi (then East Bengal) refugee crisis. An original script, *Head Start,* by Vijay Padaki, was produced for CRY in January 1996. Since then BLT has made a constitutional commitment to dedicate one production for a charity every year. The group also provides various kinds of help to theatre projects in colleges, schools, clubs and other institutions.

With the high repute in training and outreach activity, it was only logical for BLT to set up an Academy of Theatre Arts in 2008. The stated mission of the Academy is to enrich the theatre institutional system through the thrust programme of *Theatre Education,* thus building the societal base for the true appreciation of the theatre and, indeed, all of the performing arts.

# THE SERIES EDITOR

**Vijay Padaki** is a Theatre Educator based in Bangalore. He has worn two caps for most of his life with equal facility. He has been active in the theatre for sixty years. He has been a management professional for over forty-five years.

Vijay is a psychologist and behavioural scientist by training, and founder-director of The P&P Group, a management resource centre that has programmes of research, consulting and training in the areas of Organisation and Institutional Development. A good part of the work of The P&P Group is devoted to the effectiveness of large development programmes. Among his earlier assignments, he headed the Human Resources Division of India's oldest cooperative R&D institution, Ahmedabad Textile Industry's Research Association (ATIRA), which also helped set up the first Indian Institute of Management in Ahmedabad. Later, he was a member of the founding faculty at Indian Institute of Management, Bangalore, the founder of a Centre for Management for the textile industry in Ahmedabad, and a Visiting Professor at Indian Institute of Science, Bangalore to initiate a programme in R&D Management. He was a Senior Associate at the National Institute of Advanced Studies in its early years.

Vijay joined Bangalore Little Theatre in 1960, the year of its inception, and later served the company in many capacities – as actor, director, trainer, writer, designer and administrator, including two stints each as Secretary and President. In 2008, the institutional set-up was restructured. Bangalore Little Theatre Foundation was created as a Public Charitable Trust. It was done with the purpose of reinforcing the organisation's strengths in outreach activity, and thus *rededicating the commitment to social development goals beyond performance.* The Trust requested Vijay to provide the leadership to a newly-created Academy of Theatre Arts in its formative years. The Academy is developing long-term programme thrusts to strengthen the institution of theatre education and practice in India.

Vijay has been responsible for institutionalising several activities of BLT, such as the annual summer workshop for newcomers to the theatre (SPOT), from which have emerged a large number of the theatre personalities in Bangalore, the History of Ideas programme of biographical plays, the Courtyard Theatre programme, and the Children's Theatre programme, which includes the annual flagship children's play as a partnership production to support a charity. Vijay conceived and initiated the highly successful Trainer-Training programme and the Directors Training programme in Bangalore.

He has forged several international partnerships with BLT over the years. The John F Kennedy Centre for Performing Arts in Washington invited him to serve as an advisor to the India Festival in 2011. The same year, he gave the Harold Clurman lecture at the Stella Adler Studio in New York. More recently, the Ministry of Culture invited Vijay to initiate a programme of Arts and Heritage Management in India.

Vijay has written over 50 original plays. He has also adapted or translated several play scripts. Seagull Books has published a volume of two Gujarati plays translated by him. In 1993, Vijay won the award for the best contemporary play script instituted by *The Hindu* for the play *Credit Titles.*

## PUBLICATIONS IN THE SERIES

### Volume 1: FOUR CLASSICS on the Indian Stage

Contains original English language adaptations of Indian classics. These include ***The Toy Cart of Clay,*** an adaptation of the Sanskrit Classic ***Mrichhakatika*** by Sudraka; ***The Anklet,*** an adaptation from Ilango Adigal's Tamil Classic ***Silappadikaram***; ***Kurukshetra Burning!*** based on ***Smashana Kurukshetra*** in Kannada by Kuvempu; ***The Echo,*** an adaptation of ***Chomana Dudi*** in Kannada by Shivarama Karanth.

### Volume 2: THE HISTORY OF IDEAS Programme of new plays

From BLT's highly acclaimed History of Ideas programme, plays include ***The Prophet and the Poet,*** based on the Gandhi-Tagore exchanges; ***Finding Ananda***, rediscovering the life and work of Swami Vivekananda, with the Bengal Renaissance as the backdrop; ***Tiger! Tiger!*** revealing the humanistic side of Tipu Sultan; ***Monsters in the Dark,*** an original adaptation of the Pulitzer award book ***The Emperor of All Maladies*** by Siddhartha Mukherjee, sub-titled A Biography of Cancer; ***Einstein's Dreams,*** an original dance theatre adaptation of the novel by the same title by Alan Lightman.

### Volume 3: CHILDREN'S THEATRE Programme of new plays

Containing plays from BLT's hugely successful Children's Theatre programme, this volume includes ***The Ungrateful Man,*** a tale from the Panchatantra; ***The Magic Drum,*** a collection of stories from the book by the same title by Sudha Murty; ***Ali Oh Baba,*** a retelling of the tale from the 1001 Arabian Nights; and ***The Court Jester,*** the tales of Tenali Rama.

## Volume 4:
## FOOTPRINTS and other plays

These plays were written by ***Vijay Padaki*** in the period 1986 to 2002 and represent explorations in combining form with content. There is a humanistic undercurrent in the plays, an affirmation of the human spirit, the innate ability to question the given, so often remaining suppressed, and the ability to find alternatives. It is known that a lot of his writing has been influenced by field experiences in his professional engagements. The content of the play has often (not always) begun as a case study, intriguing in itself, but demanding an alternative perspective. The alternative perspectives have provided the raw material for the play scripts. The play scripts should explain themselves. Footprints is presented as 'fictional science', raising the serious question of the human species being Nature's mistake, the price to be paid by the rest of the earth.

## Volume 5:
## MANDAP and other plays

The plays included in this Volume represent two main periods of Vijay Padaki's writing. The first is when he was deeply involved in social-development programmes that had field projects in rural areas. They were all addressing the issues of human rights and social justice, although from different 'sectoral' perspectives. It was the absence of rights and justice that was coming in the way of development in real terms. Violence was not ruled out. ***Mandap*** is the play from that period. The dynamics of rights and justice are seen in the urban setting too. The next five plays in this volume represent a period of writing in which the writer was increasingly drawn to developmental issues in the urban setting. The plays form a set that came to be called ***Tales From the City***. They are grouped in this Volume as two double-bills and one play by itself. Violence is the recognizable undercurrent in all these plays. ***Second Shift Muster*** is the oldest of the play scripts appearing in this volume. The one-act play is included in this volume for a variety of reasons. As with the other tales, this play explores a lesser known city-based occupation in changing times, with changing value systems.